A level year 1 and AS
AQA Psychology

Nigel Holt and Rob Lewis

Crown House Publishing Limited
www.crownhouse.co.uk

First published by
Crown House Publishing Ltd
Crown Buildings, Bancyfelin, Carmarthen, Wales, SA33 5ND, UK
www.crownhouse.co.uk
and
Crown House Publishing Company LLC
6 Trowbridge Drive, Suite 5, Bethel, CT 06801, USA
www.crownhousepublishing.com

An extension of this page appears on page 274.

British Library of Cataloguing-in-Publication Data

A catalogue entry for this book is available from the British Library.

Print ISBN 978-184590974-1

LCCN 2015947711
Printed and bound in the UK by Bell & Bain Ltd, Thornliebank, Glasgow

contents

INTRODUCTION

AQA Psychology: A level year 1 and AS

Authors: Nigel Holt and Rob Lewis

Nigel Holt works in the Department of Psychology at Aberystwyth University, and Rob Lewis works in the School of Education at Cardiff Metropolitan University. They are always happy to hear from students and teachers, so if you have any questions or would just like to say hello, please feel free to get in touch – their email addresses can be found on their respective institutional websites.

ACKNOWLEDGEMENTS

Nigel and Rob would like to thank Kate and Nic. We could not possibly engage in ridiculous tasks like writing textbooks without their continued good humour, patience and support.

Rob would like to dedicate this book to his friends and travelling companions – Bryan, Malcolm and Rhys. Many happy returns!

HELLO STUDENTS

Psychology is one of the broadest and newest of the sciences. It is extremely popular in schools and colleges and at university – it is one of the largest A levels and undergraduate degree programmes. This book is, first and foremost, for students. We know teachers and those interested in psychology from other professions read textbooks like this, but this particular book is designed carefully with students in mind. Specifically, it has been written for students preparing for the AS and A level psychology with the AQA examining board.

This is not a book with the bare minimum of information. We know from experience that textbooks are often written with teachers in mind, and frequently contain content more suited to teachers than students. Textbook authors know that teachers help students to understand difficult material in the classroom and so are often guilty of not explaining things as carefully and as thoroughly as they might. We are teachers ourselves and know how vital a good teacher is to education. However, we also wanted to help student understanding by providing a textbook which thoroughly covered the specification and which was accessible outside the classroom.

Everything required to get a top grade in the AQA AS and A level exams is included in this book. We have taken an approach which we hope will encourage students to *read*, and allow them to access ideas that are often hard to understand. We know from our work at university how important reading is to a rounded and successful education, and we also know that this wonderful 'habit' begins before university. We have not designed this book as a scattered assembly of facts or as something which resembles a comic. In fact, we have been terribly traditional in our approach. Sometimes, things were done a certain way in the past because that way was just better.

USEFUL FEATURES

The AS and A level Year 1 specifications are slightly different. If you are doing Year 1 of a full A level then *all* of this book is for you. If you are an AS level student then you *do not* need to cover the material indicated by the pale yellow highlights. We have indicated this content on the 'What you need to know' pages of each chapter, and down the sides of the A level *only* pages.

> Watch for the pale yellow bars and highlighting. This tells you which content is A LEVEL ONLY.

We have minimised features which break up text, but we have added boxes which we hope will help understanding and enrich the reading experience. Sometimes these boxes expand on research in order to give a little more detail about studies we think are particularly important. Another kind of box expands a featured point made in the text to aid understanding and to give greater context, or occasionally because we think it is just relevant and interesting.

Sometimes, seeing and hearing can do more for understanding than mere words on a page. There are many useful video clips on the internet, and we have included QR links to some of the more useful ones in this book. If you do not have access to a smartphone with a scanner app, you will find their URLs in an appendix at the back of this book.

An expert perspective is always useful, and at AS/A level the experts are the examiners, so we have included occasional 'Ask an Examiner' boxes to focus the reader on examination issues.

Internet forums are a notorious source of misinformation and bad advice - best avoided or, like anything else on the internet appearing helpful to your studies, approached with extreme caution …

Section 1
Introductory Topics in Psychology

Social Influence

WHAT YOU NEED TO KNOW ☑

Types of conformity: ❑

Internalisation ❑

Identification ❑

Compliance ❑

Explanations for conformity: ❑

Informational social influence ❑

Normative social influence ❑

Variables affecting conformity as ❑
investigated by Asch:

    Group size ❑

    Unanimity ❑

    Task difficulty ❑

Conformity to social roles as ❑
investigated by Zimbardo

Explanations for obedience: ❑

Agentic state ❑

Legitimacy of authority ❑

Situational variables affecting ❑
obedience as investigated by Milgram:

Proximity ❑

Location ❑

Uniform ❑

Dispositional explanation for ❑
obedience: the authoritarian personality

Explanations of resistance to social ❑
influence:

Social support ❑

Locus of control ❑

Minority influence: ❑

Consistency ❑

Commitment ❑

Flexibility ❑

The role of social influence processes ❑
in social change

Social Influence

Every aspect of our lives is affected by social influence. What others think, feel and do is very important to us. We use this information as a guide to our own thoughts, feelings and actions. We want to feel part of social groups, to believe we hold the 'right' views and opinions, and to behave in 'appropriate' ways. Such social forces are well understood and can be used to explain, for example, why some songs become more successful than others without necessarily being better. It also explains the attempts by companies to manufacture popularity for products by creating videos that they hope will go 'viral'.

Humans are social creatures so it should not be surprising that we influence one another's behaviour, why sometimes we go along with what others do and why, on other occasions, we behave in ways that convince others to follow our lead. Social psychologists have long been interested in how groups reach agreement and why their members so readily accept the influence of others, why people are prone to do improper things when authority figures tell us to and even how some hardy individuals champion a minority view and, in the face of enormous social pressure, change the views of society.

CONFORMITY

Altering our behaviour to match more closely the behaviour of the majority of others around us is a normal and everyday occurrence. So normal in fact that we hardly even notice it happening. This is *conformity* – what Aronson (1976) defines as 'yielding to group pressure'. This pressure to 'give in' and do as others do might be real (perhaps a group of friends encouraging a person to join in with their smoking) or it might be unspoken or imagined. For instance, you might regard it as 'expected' by society to behave in a certain kind of way. These expectations, or norms, are seldom written down. We just 'know' how to behave, and often feel a pressure to conform to the behaviour of those around us.

Conformity is part of the glue holding society together and it can be seen as highly functional. If we did not conform to social norms the world around us would be very difficult to live in – we would be unable to predict how others were going to behave and this would result in a high degree of uncertainty. So conformity is not always a bad thing: any cost of conformity is ultimately small given the important benefits to the wider social group. To conform is not necessarily a sign of weakness – rather, it can be seen as a sign of trust and of relying on others for information and support.

TYPES OF CONFORMITY

According to Kelman (1958) there are three types of conformity: *compliance*, *identification* and *internalisation*.

1. Compliance: This involves going along with the group without a change in attitude. We might behave as others in a group are behaving but we don't necessarily agree with or believe in the group behaviour. This is not necessarily a long-lasting change in behaviour – basically, it lasts for as long as the group pressure is exerted. For example, we may feel pressured by peers to smoke whilst in school. We may be forced or bullied until we do so.

2. Identification: This is where conformity occurs because we want to be like the primary influence. The more attractive the influence, the more long term the conforming behaviour. In effect, we see others in a group as role models and try to be like them. We may want to be liked or accepted by a particular group who dress in a certain way, and so we too may begin to dress accordingly.

3. Internalisation: This is the most permanent form of conformity. The group opinion or behaviour is accepted as a belief by the individual and becomes part of their own thinking. Here, conformity occurs without any particular conscious effort. Religious belief could be described in terms of internalisation. The opinion of those in a person's family may be taken on board and internalised. Their views are accepted and integrated into an individual's own thinking and they conform.

ASCH'S STUDY OF CONFORMITY

An early classic experiment by Muzafer Sherif (1935) dramatically demonstrated the power of groups to affect the thoughts and behaviours of its members (see box 'Early studies of conformity'). The *social influence* demonstrated by Sherif also has long-lasting effects. Rohrer et al. (1954) replicated Sherif's study and retested the participants a year later and found that they still used the consensus distance arrived at by the group. This suggests that participants had internalised the group norm.

A problem with the Sherif study, however, is that there is no correct answer to the *autokinetic effect* – which is an illusion that produces unique responses from individuals. The distance you think the spot moves will probably be different from the distance your friends think it moves. Asch (1951) argued that because the task was ambiguous, it was not clear that Sherif was demonstrating conformity at all. Asch carried out a series of studies to demonstrate conformity when the task was unambiguous. He found a tendency to conform to the majority view in a line judgement task where the answer of the majority was clearly wrong. Asch found that nearly one-third of his participants called out the majority wrong answers and three-quarters of his participants conformed at least once. The participants appeared to be displaying compliance (i.e. although they went along with the majority view, they still believed that they were correct).

Asch's conformity study

The participant was seated at a table with a number of others (who were all confederates, instructed by Asch to respond in a certain way and make the wrong choice in the task). The group was shown three lines (Figure 1.1a), then a fourth line (Figure 1.1b), which Asch described as the 'standard'. Each person in turn was required to say which of the first three lines matched the standard line. The participant was always next to last to do this. Some 123 participants were tested in this way 18 times. On 12 of these trials the confederates gave identical wrong answers (these were the critical trials during which conformity was measured).

Figure 1.1a: Comparison lines.

Asch found that 75% of the participants gave the wrong answer at least once (i.e. conformed on at least one occasion). Overall, there was a 32% conformity rate to wrong answers, and 5% of participants conformed on all critical trials. He also found that on 63.2% of all trials, where there was a clear and unambiguous difference in lines, participants did not conform.

Asch concluded that people show a tendency to conform even though in doing so they are compromising what they know to be true. He also concluded that there is a resistance to this tendency to conform, as shown in the number of trials where a non-conforming answer was given.

Figure 1.1b: Standard line.

Evaluation of Asch's experiments

1. It has been argued that the high levels of conformity found in the Asch studies reflects the norms of US society at the time. The 1950s was a time of high conformity in the United States. For example, the Cold War with the Soviet Union was just beginning and activities regarded as 'un-American' were frowned upon and actively discouraged. People were very concerned about stepping out of line and appearing to be different. Using an Asch-type set-up Perrin and Spencer (1981) found virtually no conformity in British university students, suggesting that the changed social climate of the 1980s did less to encourage conformity than the 1950s in the United States. It should be noted though that the Perrin and Spencer study has itself been criticised on the grounds that it used engineering students as participants – individuals who are inclined to make exact measurements and so are less susceptible to social influence in these circumstances.

2. Crutchfield (1955) thought that the degree of conformity found in the Asch studies was a result of the procedures used – in particular, the closeness to others in the line decision task exaggerated the degree of conformity. Using a procedure which isolated participants, he found lower levels of conformity than Asch. Allen and Levine (1968) suggest that conformity varies according to whether participants are required to respond to objective or subjective stimuli. For example, using the type of apparatus deployed by Crutchfield, they found that participants were far less affected by the majority when the task involved expressing a political opinion (which is subjective) as opposed to a line judgement (which is objective). It has been pointed out, however, that the artificial experimental setting of Crutchfield-type studies, rather than the style of question, might contribute in some way to variations in conformity.

3. Given that social norms vary from culture to culture, it might be expected that the value placed on conformity might also vary according to culture. Smith and Bond (1996) compared 133 Asch-type conformity studies conducted in 17 countries. They found that although conformity was, on average, lower than in the Asch studies, rates of conformity were not significantly different. They also suggested that variations in conformity between cultures depend on whether the culture is collectivist or individualist.

> **ASK AN EXAMINER**
>
> *You could be asked specifically about the Asch study, so be sure to learn the procedure and findings. Just as important though is to link this learning to your understanding of research methods and ethical considerations.*

It's not what you do, it's the way that you do it

Crutchfield (1955) thought that Asch's results may have had something to do with the procedures he used. He tested this idea by requiring the participants in his study to engage in an Asch-type perceptual task whilst sitting in separate booths. Participants were required to respond to stimulus material, presented on a screen, by flicking one of five switches representing possible answers. Conformity was encouraged by giving participants what they thought were the responses of participants in other booths – in reality, all participants received exactly the same information from a 'bogus majority'. Crutchfield was able to test 600 participants in this way. Crutchfield found lower levels of conformity (30%) than those found by Asch, which is still quite high considering that participants were responding in private.

EXPLANATIONS FOR CONFORMITY

Why people yield to the will of a majority has been a matter of debate in psychology for many years. There is general agreement, however, that there are two main reasons for conformity: *normative* and *informational* influence.

Informational social influence

In some situations we lack sufficient information about how to act. Think of your first experience of a nightclub, for instance. In unfamiliar situations like this we need information about the right thing to do and we look to others for this: where to stand, where to sit and how to behave so as not to look too stupid! The behaviour of others can often provide us with very persuasive information. When it is not clear what the correct response should be, people look to others as a guide to their own responses. This idea is supported by studies which show that conformity varies according to the ambiguity of the task that participants are given – for example, Sherif's (1935) study using the autokinetic effect. Asch (1956) found that conformity increased when he made his line comparison task more difficult by reducing the differences between the lengths of the lines. It appears that the more uncertain people are, because of a lack of information, the more likely they are to conform.

Normative social influence

Normative influence occurs because of the basic need we have to be accepted as a member of a group. Interestingly, this group does not have to be meaningful to us in any way. For example, it could be a random group of people who might never meet each other again. The important thing is the need for acceptance and approval from this group, which encourages agreement with the norm, or central view, of the group. It isn't necessarily important to actually agree with

Early studies of conformity

Two of the earliest studies into conformity both clearly demonstrate informational social influence. Considered to be the first demonstration of conformity in research, Jenness (1932) gave his participants the task of estimating the number of jelly beans in a jar. Clearly, there is not an obvious answer to this task. Having made private individual estimates, participants were then required to work in groups of varying sizes to agree a group estimate. After this, they had to once again privately estimate the number of jelly beans. Jenness found that the second estimate tended to move towards the estimate arrived at as a group.

Another famous study was conducted by Sherif (1935). He used an optical illusion called the autokinetic effect (if you stare at a spot of light in a darkened room it will *appear* to move, though it doesn't actually move). His participants were first required to estimate how far they thought the light moved, then, following this, to estimate again but this time in small groups. Sherif found that individuals tended to change their estimates to more resemble those of the group.

the group, there just needs to be the appearance of agreement or harmony. This is the likely explanation for conformity in the original Asch studies. Even though the right answer in the line judgement task was clear (so informational influence could not be operating), people went along with the majority by giving the wrong answer in order to 'belong'.

It can be effective when describing explanations to link them to examples from research, e.g. Sherif's study shows informational, Asch's study shows normative social influence.

VARIABLES AFFECTING CONFORMITY

Whilst Asch's classic study clearly demonstrates the strong pressure to conform to majority views, everyday experience tells us that conformity is not inevitable in all situations or even to the same degree. Many factors have been found to influence group pressures to conform.

Group size

According to Stang (1976), rates of conformity do not rise inevitably as the group size increases. Group conformity is at its greatest when the majority number between three and five people. After that, increasing the size of the majority has little effect on rates of conformity. In one variation of his study, Asch varied the size of the group to include 1, 2, 3, 4, 8, 10 and 15 confederates. He found that conformity was very low when there was just one confederate (3%). With two confederates conformity rose to 13%, and with three confederates it rose to 33%. There was little change in conformity beyond this, and there was even some reduction in conformity with higher numbers. One possible reason for this is suspicion of collusion – after all, it is not that common for all members of larger groups to be unanimous in their views. It appears, however, that the nature of the judgement is an important factor interacting with group size. For example, there is greater likelihood of conformity increasing with group size in circumstances of *informational social influence* (i.e. when there is no objectively correct answer).

Group unanimity

It appears that if the people making up the majority do not seem to hold the same view (i.e. they are not unanimous), it is easier for individuals in the minority to resist pressure to conform. It does not seem to matter how the unanimity of the majority is broken. Asch found that just one other group member agreeing with the judgement of the participant was enough to greatly reduce conformity (from 33% down to 5.5%). However, group dissent does not have to be supportive of the minority view for conformity to be reduced. For example, an incorrect but different view from a group member reduces conformity, as does a dithering response to questioning. Even when the competence of the 'supporter' is questioned (e.g. by being visually impaired), conformity is still reduced. As soon as the unanimity of the majority group is weakened, or even in some circumstances put into question, non-conformity is more likely to emerge as a response.

Task difficulty

In one variation of his study, Asch made the comparison task more difficult by making the differences in line lengths much smaller. This increased rates of conformity, probably by adding informational social influence to the existing normative social influence – not only do participants want to be accepted as members of the group, but the ambiguity of the task causes them to seek information about the correct response from others. However, the effects of task difficulty on conformity are not straightforward. For example, it has been shown that conformity is influenced by the extent to which an individual believes they are capable of doing the task (known as self-efficacy). Individuals who have more confidence in their abilities on a task are less likely to be influenced by the wrong answers of others.

Many factors have been found to influence conformity but you only need to learn these three. Just make sure you can link them back effectively to Asch's research.

CONFORMITY TO SOCIAL ROLES AS INVESTIGATED BY ZIMBARDO

Social roles are behaviours that are expected of us in certain circumstances. These roles carry with them expectations – people expect you to behave in a way consistent with your role. They exert pressure on people's thoughts, emotions and behaviours. Roles are powerful and their influences are often subtle – we usually do not know how our behaviour is being influenced by the role we occupy. For example, there are social roles associated with being a student or a teacher, although we are rarely aware of the pressures on us to conform to the expectations of these roles.

Zimbardo et al. (1973) were interested in the power of social roles in influencing conformity, and their Stanford Prison Experiment became one of the most controversial in psychology. Zimbardo constructed a mock prison in the basement of the Stanford University psychology building. Participants were randomly assigned to one of two roles: prisoner or guard. It was found that prisoners quickly became passive and depressed, whilst the guards became harsh and frequently brutal. It seems Zimbardo's participants readily conformed to their powerful new social roles, emphasised by appropriate clothing and a realistic environment.

Zimbardo's Stanford Prison Experiment

Twenty-four men were recruited from the student population, and paid US$15 a day for up to two weeks. Each was checked carefully for both physical and psychological well-being and assigned randomly to the role of either prisoner or guard. 'Prisoners' were 'arrested' by a real police officer, blindfolded and taken from their homes to the 'prison' that had been set up in basement rooms at the psychology department. They were subjected to all the things a real prisoner would be, such as delousing to ensure cleanliness, searching and removal of their possessions, including their clothes. They were given overalls bearing their prisoner number to wear and confined to 2 x 3 metre cells for a large part of the day. The guards were given mirror sunglasses and official-looking uniforms, and carried whistles and clubs. The guards and the prisoners experienced life in these roles in the prison for 24 hours a day, with the guards working eight hour shifts. No names were used, with prisoners being referred to by their numbers and guards as 'Mr Correctional Officer'. Unknown to participants, their behaviour was closely monitored.

The behaviour of the guards towards the prisoners surprised everyone involved. They quickly became tyrannical and sadistic (what the researchers referred to as the 'pathology of power'). Prisoner 'rights' (e.g. going to the toilet) were considered privileges and frequently withheld, punishments were applied without justification and some guards became verbally aggressive. The effects of imprisonment were severe. A range of negative behaviours developed, including passivity (being overly obedient) and dependence (not doing anything unless told to). Half the prisoners showed signs of depression, including crying, anxiety and anger. Zimbardo allowed one prisoner to leave during the experiment because he feared for the participant's psychological well-being. Despite being timetabled to run for two weeks, the experiment was stopped before it got too out of hand after only six days.

It was clear that it was the situational factors (where they were) that influenced behaviour more than the disposition of the participants (what kind of person they were), with ordinary, otherwise good-natured and intelligent young people behaving in a very unexpected way once given powerful social roles to which to conform.

Evaluation of Zimbardo's experiment

1. The Stanford Prison Experiment has been criticised for not being realistic. For example, unlike real prison guards, the participants in this study were not given a code of conduct which real prison guards would have been. Without these rules, the 'guards' were not limited and could behave in more extreme ways. Similarly, they knew they were taking part in a study and allowed the researchers to take responsibility for their actions instead of themselves, so an 'If I'm not being stopped I can't be doing anything that bad' mentality began to emerge. It was almost as if the lack of interference amounted to approval of the behaviour by the researchers.

2. In 2002 the BBC broadcast a TV series called *The Experiment* which could be described as a partial replication of the prison simulation study. Their results tended to contradict Zimbardo's – for example, guards refused to show punitive authority and the prisoners soon took charge of the prison. Psychologists Haslam and Reicher, who led the study, point out that whilst, as Zimbardo claims, the situation is important, other things must be taken into consideration also, such as social and cultural factors. For instance, brutality in prisons is sometimes focused on particular groups – something which might be expected if the situation (i.e. prison) was the only factor. Also, Haslam and Reicher argue that people don't react mindlessly to situations – they often think and reflect before acting. This can result in resistance rather than oppression, as seen in their study.

3. It has been claimed that the findings are not necessarily related to the researchers' careful design, but have more to do with an expectation of how the participants should behave. Making some participants 'prisoners' and some 'guards' introduced strong demand characteristics. The participants knew how they were supposed to behave, so the observed behaviour may have been a reflection of this expectation rather than a display of real behaviour. This puts the validity of the experiment into question. Also, Zimbardo was closely involved in the experiment, playing the part of prison warden. He was not, perhaps, ideally placed to be impartial in decisions relating to the conduct of participants in the study. He could not be said to be truly impartial.

4. The ethical issues surrounding the prison study are clear to see. The 'prisoners' experienced psychological harm and were clearly distressed. It seems likely that the experiment will also have caused the 'guards' distress – for example, that they were capable of brutality. In his defence, Zimbardo could not possibly have foreseen the extremely unusual result. He also followed up on the participants over the years that followed and found no long-term effects.

'What's bad is the barrel'

In 2004 news broke that prisoners in Abu Ghraib, Iraq had experienced beatings, sexual abuse and psychological torture at the hands of some of their American military guards. Zimbardo (2007) directly compared the events at Abu Ghraib to his own prison study. In both situations the guards were poorly trained but in very powerful and stressful social roles. There was a lack of an authority figure to control the guards' behaviour and uniforms dehumanised the guards and prisoners. Zimbardo pointed out that the guards were no different to the rest of us. They were not 'bad apples' but rather the barrel was rotten – the situation they found themselves in made it impossible for some guards to resist the power of the social role.

OBEDIENCE

Whilst some social influence appears subtle and indirect, it can also be straightforward and direct. For example, a teacher instructs her students to do a particular piece of work and they do as they are told, or a parent tells a child to behave and she does so. These are examples of *obedience* – individuals are acting in direct response to an authority figure.

For the most part, obedience to authority is benign and can be viewed as another of the norms that glue societies together. However, obedience is a very powerful social influence and sometimes people are urged by an authority figure to do things which are actually or morally wrong. History gives us many examples of the destructive effects of obedience authority. For example, Nazis and concentration camp guards during the Second World War used the defence that they were 'only following orders' to justify or excuse their terrible actions. It was this example of apparent blind obedience which influenced Stanley Milgram to design a now notorious series of experiments in the early 1960s. Milgram thought that if a figure had legitimate authority then ordinary people would obey their demands to do extraordinary things, even though these demands were clearly morally wrong. Moreover, he believed acts of evil were not necessarily carried out by evil people, but the acts were, at least in part, due to the situation in which individuals found themselves. A person's personality (i.e. their disposition) might influence their decision, but their actions depend on the context in which an authority figure has given them what they believe to be a legitimate order. These *situational* and *dispositional* factors are both important influences on whether people obey authority.

SITUATIONAL VARIABLES AFFECTING OBEDIENCE

Milgram's initial study demonstrated the power of an authority figure. He did, however, carry out a further 18 variations of the obedience experiments in order to discover what it was about the situation a person finds themselves in that influences their obedience to authority. The effects of varying proximity, location and uniform (authority) are summarised in Figure 1.2.

Proximity
In Milgram's original experiment, the teacher and learner were in different rooms, meaning that the learner could be heard but not seen. In one variation Milgram put the learner in the same room as the teacher. The obedience

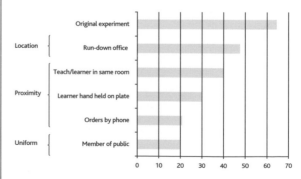

Figure 1.2: Percentage of fully obedient participants in experiment variations relating to location, proximity and uniform.

Milgram's experiment into obedience

Milgram (1963) recruited his participants by advertising for volunteers to take part in a study to see how punishment influenced learning and memory. They would be paid for their time and were told that even if they quit the study they would still receive the money. The procedure was relatively simple. Milgram employed two confederates whom he called an 'experimenter' (the authority figure dressed in a lab coat) and a 'learner' (who looked like a perfectly normal individual). The learner was wired to an 'electric shock machine'. The participant (the 'teacher') sat in an adjacent room beside the controls for the machine. The participant (who would be administering the shocks) was required to give shocks of increasing intensity to the learner each time they got a question wrong. Of course, the shocks were fake and the fake learner would receive no shock at all, but the participant would believe that he had administered a real voltage.

Milgram had instructed the learner to give wrong answers and to remain silent in response to the fake shocks until they reached 300 volts (V). At this level the learner then banged on the wall between himself and the participant. The learner gave no response after 315 V, but the teacher was required to continue asking questions and administer electric shocks up to 450 V. If at any time the participant demurred or asked to stop, the fake experimenter would tell the participant, 'You have no choice', 'You must go on' or 'It is essential that you go on'.

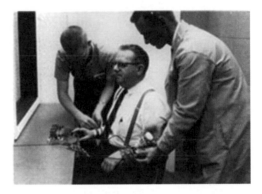

Despite a line marked 'Danger: severe shock' on the apparatus at 420 V, 65% of participants went past this to the machine's maximum voltage – 450 V. A small proportion (12.5% – just 5 of Milgram's 40 participants) stopped at the 300 V level, where the learner had begun to object to the shocks.

Prior to the experiment, it had been estimated that only 3% would go to the maximum shock level. Milgram's obedience studies clearly demonstrate how much impact an authority figure can have on our behaviour and the destructive potential of blind obedience.

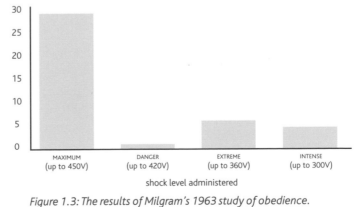

Figure 1.3: The results of Milgram's 1963 study of obedience.

rate (i.e. the number of participants who went to the maximum shock level) fell to 40%. In another variation the learner and teacher were brought into even closer proximity. Here, the teacher was required to hold the learner's hand on the metal plate that delivered the shock.

Puppies have feelings too

Criticisms of Milgram's findings, such as 'pact of ignorance' and weak ecological validity, led Sheridan and King (1972) to wonder what participants would do if they actually had to deliver a real electric shock. Of course, they couldn't electrocute a human so instead they used what they described as 'a cute fluffy puppy'.

The participants (the 'teachers') were 13 male and 13 female undergraduates. They were told that the 'learner' (the puppy) was being trained to discriminate between a steady and a flickering light. If the puppy failed to move as it should in response to each type of light, then it was to receive increasing shocks via the metal cage floor. The puppy was on the other side of a one-way mirror in full view of the teacher and really did receive the shocks. The shocks had limited amperage so whilst very painful (predictably causing howling, crying, yelping, jumping, etc.), no lasting physical damage was caused.

They found that six of the male participants refused to continue before reaching the maximum 450 V, whilst all female participants obeyed the authority figure and went to the maximum level. All participants showed distress during the procedure – for example, puffing, pacing and crying. Some participants attempted to coax the puppy to escape the shock (even though they could not be seen) and some attempted to secretly limit the duration of the shock. The findings clearly support Milgram's conclusions that, under certain conditions, people are willing to follow what are obviously 'repugnant' commands.

Obedience rates fell to 30%. Milgram also manipulated the proximity of the authority figure. In one variation the experimenter did not stay within a few metres of the teacher as in the original experiment, but left the room and gave orders by telephone. The obedience rate fell to 21%, and it was noted that some participants secretly gave weaker shocks than they should have. These findings suggest that people are less compelled to obey when the order from an authority figure is less direct and the consequences of obeying the order are less immediate.

Uniform
Authority figures are often identifiable by how they dress – for example, a head teacher may wear a smart suit or a police officer a uniform. In Milgram's original study the authority figure wore a white lab coat. To investigate the importance of uniform, Milgram conducted a variation where the experimenter received a phone call at the start of the procedure that required them to leave. Their place was taken by what the participants thought was an ordinary member of the public, wearing normal everyday clothes and no lab coat. He was, of course, a confederate. Obedience levels fell to 20%, the lowest of any of the variations.

Location
Milgram noted that the location of the experiment may have influenced level of obedience as it gave the impression that the authority was legitimate. After all, Yale is a prestigious university so its scientists are bound to know what they are doing! To test this, Milgram conducted the obedience experiment in a run-down inner city office building. Finding that obedience dropped to 47.5%, Milgram concluded that location contributed to but did not entirely explain the occurrence of obedience.

Evaluation of Milgram's experiments

1. It has been claimed that the 'teachers' (i.e. the real participants) did not really believe that the 'learner' was receiving electric shocks. Orne and Holland (1968) called this a 'pact of ignorance'. On the face of it, this criticism seems reasonable. For example, how could an employee of Yale University, a prestigious institution, allow such harm to be inflicted? Or why was the teacher needed at all? A researcher could easily have conducted the memory test and administered the shocks without the need for an intermediary. However, films made of some of the studies and post-experimental interviews show participants under extreme stress which suggests the reality of the situation for participants.

2. It has been claimed that the extreme levels of obedience seen in Milgram's study were in some way due to the artificial nature of the laboratory setting (i.e. it lacked ecological validity). However, research by Hofling et al. (1966) suggests that obedience is observable in settings other than the laboratory. Their participants were 22 nurses working at different hospitals who were not aware that they were taking part in a study. The nurses were telephoned by a fictitious 'doctor' and instructed to administer a potentially dangerous medication. Despite the fact that the telephone instruction clearly broke several hospital rules, all but one of the nurses were willing to carry out the order.

3. Evidence in support of Milgram comes from Burger (2009). He attempted to replicate Milgram's study and found comparable levels of obedience (see box 'Obedience lite' – a replication of Milgram's study).

'Obedience lite' – a replication of Milgram's study

Milgram's research was strongly criticised on ethical grounds, something which prevented replication of his procedure. Burger (2009) conducted the first obedience study in the US in 30 years, only altering the procedure to bring Milgram's experiment within the bounds of current ethical standards. Like Milgram, Burger recruited participants through advertisements in newspapers and leaflets. He filtered out those with knowledge of psychology and Milgram's research in particular. Burger found that obedience rates were only slightly lower than in Milgram's study conducted decades before.

ETHICAL ISSUE: PREVENTION FROM HARM

Whilst Milgram did follow-up interviews which satisfied him that there were no long-term psychological effects on participants, he did not ensure that vulnerable individuals were excluded from participation. Burger addressed this by screening all participants and excluding anyone who might have a negative reaction to the experience. He also limited distress by stopping shocks at 150 V – his logic being that Milgram's participants went all the way once they got that far anyway, so in all likelihood his participants would too. Burger also ensured that a thorough debrief was provided as quickly as possible following the experiment.

ETHICAL ISSUE: RIGHT TO WITHDRAW

Whilst Milgram's participants were told they could leave the study and keep their money, the orders of the authority figure clearly indicated that participants could not simply stop. Burger informed participants on three separate occasions during the procedure that they could withdraw at any time.

EXPLANATIONS FOR OBEDIENCE

The findings of Milgram's experiments cannot be explained by arguing that the participants were somehow uncaring and heartless individuals. On the contrary, they pleaded to be allowed to stop and expressed concern for the learner's suffering. Neither were participants seeing through Milgram's deception. They appeared to show a great deal of emotional distress during the procedure. A number of possible explanations have been proposed – just two are outlined here.

Legitimacy of authority

Society assigns legitimate authority to certain individuals, and Milgram (1974) believed that the norm of obedience to authority compels us to act upon their commands. We are, in effect, socialised to obey the orders of individuals that society has given the right to demand obedience – for example, teachers, police officers and parents. However, an authority figure must somehow send the message that they are the one with the status and power and should be obeyed. This can be conveyed by things like posture, tone of voice and facial expression. This is also done through more overt symbols, such as formal dress (e.g. a suit) or a uniform (e.g. a police uniform). The effect of legitimate authority can be seen in Milgram's experiment, with the increased obedience when the experimenter wore a white lab coat. When the orders were given by someone without this symbol of scientific authority, obedience rates fell. He also found that obedience was highest when there was the greatest credibility and legitimacy – for example, when the experiment was conducted at the prestigious Yale University rather than a shabby office. The power of outward signs of authority like uniforms was demonstrated in a field experiment by Bickman (1974) (see box 'The uniform – a symbol of legitimate power').

Normative and informational social influences

Normative social influence made it difficult for participants in Milgram's study to refuse to continue. By agreeing to take part, participants had entered into a social contract – a norm of which required them to continue doing what they had agreed to in order to please the experimenter. Informational social influence also played a part. Participants found themselves in a confusing situation they had never experienced before. We know that informational social influence is especially strong in ambiguous situations. Unsure about exactly what was going on, participants used others to guide their behaviour – the expert who was instructing them to continue administering shocks.

The uniform – a symbol of legitimate power

Bickman (1974) had a researcher approach people passing by on the street and ask them one of three things: to pick up a piece of litter, to give a dime (the equivalent of a 10 pence coin) to a stranger or move away from a bus stop. The researcher was dressed either as a civilian, a milkman or a guard. Bickman found that 14% obeyed the milkman, 19% the civilian and 38% the guard. In order to further investigate the power of the guard, he conducted another experiment where the guard, after having made the request, either stayed to watch what the passer-by did or walked away. Bickman found that people continued to obey the guard even when he was not there to see them comply. For Bickman, this demonstrated the power of a visible symbol of authority – the uniform.

Agentic state

Milgram proposed that individual social consciousness can operate in two ways: the *autonomous state* is when individuals assume responsibility for their actions. Because an individual's own values and beliefs are guiding their behaviour they are more likely to behave in moral and pro-social ways. The *agentic state* is when individuals feel they have diminished personal responsibility because they are the 'agents' of others (i.e. they act on someone else's behalf). In this state of mind they are likely to feel less conscience and guilt about the consequences of their own actions, and are more likely to engage in antisocial acts. Milgram (1974) called the move away from autonomy to agency the 'agentic shift'. It is triggered by the presence of someone perceived to have greater legitimate power.

The agentic state has probably evolved because it serves useful social functions. For example, it allows us to live successfully in hierarchical societies where we give up control over aspects of our lives to other legitimate authorities, such as teachers or police officers. The agentic state is something which develops early in life. Parents encourage their children to obey, follow rules and respect other's authority. As we grow we are encouraged to take more responsibility for ourselves, thus to be autonomous. In the context of obedience studies, people who are obeying the authority figure, the experimenter, are in an agentic state – they are agents of an external authority. Those who remain independent, and thus disobedient, are consequently expressing autonomy rather than agency.

Dispositional explanation for obedience: the authoritarian personality

Milgram (1974) suggested that individual differences in obedience can be linked to an aspect of an individual's disposition called an *authoritarian personality*. People with an authoritarian personality are most likely to obey orders and give the largest shocks. Often resulting from an upbringing by dogmatic and distant parents, the authoritarian personality tends to be intolerant of others, feels secure in their opinions and beliefs, and is obedient and submissive to those they see as being in authority (Adorno et al., 1950). The attitudes towards authority formed as a child (i.e. that people with more power and authority have to be obeyed) continue into adulthood and form part of a person's disposition. It is clear why the theory of the authoritarian personality was so attractive to those seeking a dispositional explanation for acts of obedience.

The concept of an authoritarian personality has been widely criticised, however, and many psychologists consider the authoritarian personality as proposed by Adorno et al. to be fundamentally flawed. Milgram himself said, 'I am certain that there is a complex personality basis to obedience and disobedience. But I know we have not found it yet' (Milgram, 1974, p. 205). Decades later and research has yet to demonstrate a convincing association between obedience and the authoritarian personality, or indeed between obedience and any personality variable. Sutton and Douglas (2013) suggest that the situational forces at play are usually powerful and therefore overwhelm any dispositional factors that may influence individual responses. Where a person's disposition might influence behaviour is in situations where social influence is particularly weak. Whilst personality is unlikely to be an important factor influencing behaviour in specific instances of social influence (e.g. an experiment into obedience), it might emerge when behaviour is considered as an average across a range of different situations.

EXPLANATIONS OF RESISTANCE TO SOCIAL INFLUENCE

Locus of control

Locus of control refers to where an individual perceives 'control' to be. An individual might believe that they themselves are in control of events, in which case they are said to have an *internal locus of control*. People with an internal locus of control have a certain confidence and security, a positive outlook and no real need for external approval. Alternatively, an individual might feel that they have no control over events, in which case they have an *external locus of control*. Such people tend to be less confident, more nervous and more insecure. Rotter (1966) developed a scale intended to measure a person's locus of control. According to Rotter, locus occurs along a continuum of high locus of control to low locus of control, and we all lie somewhere between the two extremes.

Some characteristics of locus of control

Internal locus of control ←——————→ External locus of control

High internal locus of control:

- Take responsibility for their actions.
- Less influenced by the opinions of other people.
- Confident when confronted with challenge.
- A strong sense of self-efficacy.

High external locus of control:

- Successes often credited to luck or chance.
- Believe that nothing they do will change the situation.
- Feel hopeless, helpless or powerless in difficult situations.
- Outside 'forces' blamed for their circumstances.

Those with a high internal locus of control are less likely to be obedient. Because they feel in control they are more likely to remain autonomous and take responsibility for their actions than become agentic and defer responsibility to someone else. Someone with an external locus of control is much more likely to conform. Their insecurity and need for approval means that they are especially susceptible to normative social influences – they have a stronger need to appear part of the majority.

Social support

When, in one of the variations of his experiment, Milgram gave his participants an ally (i.e. someone else in the room who also disagreed with the authority figure) obedience levels were found to significantly reduce. Rank and Jacobsen (1977) demonstrated the same effect. Their study was similar to the Hofling et al. (1966) study, in which a researcher pretending to be a familiar doctor telephoned nurses at work telling them to give patients Valium at three times the recommended dose. Only 2 out of 18 nurses who were able to discuss the order with other nurses carried it out. This suggests that obedience is lowered when there is another dissenting person present. A similar phenomenon occurred in the Asch studies. Just one extra dissenting voice caused the rate of conformity to plummet to 5%. It appears that the presence of others enables a group norm of resistance to form, so providing group members with an alternative normative influence. It might also be that the social support provided by another person might make individuals feel less at risk of negative consequences from resisting the majority or the authority.

You can draw information from any social influence research which is relevant to social support, but remember to learn why social support helps resistance – don't just list examples.

MINORITY INFLUENCE

Whilst the majority exert a significant influence, minorities can and do influence the majority. However, much less is understood about the processes which bring about change through *minority influence*, although it is clear that the process of changing the opinions of a majority occurs at a slower pace. The first person to experimentally investigate minority influence was French psychologist Serge Moscovici.

Moscovici et al. (1969) experimentally investigated the effect of a minority on a majority opinion. In his study he asked participants in small groups to judge a colour – whether a slide projection showed blue or green. There were two confederates in each group who were instructed to consistently say that the colour was green, regardless of the actual colour. When the minority called the colour green on only 24 of 36 trials the majority was not swayed in its view. However, when the minority called the colour green on all trials nearly a third of participants agreed with the minority opinion at least once. It appeared that if the two confederates consistently agreed with each other, and were confident in their answers, then they were able to persuade a majority that blue colour slides were in fact green. A number of characteristics appear to make a minority more influential:

Figure 1.4: When does blue become green?

Consistency

This is the key factor. A minority must maintain a clear position over time and resist pressures from the majority to change (i.e. it must be consistent). For Moscovici (1976) consistency has two components. First, there must be *diachronic consistency*, which means that individuals must hold stable views over time. Second, there is *synchronic consistency*, which means that individuals within a minority should hold the same views and thus show stability across the group.

Commitment

Having a consistent view will give the majority a signal that the minority is committed to its position. Any dissent is likely to weaken the minority position, in that members of the majority are likely to exploit this inconsistency as a demonstration of the doubtfulness of the position. By demonstrating commitment, which can often involve considerable personal sacrifice, a minority is harder for the majority to ignore and sends a message that an alternative view to that of the majority is available.

Flexibility

It appears that the influence of a minority also depends on how the majority interpret the consistency of the minority. According to Mugny and Papastamou (1982), a minority will have a better chance of changing the majority view if it is seen to be flexible and willing to compromise, since dogmatic views exert less influence. This was demonstrated by Nemeth and Wachtler (1974). In a study similar to Moscovici et al. (1969), they had confederates either respond in a consistent, rigid way or alternate between two responses. They found that the rigid minority were viewed as less confident and competent and produced less change in the majority. However, they also found that the flexible minority must have a credible view to be perceived as consistent – they were more influential when there was a pattern in their responses (e.g. always saying 'green' to dim slides) than when the responses were random.

SOCIAL CHANGE

Sometimes the actions of a small number of people, or even a single individual, can have an enormous influence on society. In 1955 Rosa Parks refused to give up her bus seat to another passenger. The passenger was white and she was a black woman. In Montgomery, Alabama at that time, she was obliged to make way for the white person. Her refusal began a campaign of civil disobedience. The action of this single woman lit a fuse in the black community. Her refusal to obey led to the rise in prominence of Martin Luther King. The Civil Rights Movement gathered steam and the rights of those in the black community were finally regarded as important.

Nine years later, segregation was banned across the United States. That segregation was the norm, and had been for many years, tells us something about the powerful influence of norms and authority figures in society. However, the example of Rosa Parks also tells us that a minority can exert an influence so as to bring about *social change*.

MAJORITY INFLUENCE: THE ROLE OF CONFORMITY IN SOCIAL CHANGE

Given that humans are fundamentally social in nature, it is perhaps not surprising that we conform in order to be liked and gain acceptance. Our interactions with others provide us with experiences essential to our well-being, such as affection, love, emotional support, approval and social stimulation. Indeed, society uses social isolation (i.e. jail) as a threat to members who might be tempted to deviate from the norms of society, and social groups also have their own penalties (e.g. ejection from the group). Asch (1956) demonstrated

the power of social approval in one experiment where he had participants write down their answers rather than say them out loud. Now that the concern about what others thought was removed, conformity dramatically reduced. These normative pressures reduce the impact of non-conformists and have the cumulative effect in society of maintaining the status quo (the stable order of things). People are persuaded to go along with the majority view.

Smith et al. (2015) point out that a number of conditions exist that ensure majority views remain the most persuasive, which in turn strengthens the position of the majority.

1. Majority arguments are more frequently heard: The majority (obviously) has more people in it so there are going to be more individuals sharing a particular majority view. This makes it more difficult for dissenting opinions to be heard.

2. Majority arguments are discussed more frequently: People are more likely to express their views when they think others share them.

Also, opinions shared by a group are more likely to be discussed. This means that there is a bias towards discussing the majority view.

3. Majority arguments seem more compelling: The more people there are making the same argument, the more impact it has. Different people reaching the same conclusion makes the view even more compelling.

4. Majority arguments are presented in more compelling ways: When people seek information about something, they generally select that which is both shared and familiar. Such information is likely to be expressed confidently by the majority.

THE ROLE OF MINORITY INFLUENCE IN SOCIAL CHANGE

The success of society and its democratic systems depends to some degree on having smaller groups of people (minorities) holding often unpopular views and attempting to exert non-violent influence on the majority. These smaller groups that hold often radically different views from the majority are often referred to as 'pressure groups', and there are many examples of such groups bringing about positive social change.

In the 1970s, a minority began to voice concerns about human-caused climate change. This group could not exert normative social influence – individuals are unlikely to abandon a majority view (i.e. humans have not caused climate change) in favour of radically different views held by far fewer people. However, the view was expressed consistently over time, with confidence and with persuasive evidence to encourage defections from the majority. Eventually, as more and more individuals changed their opinion, the minority grew in size, it took on a momentum of its own (the 'snowball effect') and the minority view slowly became the majority view. This is a process Moscovici (1976) called 'conversion'.

The role of obedience in social change
Turner (1991) says that for a group to function effectively, individuals must give up responsibility and defer to others of higher status. This 'legitimate authority' then replaces a person's own self-regulation, consequently increasing obedience. This has implications for social change. A strong form of authority encourages the norm of obedience, and when this idea is applied to the wider social group, power can be exerted in order to maintain the status quo.

Research also tells us, however, that power needs to be wielded carefully. If the authority is not perceived to be legitimate, or people feel that they are not free to make their own decisions, then there may be *reactance*. Research into reactance shows that people actively rebel against the restriction when they feel their freedom is threatened, often by doing exactly what they have been told *not* to do. This is especially the case when they feel that the restriction is arbitrary or illegitimate.

Voting rights for women

A frequently cited example of social change through minority influence is the suffragette movement of the 20th century. Suffrage means the right to vote, and the suffragettes campaigned during the early 1900s, against all the odds, to bring the vote to women in the majority of Britain, eventually gaining the same suffrage rights as men in 1928. Women like Emmeline Pankhurst carried out extraordinary acts of bravery that saw them excluded socially. Women at the time were not expected to be politically active in this way, and the majority felt that the suffragettes' behaviour was not 'becoming of their gender'.

KEY TERMS

Agentic state Where individuals feel that they have diminished responsibilities for their actions because they are the 'agents' of others.

Autokinetic effect An optical illusion used by Sherif (1935). If you stare at a spot of light in a darkened room it will appear to move. He had participants in groups estimate how far they thought the spot had moved in an investigation of *conformity*.

Autonomous state An autonomous state is where an individual feels independence and assumes responsibility for their own actions.

Compliance Where we conform even though our attitudes and opinions have not changed. It lasts for as long as group pressure exists.

Conformity The act of altering one's behaviour to match more closely the behaviour of a majority of others.

Identification *Conformity* occurs because we want to be more like those in the group influencing us. *Conformity* lasts as long as the influencing group remains attractive.

Informational social influence *Conformity* may be influenced by the information available to us. For instance, what others are doing can significantly impact on whether we comply or not.

Internalisation The most permanent form of *conformity* where the group opinion is accepted as a belief.

Legitimacy of authority We are more likely to obey people who we regard as having legitimate authority. This might include the police, doctors or even teachers and lecturers!

Locus of control An aspect of personality whereby we see ourselves to be either in control of events (internal locus of control) or at the mercy of other outside forces (external locus of control). People are usually somewhere between the two extremes.

Majority influence The influence over a smaller number of people by a larger, more powerful group.

Minority influence The influence of a larger group of people over a smaller, less powerful group.

Normative social influence *Conformity* may be influenced by our basic need to be accepted as a member of a group.

Obedience A direct form of *social influence* where people do as they are told by an authority figure.

Social change Changes in society. This can often come about because of the actions of a minority.

Social influence The study of how social situations influence how we feel, think and behave.

PAGE 11

Discuss research into conformity. (8 marks)

There are two things to know here – what research to discuss and what the discuss command requires from you. The obvious way to answer this question is to select Asch's study. *Discuss* means to present key points and provide some strengths/weaknesses. So, 4 marks worth of detail – e.g. what Asch did and what he found, followed by a strength (e.g. although lower, conformity was also found by Crutchfield) and a weakness (e.g. cultural limitations) for another 4 marks.

PAGE 15

Many factors have been found to influence group pressures to conform. Outline two variables that Asch found affected rates of conformity. (4 marks)

The key thing to note here is how few marks are available – only 2 marks for each variable. Don't do any more than correctly identify the variable and briefly state how it affects conformity.

PAGE 16

Discuss conformity to social roles. Refer to research in your answer. (12 marks)

You will often find questions which give further instructions about how you should go about answering the question. Here, you are told to refer to research in your answer. This is not a polite request, it is an instruction! The research is clear – it is Zimbardo's Stanford Prison Experiment. This should be straightforward enough, but there is a real danger in you giving endless detail about procedure and findings. This will only get you half marks, no matter how brilliant it is. Try to get some balance between outlining the research and your strengths/weaknesses, which gets you the other half of the marks.

PAGE 22

Outline one explanation for obedience. (3 marks)

An outline is a brief answer. You get a mark for identifying one explanation. The other marks are for further elaboration – e.g. if you choose the agentic state you would say how it leads to obedience in a little bit of detail.

PAGE 24

Explain how resistance to social influence is influenced by locus of control. (4 marks)

This appears to be straightforward, and it should be. The key success here is to give an answer with enough detail for 4 marks. Here, you can outline the effects of both an internal and an external locus of control, and that will be enough. But be careful of variations in the question – if it asks you to explain resistance (e.g. Outline how locus of control explains resistance to social influence), then you would focus on external locus as this is the one that explains resistance.

PAGE 26

In 1955 Rosa Parks refused to give up her bus seat to another passenger. The passenger was white and she was a black woman. At that time in Montgomery, Alabama she was obliged to make way for the white passenger. Her refusal began a new era for freedom and equality and an end to segregation.

Explain how social influence processes can help us to explain this example of social change. (6 marks)

In this question you need to relate psychological theories and concepts to the specific issue – in this case to an example of social change. First of all, describe the relevant social influence processes (e.g. minority influence and the process of conversion). It is vital to relate what you say to the example. Your marks will be limited if you don't, regardless of how good your knowledge of minority influence is.

Memory

WHAT YOU NEED TO KNOW ☑

The multi-store model of memory ❑

Sensory register: ❑

    Coding ❑

    Capacity ❑

    Duration ❑

Short-term memory: ❑

    Coding ❑

    Capacity ❑

    Duration ❑

Long-term memory: ❑

    Coding ❑

    Capacity ❑

    Duration ❑

The working memory model ❑

Central executive: ❑

    Coding ❑

    Capacity ❑

Phonological loop: ❑

    Coding ❑

    Capacity ❑

Visuo-spatial sketchpad: ❑

    Coding ❑

    Capacity ❑

Episodic buffer: ❑

    Coding ❑

    Capacity ❑

Types of long-term memory ❑

Episodic ❑

Semantic ❑

Procedural ❑

Explanations for forgetting ❑

Proactive interference ❑

Retroactive interference ❑

Retrieval failure due to absence of cues ❑

Factors affecting the accuracy of eyewitness testimony ❑

Misleading information, including leading questions and post-event discussion ❑

Anxiety ❑

Improving the accuracy of eyewitness testimony ❑

The cognitive interview ❑

Memory

Where would we be without memory? Who we are and what we are is largely the result of our memory. It gives us our sense of self, it guides what we already know and it determines what and how we will learn. Our knowledge base is composed of all that we have in our memory: memory is, in effect, the sum total of all that we can remember. Memory clearly plays a vital role in every aspect of our lives. Indeed, it could be argued from an evolutionary standpoint that without the capacity to learn and remember we would not have survived as a species. It is perhaps not surprising, therefore, that memory has always been an important topic in psychology.

THE MULTI-STORE MODEL OF MEMORY

Atkinson and Shiffrin's (1968) three-stage model of memory remains the leading theory of how memory operates. It proposes that memory is not a single process but involves more than one stage and more than one kind of memory that operate together to give us the rich memories nearly all of us are lucky to have.

According to this model, there is a flow of information through a series of discrete memory systems, each serving a different function. First, information from the environment enters our *sensory memory*. We receive an enormous amount of sensory information, too much to process and not all of it immediately important. Information selected out by an *attention* mechanism is then passed on to a temporary store called *short-term memory*. Rehearsal ensures that information is retained here or transferred to a more permanent long-term store.

At each stage, information can be lost (forgotten) and during transfer between each stage information is coded. *Coding* (sometimes called encoding) is the process of changing information into a form suitable for memory to deal with. Each stage also varies in terms of its *capacity* and *duration*.

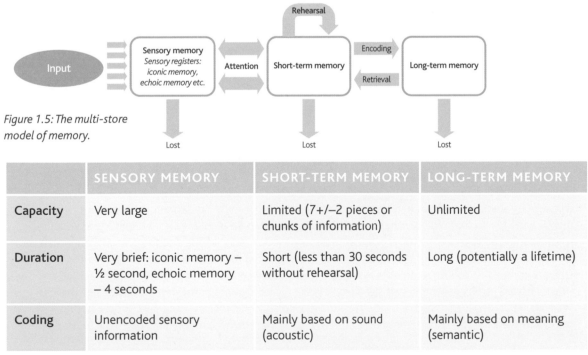

Figure 1.5: The multi-store model of memory.

	SENSORY MEMORY	SHORT-TERM MEMORY	LONG-TERM MEMORY
Capacity	Very large	Limited (7+/−2 pieces or chunks of information)	Unlimited
Duration	Very brief: iconic memory – ½ second, echoic memory – 4 seconds	Short (less than 30 seconds without rehearsal)	Long (potentially a lifetime)
Coding	Unencoded sensory information	Mainly based on sound (acoustic)	Mainly based on meaning (semantic)

Table 1.1: Capacity, duration and coding for stores according to the multi-store model.

SENSORY MEMORY

Sensory memory system is the first stop for all sensory information. It receives information from the environment and holds on to this information very briefly – only until it can be attended to and selected for further processing. Everything we hear, see, taste, touch and smell arrives as data and is held in a *sensory register*, a memory system for a specific individual sense. For example, a visual register (sometimes referred to as *iconic memory*) holds on to images, and an auditory register (or *echoic memory*) holds on to sounds. Historically, research has focused almost entirely on these two registers, but there is likely a sensory register for each of our senses. Recently, psychologists have become more interested in the workings of *haptic memory*, which is our sensory register for touch.

Capacity

It is likely that everything the body is capable of sensing is stored in a sensory register – iconic, echoic, haptic, gustatory and olfactory. It follows, therefore, that sensory memory must be capable of holding a great deal of information at one time. However, because information is held on to briefly and below conscious awareness, it seems from experiments as though it is limited. Sperling's studies, for example, suggested that between 9 and 12 items could be recalled from iconic memory before information is lost.

Duration

Research suggests that information in iconic memory lasts only a very brief time (up to half a second), after which the information is permanently lost (Sperling, 1960). Echoic memory is similar, but a weaker 'echo' extends the time to about 4 seconds (Darwin et al., 1972). This increase in duration of echoic memory may be related to our need to hold on to sounds longer for language processing.

Coding

Each sensory register contains an exact reproduction of the sensory stimulus (i.e. it holds the information received more or less in its original unencoded form). For example, some researchers believe that the basis of iconic memory is at least in part the activity of cells in the retina of the eye.

Sperling's experiments into iconic memory

Having asked participants to fixate their eyes on a particular part of the display screen, Sperling displayed an array of letters for a twentieth of a second (about the blink of an eye). The participants could only remember four or five letters, which for Sperling was evidence for the limited duration of sensory memories – most of the letters had faded from the iconic register faster than the participants could recall them. Interestingly, however, participants recalled being aware of more letters than they could remember. Sperling set about investigating this phenomenon. He did the same thing again, but now asked participants to recall only the row associated with a particular tone: when a high tone sounded participants had to recall the top row, the middle row with a medium tone and the bottom row with a low tone. The performance of these participants was compared to a control group which did not hear any tone and were just told to remember as many letters as they could. Sperling found that all four letters were recalled in whichever row was signalled. It is significant that the participants did not know which row would be signalled ahead of time – this means that an iconic memory had been stored of the whole array but then the tone had focused attention to a particular row which they now had time to recall.

F	Q	C	B
R	D	G	X
T	M	P	E

SHORT-TERM MEMORY

In order to keep information longer in memory, it needs to be transferred from sensory memory into *short-term memory* (STM). This is the part of the memory system which holds the information an individual is thinking about at any one time.

Capacity

Capacity of STM refers to the amount of information that can be held at one time. In his famous paper, 'The Magical Number 7+/–2', Miller (1956) suggested that STM could hold between five and nine items of information. For example, whilst we would have no difficulty remembering a six-digit telephone number, we would have difficulty remembering it if the number also included the dialling code, increasing the number to 11 digits and thus outside the capacity of STM. One problem with this, however, is that it is not always clear what constitutes an 'item' in memory. It could be each digit in a telephone number or it could be a verse in a song. The size of an item depends on how we organise information, a process called *chunking* (see box 'How chunking affects capacity').

Duration

The length of time, or duration, that information can be held in STM is limited. If the information in STM is not being used then it will quickly disappear. One way to keep information in STM is by rehearsing it – by repeating information we are in effect re-entering it into STM. Research suggests that without rehearsal information can be lost from STM within seconds. Peterson and Peterson (1959) presented their participants with a trigram (three letters, e.g. PMW), and then asked them to count backwards in threes to prevent rehearsal of the trigram. They found that after 18 seconds of counting backwards the participants could not remember the

How chunking affects capacity

Chase and Simon (1973) gave their participants five seconds to review pieces in a chess game. The participants who were chess experts remembered the position of nearly all the pieces, whilst non-experts remembered an average of 9 out of 32. There was no difference in the experts and the non-experts when they were given the same time to view chess pieces arranged randomly. The better memory of chess experts was due to them grouping chess pieces into meaningful 'chunks' of playing pieces. Non-experts did not have the knowledge to chunk in this way. Experts did not have the advantage when the pieces were arranged randomly so their STM capacity was limited to that of non-experts.

trigram. This classic study demonstrates clearly that STM has a limited duration – unless we recall information it will quickly decay and be permanently lost.

Coding

STM prefers to code information according to sound. Even when we code something visually we also code acoustically, by explicitly verbalising what we see or subvocally verbalising it (speaking it silently to ourselves or even below conscious awareness).

This preference for acoustic coding was demonstrated by Conrad (1964). He presented strings of letters (e.g. PVJTSL) to participants for approximately three-quarters of a second and asked them to recall what they had seen. The pattern of errors revealed acoustic encoding in that errors were based on the sound of the letters not visual features (e.g. T and V were muddled with P, but very rarely were any of these muddled with S). Even though the letters were presented visually, information must have been changed (coded) to sound in STM for these errors to have occurred.

LONG-TERM MEMORY

Long-term memory (LTM) is where information is held for some period of time longer than it is held in sensory memory or STM. This could be anything from seconds to a lifetime. Your long-term memory holds everything you know about the world – all the facts, all the personal experiences, all the skills. Without the ability to hold on to information for a period of time, we would not be able to easily perform even the most simple everyday task.

Capacity

The capacity of LTM appears unlimited. Estimating an upper limit is impossible – the amount of information that LTM can hold is certainly greater than the physical size of the brain suggests. What is certain is that, under the right conditions, people can store and recall a great deal of information, far more in fact than they would ever predict they could.

Duration

Although described as our 'permanent' memory store, duration is better described as 'relatively permanent'. Whilst many researchers believe that it is normal to lose information from LTM, others have suggested that information never really disappears but just becomes inaccessible (i.e. harder to locate).

Coding

Information in LTM is mainly coded in terms of meaning. Another word for meaning is 'semantic', so this is usually referred to as *semantic coding*. This coding can be seen in the kinds of LTM errors we make. For example, if we are trying to remember the word 'barn', we are much more likely to make the mistake of saying words that are meaningfully related than are sound related – 'shed' (which sounds very different) rather than 'born' (which sounds very similar). It is very unusual to make sound-based errors like this when recalling from LTM, but it is very common to make semantic errors. Whilst semantic coding is predominant we do, however, use other codes in LTM: we recall images (visual coding), remember sounds (acoustic coding) and we remember how things feel to the touch (haptic coding).

How long is long-term memory?

There is a tradition in the United States of producing a 'yearbook' with pictures of and a statement about all the students who left school in the same year. Bahrick et al. (1975) used these yearbooks to test for what they referred to as 'very long-term memory' (VLTM). Their experiment involved three main tasks. First, participants had to remember as many names of their ex-classmates as they could (free recall). Second, some pictures were taken from their yearbook and mixed with others that the participant would not previously have seen. Participants had to identify those they recognised from school (visual recognition). Third, participants were asked to recognise the names of people from school (verbal recognition).

They found that free recall was poor, with those having left school within 15 years being only 60% accurate and only 30% accurate for those having left 48 years ago. They found that verbal and visual recognition was highest (about 90% accurate) in those who had left school less than 15 years ago. At 48 years after leaving school, accuracy had dropped off to 70% for verbal (names) and 80% for visual (faces). We can conclude from this that long-term memories are not permanent since, with the passage of time, they get worse.

Evaluation of the Multi-store model

1. Evidence from brain-damaged people seems to clearly support the idea that STM and LTM are separate stores. There is evidence of people losing their ability to use short-term memory but retaining their long-term memories from before the damage. Shallice and Warrington (1974) found that patient KF could hold no more than one or two items in STM but appeared to have no problems with his LTM. An LTM/STM distinction can also be seen in people with Wernicke–Korsakoff's syndrome (a memory disorder caused by long-term alcohol abuse). People suffering with this condition have problems with their LTM but have a reasonably intact STM. For example, they might hold perfectly normal conversations but have no memory of them a short time later.

2. The multi-store model offers a good explanation for the *serial position effect*. Murdock (1962) found that when asked to remember a list of words, participants can generally remember the first few words (this is called the *primacy effect*) and the last few (the *recency effect*) more easily than those in the middle. The multi-store model explains the primacy effect because the words learned at the start are more likely to have been rehearsed and transferred into LTM, whilst the recency effect occurs because the words are still available for recall in STM.

3. Many of the features of the three stores are supported by research. For example, Conrad (1964) supports the idea of acoustic encoding, Peterson and Peterson (1959) support the idea of a limited duration in STM, whilst Bahrick et al. (1975) support the relative permanency of LTM.

4. The assumption that there is one single short-term store underestimates the complexity of STM. Shallice and Warrington (1974) found that KF's problem with STM was restricted to verbal material, such as words and letters. His

We can recall later in the day something from earlier even though we did not rehearse it at the time. It seems that information from STM occasionally creates long-term memories without using STM.

performance in short-term memory tests for non-verbal sounds, such as doorbells and a ringing telephone, was normal. This suggests that the short-term store must have at least two different sound-based mechanisms – one for dealing with verbal and one for non-verbal sounds.

5. According to the multi-store model, rehearsal in STM is essential for information to be encoded into LTM. However, the model may be exaggerating the role of rehearsal. Shallice and Warrington (1970) showed that some brain-damaged people who have lost STM can still have memories of events that occurred after the damage, so information must be reaching LTM without passing through STM. Everyday observations of how our memory works also suggest that rehearsal is not necessary for information to become established in LTM. For example, we often seem to be able to recall information at a later date with no obvious rehearsal having taken place earlier. You might remember something you heard on the radio in the morning or a conversation you had with a friend on the bus last week. It appears that STM does not have to come between sensory memory and long-term memory for material to be retained long term.

TYPES OF LONG-TERM MEMORY

Psychologists have made a basic distinction between two different types of long-term memory. One is the kind of memory that can be explicitly recalled and verbalised – that is, memory for facts and events. For example, knowing the largest city in England or what you had for dinner yesterday. This is called *declarative memory*. The other type of long-term memory is called *procedural memory* and relates to our unconscious memory for skills (because this does not involve explicit awareness it is often referred to as non-declarative or implicit). For example, riding a bicycle is straightforward to do if you have the skill, but explaining (i.e. declaring) how to do it is very difficult.

Evidence for there being two such separate types of long-term memory comes from studies of brain-damaged patients. Following surgery for severe epilepsy, HM (Milner, 1962) had severe amnesia and was unable to learn new facts or people's names or remember events. For example, he couldn't remember his last meal or the names of researchers after many years of being tested by them. His explicit, declarative memory was impaired. However, he could learn new motor skills. For example,

he eventually became skilled at mirror drawing (copying an image from its reflection is very difficult!), even though he had no explicit memory of ever having done mirror drawing before. His ability to do things like mirror drawing shows that his procedural memory was intact. Classically conditioned responses also reflect procedural memory (Holt et al., 2012). HM was conditioned to blink to a tone by pairing a tone with a puff of air to the eye. HM had no memory whatsoever of having been conditioned (he could not form a declarative memory). He did however blink whenever the tone was played, showing that he had formed a procedural memory. This and many other examples of people who have suffered brain damage points to a clear distinction between declarative and procedural memory. Further evidence for a distinction comes from studies investigating the effects of stress on memory. Kirschbaum et al. (1996) gave participants 10 mg of cortisol (a major stress hormone). An hour later they were given a test for procedural and declarative memory. It was found that the

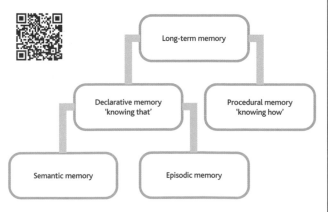

Figure 1.6: Types of long-term memory.

Tracing an image that can only be seen in reflection is really difficult! It is easy to set up – just make sure that you can only see what you are doing by looking in a mirror. HM did this task many times and became very skilled at it, but each time claimed never to have done it before.

cortisol impaired declarative memory but not procedural memory, which ties in with what we already know about the negative effects of psychological stress on memory.

Episodic and semantic memory

Psychologists have identified further subtypes of types of long-term memory within declarative memory. Tulving (1972), for example, distinguished between *semantic memory* and *episodic memory*. Semantic memory is a vast store of information containing all our facts, concepts and associations. Whilst semantic memory gives us our knowledge – for example, that the chemical symbol for water is H_2O – episodic memory is our recall of specific things we have done, such as when it was we learned the chemical symbol for water. Whilst these two types of LTM appear to be quite different, the distinction between them is not always clear. For instance, whilst you know the symbol for water is H_2O (semantic memory), you probably don't remember the event of learning this (episodic memory). At some point, the fact about H_2O was lost as an episodic memory and became a semantic memory. Quite how or why this transformation occurs is not clearly understood. This has led some researchers to suggest that the episodic and semantic distinction actually refers to two types of remembering rather than two distinct types of long-term memories. However, research has established that brain damage can impair both episodic and semantic memory together or either of them independently. HM could not remember any new personal experiences and neither could he remember any new facts. For example, he retained his memory for words he had learned prior to his operation but could not retain the meaning of new words that he encountered for the first time after his operation, such as 'biodegradable', no matter how many times he came across them or had them explained (Holt et al., 2012). This shows that HM had impaired episodic and semantic memories.

Rosenbaum et al. (2005) studied patient KC who had suffered brain damage in a motorcycle accident. His semantic memory appears normal, including his store of semantic memories about himself. Although he has no explicit memory for it, KC can learn new skills. His episodic memory, however, is severely impaired. He cannot remember details of life events, such as previous illnesses and family tragedies. Nor is he able to form new episodic memories. For example, when he is informed of events like the 9/11 attacks he responds each time with shock as though he was hearing the news for the first time.

Semantic and episodic memory are forms of declarative memory so it makes sense to mention it, but you could only be asked specifically about episodic, semantic and/or procedural memory in your exam.

THE WORKING MEMORY MODEL

The working memory model was developed by Baddeley and Hitch (1974), partly in reaction to what they saw as an underestimation of the complexity and importance of short-term memory in the multi-store model. They claimed that STM is not just a passive storehouse of information; it is more complex and active than a temporary 'waiting stage' for information before LTM. Working memory is that part of the memory system where new information is held temporarily and combined with knowledge from LTM. Roughly speaking, working memory holds all the material that you are thinking about at any one moment, and so for many psychologists working memory is our 'consciousness'.

The working memory model is multi-component. Unlike the single STM of the multi-store model, working memory has several separate, but connected, parts (or modules). This means that the components can either work together or independently. If two tasks make use of the same component they cannot be performed successfully together. If two tasks make use of different components it should be possible to perform them as well together as separately.

capacity (i.e. it can't do much at one time), it directs attention towards the most important information at the expense of other, less important information. It is also modality-free – that is, it works independently of the senses and information is not coded. It integrates the actions of the other systems so that our thinking processes appear coordinated. In effect, the other modules are 'slaves' to this one and are often called *slave systems*.

The central executive

The *central executive* controls the activity of working memory. It has a 'supervisory' function, hence the name 'executive'. It 'manages' what goes on, just as a manager in an office prioritises and decides what work should and should not be done at any one time. As it has a limited

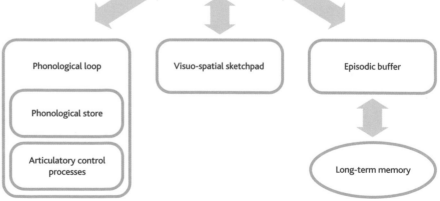

Figure 1.7: The working memory model.

The phonological loop

The *phonological loop* component is a limited capacity auditory store which rehearses sound-based information to prevent the rapid decay (loss) that would otherwise occur. It has two subdivisions, both of which hold a limited amount of information for a short amount of time. The phonological loop has two parts:

1. Phonological store: This is often referred to as the 'inner ear' and, as this suggests, it deals with the perception of sounds and, in particular, speech.

2. Articulatory loop: This is linked to speech production, often referred to as the 'inner voice'. It is a sub-verbal rehearsal system which is used to prevent the decay of verbal material by repeating it until it is used. According to Baddeley (1986), the articulatory loop is a rehearsal system of up to about two seconds in duration, which means that we can hold as much information as we can rehearse in two seconds.

The visuo-spatial sketchpad

The *visuo-spatial sketchpad* (sometimes called the 'scratchpad') is often referred to as the 'inner eye'. This component can be considered a visual and spatial version of the articulatory loop. For example, it is the mental rough paper we conjure up in our mind's eye when we do a mental sum, or it is the mental map we use when we want to find our way around. It maintains a limited amount of visual information in working memory (see the box 'The limits of the visuo-spatial sketchpad' on page 42).

Episodic buffer

The function of this limited capacity temporary store is to integrate information from the phonological loop, the visuo-spatial sketchpad and long-term memory. This component was added in order to account for the interface between working and long-term memory – we must draw information from our long-term memory store to use in working memory and, likewise, must be able to transfer information back for long-term storage. It also explains a theoretical problem with working memory of how information from different modalities is integrated – for example, if someone asks us directions we would likely use verbal and visual modalities and information extracted from our long-term store to answer.

Un, dau, tri, pedwar, pump

It is easier to recall a list of short words than a same-sized list of longer words – the word length effect. Ellis and Henelly (1980) found that Welsh–English bilinguals who rated themselves more proficient in Welsh had a better immediate recall for digit sequences presented in English than Welsh. Generally, words in Welsh take longer to say than words of the same meaning in English, so more of the shorter English words could be held by the time-limited articulatory loop. Further research has shown that the word length effect disappears with articulatory suppression, e.g. saying 'the, the, the, ...' repetitively at the same time as a verbal task. This occurs because both tasks are trying to use the same component – the articulatory loop.

	CENTRAL EXECUTIVE	PHONOLOGICAL LOOP	VISUO-SPATIAL SKETCHPAD	EPISODIC BUFFER
Coding	Modality free	Auditory	Visual	Multi-modality
Capacity	Limited	Limited	Limited	Limited

Table 1.2: Capacity and coding for components of working memory.

Evaluation of the working memory model

1. Brain imaging studies have suggested that tasks needing different parts of the working memory model use different areas of the brain, giving us evidence that there really are separate systems as suggested by the working memory model. For example, the phonological loop is related to activity in completely separate parts of the brain that deal with two different parts of our language system: *Wernicke's area*, which is involved in speech perception, and *Broca's area*, which is involved in speech production. Also, the regions of another part of the brain, the *occipital lobe*, which is involved in visual processing, become active during tasks which require the visuo-spatial sketchpad.

2. The role of the phonological loop in verbal rehearsal has been supported by studies of the word-length effect. This refers to the tendency to immediately recall short words better than long words. The explanation for this phenomenon is that the articulatory loop has a very limited time-based capacity (i.e. as much as we can rehearse in two seconds), and because small words take less time to say, we therefore remember more of them than longer words. This is supported by Baddeley et al. (1975) who found that they could make the word-length effect go away by using up the articulatory loop – that is, preventing it giving an advantage to short words. They did this by getting participants in their study to repeat simple word sounds over and over ('the the the …') whilst learning short word or long word lists. This repetition fully occupied the articulatory loop, so that no advantage was gained by a word being short.

3. Most of the research into the working memory model has focused on the 'slave' components rather than the central executive. The result is that the central executive (which, remember, governs the whole system) has relatively little experimental support. For example, the central executive is said to have limited capacity but the actual capacity has not been established. Also, it is not clear how it functions 'modality free'. Much of the terminology used to describe the central executive is vague and it may turn out that the complexity of it has been greatly underestimated.

The limits of the visuo-spatial sketchpad

Brooks (1968) asked participants to mentally visualise a letter. They were then asked questions about it (e.g. what kind of angles it had). Participants were required to respond in one of three ways:

1. Speaking out loud.

2. Tapping (one for yes, two for no).

3. Pointing to y or n on an array of y's and n's.

Brooks found that participants were more accurate and faster when they had to speak or tap their answer.

Maintaining and manipulating a mental image of a letter requires the visuo-spatial sketchpad, as does the pointing response. Because they are using the same limited capacity component in working memory, the two tasks are interfering with one another, affecting the performance of the participants required to point their responses.

EXPLANATIONS FOR FORGETTING

Forgetting suggests that a memory is in some way 'lost'. It can be lost from sensory memory, from short-term/working memory and from long-term memory. Quite *why* forgetting occurs is much debated. It could be that forgetting occurs because one memory somehow gets in the way of another, or it could be that memories are misplaced or become difficult to locate. We will consider these two possible explanations in more detail.

INTERFERENCE

Interference can be used to explain forgetting in both long-term and short-term (working) memory. In a classic early study, Jenkins and Dallenbach (1924) had participants memorise a list of 10 nonsense syllables (e.g. MUW). They were then required to recall them after a delay during which they either went about their normal daily business or they slept. They found that those participants who slept remembered the most syllables. They said this was because, in being awake, new memories were created which interfered with the memory of the syllables. The findings could not be due to memories naturally fading over time, since if this was true then there should be no difference in memory performance between the two conditions.

Whilst demonstrating interference as an explanation for forgetting, this study does not explain *why* interference *caused* forgetting. One likely explanation is *retroactive interference* (RI). This is where later memories interfere with existing ones (retro means backwards). For example, consider two groups of students, both studying French and German:

Interference theory would predict that group A would experience RI (learning German interferes with earlier learning of French) and as a result would do worse in the French test than group B, who did not experience this interference. What's more, the greater the similarity between the two memories, the more RI there will be. So, one would expect greater interference between French and German than, say, French and maths. RI can be seen in misinformation effects related to eyewitness testimony (see page 46). For instance, a police officer may supply some misinformation when interviewing someone about an earlier crime they had witnessed. Later recall is likely to be affected because this misinformation has created RI.

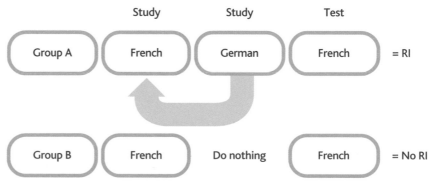

Figure 1.8: An example of retroactive interference.

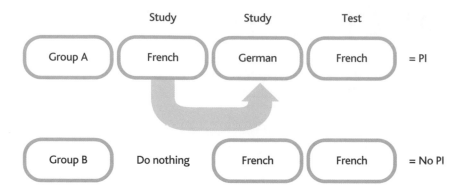

Figure 1.9: An example of proactive interference.

Another explanation is *proactive interference* (PI). The effects of PI are seen frequently in everyday life – for example, when you give someone your old mobile number rather than your new one, or after reorganising a room you look for something where it was rather than where it now is. The old information is interfering with recalling and learning new information (pro means forwards). In terms of learning French and German, group A would do worse than group B because the earlier learning of German would cause PI with the later French. Group B have avoided this by avoiding learning German before they learn French.

PI can be seen in the results of a study by Wickens (1972). He gave participants four trials, using the same procedure as Peterson and Peterson (1959) (see page 35). The nature of the to-be-remembered information was the same on the first three trials (e.g. letter trigrams). The material in the fourth trial was different (e.g. three digits). Wickens found that performance gradually declined over the first three trials, indicating a PI effect (earlier trials were interfering with later trials). Interestingly, however, performance on the fourth (different) trial returned to almost 100% – because the material was different than in prior trials there was no PI. Wickens called this phenomenon *release from PI*.

Whilst there is a great deal of research showing evidence of interference effects in memory, some psychologists believe that all interference effects are actually retrieval failures. Anderson and Neely (1996) argue that interference is caused by competition amongst *retrieval cues*. Cues are bits of information provided by the external environment or by internal states that can help the recall of information associated with them (see the next section on retrieval failure). Forgetting occurs because of difficulties distinguishing between relevant and less relevant cues whilst attempting to retrieve the memory.

The smell of Vikings

Visitors to the Jorvik Viking Centre settlement are met with distinctive smells to give a sense of what life was like in Viking York a thousand years ago. Aggleton and Waskett (1999) contacted people who had visited the museum six or seven years earlier to assess how much they remembered of their visit. One group of participants completed a questionnaire testing their memory whilst exposed to a strong smell not associated with their visit. Another group completed it without being exposed to an odour. A third group, who were given the Jorvik smells whilst completing their questionnaire, recalled 20% more details of their visit. It seems that distinctive smells can serve as retrieval cues and help us remember things.

RETRIEVAL FAILURE

Retrieval is the process of recovering information from memory. It is important that this retrieval is both accurate and fast. For this to happen memories need to be accessible, and the key to making the right memory quickly available for recall is having an effective retrieval cue. Tulving and Thomson (1973) found that retrieval of information from memory will be maximised when the cues at retrieval match cues at encoding. They called this the 'encoding specificity principle'. Subsequent research has shown that it doesn't seem to matter what type of cues are used, as long as they are present both at encoding and retrieval. Indeed, this helps to explain many everyday memory experiences. For instance, have you ever heard a song on the radio and suddenly remembered things not thought of in years associated with that song? The song reinstated the cue present at the time of encoding, giving access to that long-neglected memory.

So, it seems that whenever we encode new information we also encode something of the environmental context in which the information occurs (e.g. sounds and sights). This was demonstrated by Smith (1979). He asked participants to memorise 80 unrelated words whilst sat in a basement room. When the next day they were required to recall these words, some participants were put in the same room whilst others were put in a room which looked very different. Participants tested in the same room recalled 50% more words than those participants without these retrieval cues. This suggests that a student's memory for information depends to some extent on the room in which the learning took place. Smith also found that just *thinking* about the original study room enhanced recall – students didn't actually have to be *in* it. Clearly, cues from the room had become part of the memory for the words, showing that memory is best if cues at learning and recall are the same. This phenomenon is sometimes referred to as *context-dependent memory*.

In addition to environmental, we also encode aspects of our internal state at the time of learning, such as how you feel (e.g. mood, stress) or physiological state (e.g. the effects of alcohol or marijuana). Research has demonstrated that recall is best when the mood state at encoding matches the mood state at retrieval. Eich and Metcalfe (1989) induced either a happy or sad mood in their participants by having them listen to happy or sad music. When in the appropriate mood, participants were asked to learn a list of word pairs. Their memory for the word pairs was assessed two days later. Prior to recall, half the 'sad' participants were put in the same mood again, but the other half were made happy with happy music. Similarly, half the 'happy' participants were again made happy and the other half made sad with sad music. Eich and Metcalfe found that performance was best when the mood during recall matched the mood during learning – that is, happy when learning and happy when remembering, and sad when learning and sad when remembering. This is very consistent with findings from other context effects, offering strong support for the encoding specificity principle.

One too many

Some people claim to have a poor memory for what they got up to after a few too many drinks. This might be an example of *state-dependent memory* – they can't remember because they are not in the same physical state as when the memory was formed. Or it could be that they would rather not remember ...

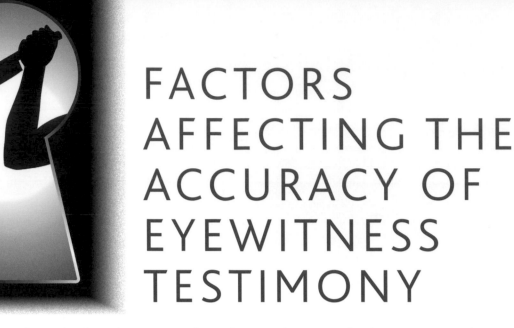

FACTORS AFFECTING THE ACCURACY OF EYEWITNESS TESTIMONY

It is crucial to the legal process that the testimony of witnesses to crimes is both accurate and reliable, otherwise there are major consequences.

According to the US-based Innocence Project, 'Eyewitness misidentification is the greatest contributing factor to wrongful convictions ... playing a role in more than 70% of convictions overturned through DNA testing nationwide.' In the United States, eyewitness misidentification is recognised as the main cause of wrongful convictions, adding up to more than all other causes combined (Gross et al., 2005).

POST-EVENT DISCUSSION, MISLEADING INFORMATION AND LEADING QUESTIONS

Human memory is not a passive system that simply records events, but is an active and dynamic one, constantly changing and updating itself. Stored material is reorganised and transformed because of new knowledge and the passage of time. Fresh information is encoded and re-encoded for storage, and memories can be modified and changed as a result. Cognitive psychologists agree that most memories are, at least in part, reconstructions of events rather than exact versions. It seems that when we remember something we do not replay in our minds a faithfully recorded version of it. Rather, we retrieve some accurate fragments and then fill in the gaps around this using common sense and logic. The reconstructive nature of memory means that information retained at the time of an event can be altered by information encountered after an event. Research consistently shows that information an eyewitness encounters after an event can become incorporated into memory and distort it. Loftus (1979) called this the 'misinformation effect'. One important source of misinformation is the kind of *misleading information* that a witness can receive as a result of post-event discussion about the event, namely through leading questions. A leading question is one which subtly prompts the listener to respond in a particular way. Loftus and Palmer (1974) demonstrated that even subtle changes in the wording of a question can produce changes in responses to a witnessed event (see box 'Is it a hit or a smash?').

Is it a hit or a smash? The influence of leading questions

Leading questions are questions that somehow, by the way that they are worded, suggest the answer that should be given. Loftus and Palmer (1974) conducted two experiments to investigate the effect of leading questions on the recall of events by eyewitnesses.

In their first experiment Loftus and Palmer investigated the effect that leading questions have on eyewitnesses' ability to recall information. They showed a series of car crash videos to 45 participants, ranging from 5 to 30 seconds in duration. Afterwards they were asked to complete a questionnaire about the video. One question was particularly important - it asked: 'How fast were the cars travelling when they .... into each other?' The blank space was filled with one of: 'smashed', 'collided', 'bumped', 'hit' or 'contacted'.

As you can see from Figure 1.10a, the word used had an effect on the estimated speed of the cars. The sentence 'How fast was the car going when they smashed into each other?' drew the fastest estimate of all. The word used in the question influenced the perception of the speed of the car.

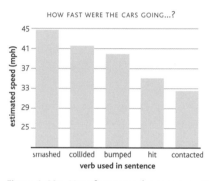

Figure 1.10a: How fast were the cars going?

Loftus and Palmer concluded that the form of a question – and just changing a single word – can markedly and systematically affect a witness's answer to that question. Not only are people poor judges of speed but their recall of an event is greatly influenced by the wording of the question. They speculated that their findings could be due to two factors:

1. A response-bias: the participant is unsure whether to say 30 mph or 40 mph and the verb used biases the estimate (i.e. 'smashed' causes a bias towards a higher estimate).

2. The leading question changes the participant's memory of the event – for example, the verb 'smashed' causes the participants to 'see' the accident as being more severe than it actually was. If this is the case, other details may be remembered that did not actually occur.

In their second experiment, 150 students were shown a short film of a multiple car crash. They were presented with a questionnaire about the accident as before, but this time using only the verbs 'hit' and 'smashed' (there were only two experimental groups). A third (control) group was not asked about the speed at all. A week after this, participants returned and were all asked another question: 'Did you see any broken glass?' There was no broken glass in the film used.

Loftus and Palmer found that participants in the 'smashed' condition were more likely to say they had seen broken glass. Although there was no broken glass in the accident, since broken glass is highly likely to occur when cars 'smash' these participants reconstructed their memory of events to include this 'fact'.

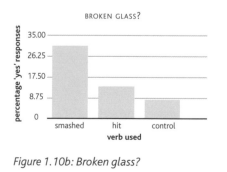

Figure 1.10b: Broken glass?

Loftus and Palmer concluded that the verb used in a leading question has an effect not only on speed estimates but also on information recalled a week later.

The influence of anxiety on eyewitness testimony

It is not surprising that people who witness a criminal event experience some degree of anxiety, maybe because it involved some threat to personal safety or maybe because they empathised with the fate of a victim. Giving evidence can also cause anxiety, not just because the witness has to recall possibly unpleasant events but also because it is a serious, pressured situation. Given that it is well-established that high levels of anxiety can impair the ability to both encode and retrieve memories, this has implications for eyewitness testimony.

Loftus et al. (1987) monitored the gaze of participants and found that, when shown a film of a crime, they tended to focus their gaze on the gun used in the robbery. When questioned later, these participants were less able to identify the robber and recalled fewer details of the crime than other participants who saw a similar film minus a gun. This phenomenon is called *weapons focus*. A number of studies support the idea that the presence of a weapon increases anxiety, focuses perception on only certain aspects of a scene and, ultimately, makes a person a less reliable eyewitness (see box 'The weapons focus'). Mitchell et al. (1998), on the other hand, suggest that, rather than being threatening and anxiety-inducing, the presence of a weapon is seen as unusual and it is this novelty that creates the weapons focus effect.

The violence of an event can also be a cause of anxiety. Loftus and Burns (1982) made participants in their study watch a film of a crime. Some participants, however, saw a version with an extremely violent scene (a young boy being shot in the face). When questioned about the events in the film, those participants who saw the non-violent version of the film recalled much more detail of the crime than those who witnessed the more violent crime. It seems that the shock of the event disrupted storage of other details, both before and after the violent scene.

The weapons focus

Peters (1988) conducted a study in a health clinic where people were receiving inoculations (an anxiety-causing event). The experience of participants was manipulated so that they met a nurse (who gave the injection) and a researcher for brief but equal amounts of time. One week later the participants were asked to identify the nurse and the researcher from a selection of photographs. It was found that the researcher was more readily recognised than the nurse. Whilst it was suggested by Peters that the anxiety of the injection directly affected the accuracy of memory, it has also been suggested that the attention of the eyewitness was drawn away from the nurse and other details of the situation by the syringe that she was holding. This indicates that witnesses to a crime might be distracted by specific aspects of a scene, in this case something that could be interpreted as a weapon.

It may be, however, that many of these findings are, at least to some extent, the result of the way in which the data were collected. These were, after all, artificial experimental situations and not adrenaline-fuelled natural conditions. Naturalistic studies have provided some contradictory evidence. For example, Yuille and Cutshall (1986) interviewed 13 witnesses to a real-life shooting incident in which someone had been killed. Despite the anxiety which the experience must have caused, their accuracy of recall did not seem to be significantly affected. The witnesses appeared to be resistant to leading questions, they stuck to their original impressions of the event and there was little evidence of memory reconstruction.

 You won't be asked a direct question on reconstructive memory, but it is important to know something about the nature of long-term memory in order to really understand EWT research.

Reconstructive memory

According to Loftus (2003), memories are the sum of what (people) have thought, what they have been told, what they believe. Cognitive psychologists have long known that memory, at least in significant part, is a reconstruction of events. When we remember something, say an event from several years ago, we do not replay in our minds a faithfully recorded version of it. We encode fragments of an experience – a sight, a sound, a feeling. When we access a memory we may retrieve some accurate fragments but these have to be put back together again (reconstructed) – the gaps between these fragments filled using expectations, common sense and logic. At times, the pieces we need to reconstruct the memory may be missing or inaccurate, and the recollection becomes a reflection of what we expect rather than how things really were. This process occurs automatically, without our awareness, and this makes us feel as though the memory is accurate and true even though they are false. Such 'memories' are often related with great confidence and conviction.

Researchers have known for some time that it is possible to implant entire false memories into the minds of people. One study found that having people simply *imagine* a past childhood event increased the likelihood of them later on believing that it had actually happened. Garry et al. (1996) called this *imagination inflation*. They suggest that this may be due to increased *familiarity* – an event, even an imagined one, is more familiar when it is revisited and this feeling of familiarity is mistaken for evidence that it actually occurred. Another possibility is *source confusion*. Information of an imagined event is stored in memory, and at retrieval the content might be remembered but not the source (i.e. that it is an imagined event).

Clearly, the reconstructive nature of memory suggests that it is possible to implant entirely false memories (called *pseudomemories*). Wade et al. (2002) showed participants photographs from their own childhood, one of which had been doctored to make it look as though they had taken a balloon ride. Fifty percent of the sample later reported a childhood memory of having taken a balloon ride, even though they had never been in a balloon. Loftus (2003) reported studies where researchers worked with the families of 24 participants to convince them that they had been lost in a shopping mall at the age of 5 or 6. Results showed that as many as 25% of participants not only 'remembered' this event but also added their own details and embellishment to the 'memory'. Further research shows that even more unusual memories such as near drowning, wild animal attacks and demonic possession have all been successfully implanted into the memories of participants.

Understanding the nature of false memory is very important because of its relevance to everyday life. The number of convictions based on eyewitness testimony but proven wrong by DNA evidence is growing. Loftus and Ketcham (1994) describe the case of tragic case of George Franklin, whose daughter claimed that she had seen her father murder her best friend when she was 8 years old – she had apparently repressed this memory for 20 years. Even though there was no other credible evidence the jury at Franklin's trial found him guilty. He served five years in prison before the decision was overturned on appeal.

Did you really take that balloon ride as a child?

IMPROVING THE ACCURACY OF EYEWITNESS TESTIMONY

It is essential in criminal investigations that accurate information is gathered. Kebbell and Milne (1998) reported that 36% of 159 UK police officers surveyed believe that eyewitnesses are 'always' or 'almost always' the most important source of leads in an investigation. However, the same survey revealed that 53% of officers believe that they 'never' or 'rarely' got as much information from witnesses as they wanted. One method developed in recent years to improve the amount of accurate recall from witnesses is the cognitive interview.

The cognitive interview

The *cognitive interview* was developed using theory and research in psychology. It recognises the *encoding specificity principle* that memory is best when cues at retrieval match those that existed during encoding. Because working memory has a limited capacity, questions are open ended with minimal disruption and distraction. It also acknowledges that memories can be retrieved in more than one way, so witnesses are encouraged to consider events from different points of view. It also avoids misinformation effects which could be caused by the nature of the questioning. Cognitive interviews have no standardised questions, they are not time limited (witnesses must feel confident that they have time to think, talk and repeat themselves as they need) and the interviewer remains silent during witness recall (i.e. the interviewee is not interrupted). Whilst the interviewer will be recording proceedings and may be taking notes, clarification and elaboration is sought only after recall has seemingly ended. Even then, this must be phrased in open-ended and non-leading ways. The interview has four distinct components which are summarised in the box 'The components of the cognitive interview'.

The components of the cognitive interview

1. Reinstate the context: The interviewee needs to be returned, in their mind, to the context in which the event occurred. If something resembling the original mood and environment can be conjured in the imagination of the interviewee, then cues might be present that will help recall. An interviewer might do this by asking the interviewer to think back to before, during and after the event, and recall their environment (where they were, what they were doing) and their mood (how they were feeling – frightened, bored, cold, hot, etc.).

2. Change sequence: Witnesses do not have to recall events in chronological order. For example, a witness might be asked to begin their witness account at any point in events, or to repeat their account but this time reversing the order of events. This ensures that the witness is not skipping details which might be important and may help to fill in any gaps existing in a story told chronologically.

3. Change perspective: The interviewee is asked to recall events from another perspective. They might be asked to think what another observer would recall of the event, or asked to consider the event from another point of view. It is important, however, that the witness is encouraged to report what they actually know and not to be overly imaginative or inventive, so as to avoid inaccurate material being inserted into the account.

4. Report everything: Regardless of how fragmented or irrelevant thoughts might seem, eyewitnesses are encouraged to report everything. Whilst it is likely that this unrestrained recall will produce a lot of irrelevant material, it is also likely to throw up details which might otherwise be inadvertently mentally 'edited out'.

Evaluation of the cognitive interview

1. According to Geiselman et al. (1985), the cognitive interview is a more effective method of gathering information from eyewitnesses than other methods that might be used. They found that the cognitive interview produced an average of 41.1 correct statements from eyewitnesses, compared to 29.4 using a standard police interview and 38.0 correct statements using hypnosis.

2. The cognitive interview can be used with relatively little training. Compared to a no-training control group, Geiselman et al. (1986) found that 35% more correct information could be obtained with relatively brief guidance on cognitive interview procedures given to the interviewer. However, to be really effective the quality of training in cognitive interviewing is crucial. Stein and Memon (2006) introduced the cognitive interview to Brazil, a developing country where witnesses are likely to have very low income and education. The interviewers were trained in cognitive interview techniques for three days and practised the techniques over a three month period. Compared to standard interview procedures, it was found that the cognitive interview produced more recall with at least as good accuracy. It seems that, even in quite challenging environments, the cognitive interview is a robust enough technique to show benefits over other methods in gaining reliable eyewitness evidence.

3. An enhanced version has been developed which, amongst other things, encourages the interviewer to use language comfortable to the interviewee and to make greater use of mental imagery. Fisher et al. (1987) found that this enhanced cognitive interview was more effective, producing more correct eyewitness statements than the original cognitive interview (57.5% compared to 39.6%). This has been replicated in naturalistic settings. Fisher et al. (1990) trained Miami police officers to use the enhanced cognitive interview and found that 46% more information was obtained, with over 90% of this material proving to be accurate.

4. Geiselman and Fisher (1997) suggest that the cognitive interview is most effective when the interview follows shortly after the event. It becomes less effective as the passage of time between event and recall increases, so to achieve the most benefit from cognitive interviewing, the eyewitnesses should be interviewed as soon as possible after the event.

Hypnosis – an alternative to the cognitive interview?

Whilst many countries have imposed a ban on witness testimony obtained under hypnosis, it is still occasionally used to help witnesses retrieve details of events. Hypnosis is basically a relaxed state during which a participant becomes highly responsive to the suggestions of the hypnotist. Despite the widely held belief that hypnosis improves memory and greater confidence in juries for information gained under hypnosis, studies have generally found no advantage to using hypnosis. Indeed, the highly suggestible state increases the risk of the hypnotist influencing memory. There is also the tendency for witnesses to have strong confidence in what they recall under hypnosis, even when this includes errors. It has been argued that any benefit from hypnosis is probably due to the relaxed and distraction-free state that occurs during hypnosis. These can be replicated without recourse to hypnosis by using skilled interviewers able to build rapport with witnesses in a quiet, calm environment.

KEY TERMS

Capacity How much information memory can hold. This varies according to the type of memory – for example, the size of *short-term memory* is significantly smaller than that of *long-term memory*.

Central executive The part of the working memory model that controls or 'supervises' activity.

Coding A term used to describe changing information in memory into a form usable to different kinds of memory. Also known as encoding.

Cognitive interview A technique employed by the police to help a witness recall witnessed events.

Encoding specificity principle The retrieval of information from memory will be maximised when the cues at retrieval match cues at encoding.

Episodic buffer A limited *capacity* temporary store which integrates information from the *phonological loop*, the *visuo-spatial sketchpad* and *long-term memory*.

Episodic memory Our memory of episodes in our lives – for instance, the first time we swam in the sea.

Long-term memory (LTM) A relatively permanent store of information.

Misleading information Information that encourages witnesses to recall events in ways in which they did not happen – for example, a leading question.

Phonological loop Part of the working memory model. A temporary auditory store containing a phonological store (the 'inner ear') and an articulator loop (the 'inner voice').

Proactive interference An explanation for forgetting in which earlier learned information interferes with the recall of later information (pro means forwards).

Procedural memory Our memory of how to do things – for example, how to make a cup of tea.

Reconstructive memory Because we don't store exact records of events in memory, when we recall information it is reconstructed based on fragments of memory plus general knowledge, common sense and assumption. Reconstructed memories therefore might not resemble the actual event.

Retrieval cue Something that helps you retrieve information from memory – for instance, a photograph of a castle may help you recall a holiday you once spent where you visited the castle in the picture.

Retroactive interference An explanation for forgetting in which later memories interfere with existing memories (retro means backwards).

Semantic memory Our general knowledge memory – for instance, whether a dog is a mammal.

Sensory memory A temporary store for sensory information which contains a register for each sense.

Sensory register A brief memory store for sensory information – for example, visual, auditory, tactile.

Short-term memory (STM) Part of the multi-store model of memory. Short duration of between five and nine items or chunks.

Visuo-spatial sketchpad Part of the working memory model. A temporary store for visual and spatial information.

PAGE 33

According to the multi-store model, memory has different stores.

Explain the difference between short-term memory and long-term memory in terms of capacity and duration. Refer to research in your answer. *(6 marks)*

The question is clearly testing your knowledge of the multi-store model. It is also being very specific, which is the tricky bit. You must know about capacity and duration in STM and LTM. Be clear how they both differ. You are only required to refer to research – it doesn't say you have to do it for both capacity and duration. Think in terms of two 3 mark questions and you will realise that not a great deal of detail is required.

PAGE 39

Distinguish between episodic and semantic long-term memory. *(3 marks)*

This question does not require you to explain what the two types of memory are, but to say how they are different. Just describing them both will not satisfy the demands of the question. Think about it and plan your answer – it's a short but tricky question, worth spending a little time pondering over.

PAGE 40

Describe and evaluate the working memory model. *(12 marks)*

The best way to remember the models of memory is to learn the diagrams. You can draw the working memory model as part of your answer. For 6 marks you don't have to write a great deal, but for top marks it has to be accurate. You will need two or three evaluative points for the other 6 marks. How much detail you give will depend on how many you've chosen – three will need less detail than two.

PAGE 43

Explain what is meant by retroactive interference. Use an example of retroactive interference in your answer. *(5 marks)*

This question is really testing your understanding. You can't just regurgitate a learned fact here – you have to know something about retroactive interference to be able to think up an example. Fortunately, this book has given you an example – all you have to do is avoid confusing it with proactive interference!

PAGE 46

Outline *and* evaluate research into the effects of leading questions on the accuracy of eyewitness testimony. *(8 marks)*

Read questions twice before you begin to answer – make sure you don't miss the key words. Research is needed here on leading questions, and the obvious choice is Loftus and Palmer. Say what they did and what they found (very briefly!), plus a couple of evaluative points (e.g. other research that supports it and/or something about the methodology).

PAGE 48

It seemed like another day working at the petrol station for Kevin. That is, until someone pulled a gun and robbed his till. As Kevin told the police officer, he was terrified and thought he was going to die.

What has research into eyewitness testimony told us about the possible effects of this experience on Kevin's memory for events? *(5 marks)*

Sometimes it is clear what we have to say in an answer; at other times we have a range of options. This is one of those latter questions! Doing the obvious is nearly always the right thing to do, so you'll probably choose either to write about anxiety caused by the violence or the weapons focus, or maybe even a bit of both. This is an application question so make sure your answer relates explicitly to the question.

Attachment

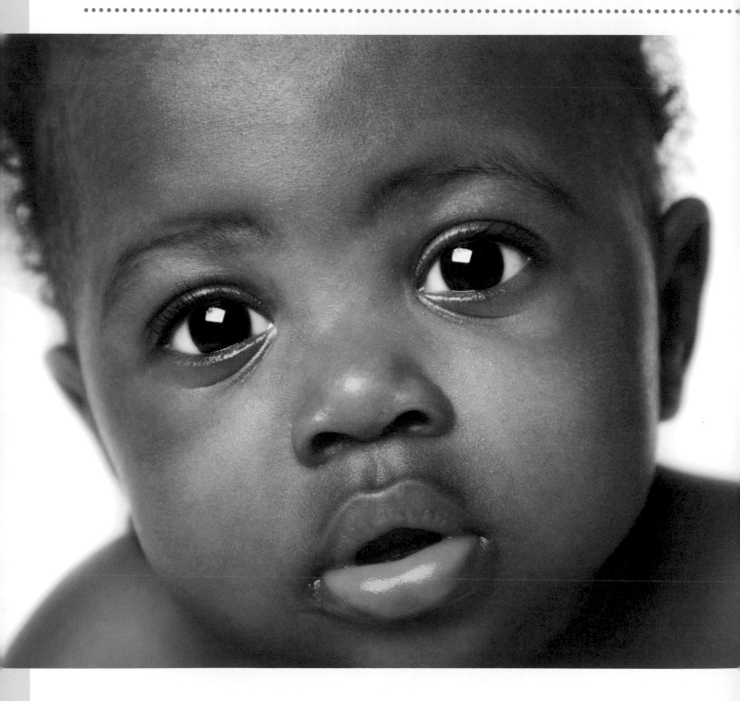

WHAT YOU NEED TO KNOW ☑

Caregiver–infant interactions in humans ❏

Reciprocity and interactional synchrony ❏

Stages of attachment identified by Schaffer ❏

Multiple attachments ❏

The role of the father ❏

Animal studies of attachment ❏

Lorenz ❏

Harlow ❏

Explanations of attachment ❏

Bowlby's monotropic theory: ❏

    The critical period ❏

    The internal working model ❏

Learning theory ❏

Ainsworth's Strange Situation ❏

Types of attachment ❏

Secure ❏

Insecure-avoidant ❏

Insecure-resistant ❏

Cultural variations in attachment ❏

Van Ijzendoorn's study ❏

Bowlby's theory of maternal deprivation ❏

The effects of institutionalisation ❏

Romanian orphan studies ❏

The influence of early attachment on childhood and adult relationships ❏

The role of an internal working model ❏

Attachment

One of the most important events occurring during the first year of life is the development of attachments. An attachment is an emotional connection or bond between the child and the principal caregiver, characterised by mutual affection, frequent interaction, a desire for proximity (to be close) and selectivity (the child wants to be with the caregiver rather than anyone else). Whilst the caregiver is usually the mother, attachments can also form with the father or some other person. Care for the physical needs of the child is obviously important (e.g. food, comfort, security) but attachments involve more than this. They are important in the emotional and social growth of the child. Children who receive consistent and responsive caregiving have been found to develop an attachment that is suggested to have advantages for intellectual, social and emotional development throughout childhood, early adolescence and even into adulthood.

CAREGIVER–INFANT INTERACTIONS

To the untrained eye, the behaviour of new-born babies seems almost entirely motivated by the avoidance of things that cause discomfort, such as hunger and being physically uncomfortable. They appear helpless and only able to communicate by crying. However, psychologists have discovered that not only is the behaviour of infants very complex but they are also far more capable than they at first appear. Vocalising is just one of a number of behaviours, including body orientation, movement and facial expression, which infants use in the turn-taking reciprocal exchanges with caregivers, known as interactional synchrony.

RECIPROCITY AND INTERACTIONAL SYNCHRONY

According to Harrist and Waugh (2002), *interactional synchrony* refers to a type of interaction that is 'mutually regulated, reciprocal and harmonious'. They suggest that interactional synchrony consists of three components:

1. Maintained engagement: Interactions take place over a prolonged period of time during which the infant and caregiver focus their attention on each other.

2. Temporal coordination: Interactions have a rhythm or pace. This 'timing' has been seen in body orientation, body movement, facial expression and vocal tone, pitch and rhythm. The fact that these interactions are coordinated suggests that they are more akin to a dance than simple mimicry.

3. Contingency: When two things are said to be 'contingent', when something happens in one, something also tends to happen in the other. Research shows that young infants respond positively to contingency and negatively when contingency rules are broken (i.e. when the caregiver doesn't respond as expected, such as keeping a 'still face'). Contingency could therefore be seen as a motivator for infants to engage in synchronous interactions.

For Harrist and Waugh (2002), the origins of these components of interactional synchrony lie in what they call 'caregiver attunement'. This refers to 'the process of reading or sensing another's state and adjusting behavior accordingly'. Brazelton (1984) believes that parents are biologically prepared to attune to their infants. Evidence for this comes from the very brief time it takes for a caregiver to respond appropriately to an infant during a phase of interactional synchrony – this is typically less than half a second. Moreover, interactions vary in intensity, timing and form, and can occur in different sensory modalities (e.g. sight, sound, touch). These interactions are far too fast and complex to be a result of conscious effort. According to Tronick and Cohn (1989), interactional synchrony accounts for about 30% of all face-to-face interactions between caregivers and infants. The other 70% of the time the interactions are *asynchronous*. During asynchrony infants can be observed putting considerable effort into drawing the caregiver back into synchrony.

From a very young age infants show an ability to imitate caregivers. In a famous study by Meltzoff and Moore (1977), babies between 12 and 21 days old were filmed as they watched an experimenter pull a range of facial expressions (e.g. tongue out, open mouth, kiss-lips). Analysis of the film showed that babies tended to match their faces to the experimenter. Whilst it is a highly complex cognitive task for the infant, this mimicry is not interactional synchrony; rather, it is likely to be an early precursor to it. For Harrist and Waugh (2002), the behaviours of infant and caregiver are complementary rather than one behaviour being an imitation of another. They point out that in interactional synchrony there is infant–caregiver 'co-action' – for example, when an adult vocalises in ever more excited tones, the infants can be seen to increasingly kick and flail.

According to Schaffer (1996), two essential characteristics of interactional synchrony are *reciprocity* and *intentionality*. Reciprocity refers to an understanding that interaction depends on the coordinated activities of both parties. It can clearly be seen by 12 months, where infants have become active participants in interactions. Before 6 months they tend to be more passive – that is, they respond to caregivers (e.g. by sticking out their tongue when a caregiver does). Intentionality refers to the ability to plan behaviour and anticipate consequences. Whilst infants communicate from birth, it is not until later that these behaviours become planned and deliberate. Reciprocity and intentionality can both be observed from about 6 months of age, at about the same time that attachments to specific individuals emerge.

The still face paradigm

That infants are active participants in interactional synchrony is demonstrated in studies using the still face paradigm (SFP), developed by Tronick et al. (1975). The SFP involves observing infants during three episodes:

1. Normal episode: Normal adult–infant interaction is observed in order to provide a baseline measure.

2. Still face episode: Interaction is interrupted by the adult becoming unresponsive and adopting a neutral expression.

3. Reunion episode: The adult resumes normal interaction.

One example of such a study is by Gusella et al. (1988). They found that 6-month-old infants showed negative reactions to the still face, such as increased grimacing, decreased smiling and gazing, and even distress. Similar responses were observed when the interaction occurred over closed-circuit television, so the still face clearly has a powerful effect on a child.

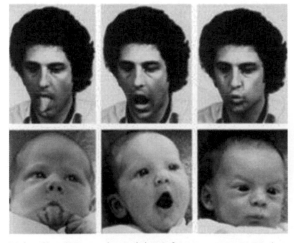

Meltzoff and Moore showed that infants as young as 12 days old actively mimic caregivers.

Reciprocity, synchrony and sensitivity

Most infants form attachments, usually to more than one person. However, who the child forms attachments with, and the strength and quality of those attachments, depends to some extent on the social interactions that take place between the child and its caregivers.

These social exchanges have been described in many different ways, using a great deal of potentially confusing terminology. Isabella et al. (1989) referred to 'interactional synchrony'. Harrist et al. (1994) used the term 'dyadic synchrony' to describe the same process. Joy-Bryant (1991) preferred the term 'reciprocal matching behaviour', whilst Belsky et al. (1984) called it simply 'reciprocity'.

Whilst there are subtle differences in how these terms are used, they all refer to the same type of infant–caregiver relationship that is a core component of what Schaffer and Emerson (1964) referred to as 'sensitive responsiveness' and Ainsworth et al. (1978) call 'maternal sensitivity'.

Schaffer (1996) further points out that each individual adult–child pair develops their own distinct *interactive style*. He identified three key influences on these interactive styles:

1. Culture: The ways that adults interact with their infants is influenced by the way of life infants are being prepared for. An example of this can be seen in the Gusii people of Kenya where mothers rarely interact playfully with their babies. For instance, the common response to a gaze from the baby is to look away in order to calm the infant, rather than treat it as an invitation to play which escalates excitement. The goal of the Gusii mother is to produce a calm and manageable infant who can be looked after by older children, so releasing her for work and further child-bearing (Kermoian and Leiderman, 1986).

2. Adult personality: Infants respond to the caregiving they receive, so that interactional style reflects the characteristics of each individual adult with whom they interact. There are many ways in which adults differ in their interactions with infants, including responsiveness, nerviness, playfulness and emotional expressiveness. An infant can thus be seen to respond differently to its various adult caregivers.

3. Child characteristics: Infants are individuals and have their own characteristics which influence how others respond to them. This includes various aspects of temperament – for example, adults will respond differently to a quiet infant that rarely seeks attention than one that is active and constantly seeking stimulation.

STAGES OF ATTACHMENT IDENTIFIED BY SCHAFFER

The emotional bond between infant and caregiver is one that develops and changes over time. Bowlby (1958) maintained that attachments emerge in a fixed sequence (see page 66). Subsequent research has supported this idea of attachment development.

A classic study into how early attachments change over time was conducted by Schaffer and Emerson (1964). They studied 60 infants, carrying out observations in the children's homes every four weeks between the ages of 12 and 18 months of age. Separation anxiety (the distress shown upon separation from the caregiver) and stranger anxiety (infant reactions to the nearness of a stranger) were measured. In addition, mothers were interviewed about the children and their care and asked to keep diaries.

Schaffer and Emerson found that the first specific attachments formed between 6 and 8 months. Stranger fear appeared about a month later, as did the period of peak attachment behaviour. About a third of the infants formed attachments to more than one person. Feeding was not the most critical factor in the formation of attachment: it was noted that infants with the strongest attachments had carers who were more responsive to their signals and needs. Schaffer and Emerson called this 'sensitive responsiveness'. The sequence of development can be seen in Table 1.3.

Subsequent research has been generally supportive of Schaffer and Emerson's ground-breaking research, although there appear to be cultural variations in the timing of events and the appearance of certain attachment behaviours. Schaffer and Emerson also underestimated the abilities of infants to distinguish their mother from other individuals. A significant amount of research has emerged to show that babies less than a day old show a preference for the sound of their mother's voice (DeCasper and Spence, 1986) and the sight of their mother's face (Bushnell et al., 1989). It has also been suggested that the development of attachment is more closely related to physical development than chronological age. For example, increased mobility and coordination allows an infant to more effectively protest at separation, seek contact with the caregiver and demonstrate preferences for other people.

STAGE	DESCRIPTION
Asocial stage (0 to 6 weeks)	Up until 6 weeks infants respond to people and objects in similar ways. They show no preference for particular individuals. Towards the end of this phase they begin to show a clear preference for people and the ability to discriminate between them.
Indiscriminate attachments (6 weeks to 6 months)	Infants are sociable and can tell people apart. They prefer human company, and as they show no fear of strangers they are happy to receive attention and comfort from anyone.
Specific attachments (7 months to 11 months)	A strong attachment to one figure (the primary caregiver) emerges. They protest when parted from this person (separation anxiety) and show distress in the presence of strangers (stranger fear).
Multiple attachments (11 months onwards)	Soon after the primary attachment, multiple attachments emerge. Attachments are shown towards people other than the primary caregiver, such as the father, grandparents, siblings and child-minders.

Table 1.3: The development of attachment according to Schaffer and Emerson (1964).

MULTIPLE ATTACHMENTS

According to John Bowlby, infants have an inbuilt bias to form an attachment to one caregiver (usually the mother). Bowlby called this *monotropy*. Schaffer and Emerson's findings directly challenged this idea. They found that infants became attached to other people soon after the primary attachment was formed at about 7 months. By 18 months, a little over 10% of infants were attached to one person and a third had five or more attachments. Whilst fathers were rarely the primary attachment figure, they were the joint first attachment figure for nearly a third of infants. The primary attachment figure is the person an infant turns to when the attachment bond is tested (e.g. when there is separation or a stranger appears). Additional (secondary) attachments can occur but appear less important to the infant. A secondary attachment figure is used when a primary attachment figure is not available. For example, Farran and Ramey (1977) placed infants in a mildly threatening situation (an approaching stranger). They found that infants chose to seek comfort from the mother (primary attachment figure) rather than a familiar day-care worker (secondary attachment figure).

Research indicates that the strength of the primary attachment in the first two years is not affected by having multiple attachment figures. Cassidy (1999) suggests that infants form an *attachment hierarchy*. Whilst most infants place the mother at the top of the hierarchy, not all infants do and some favour the father or other carer as a primary attachment figure. In the absence of the preferred primary attachment figure, it seems that infants will seek out the individuals in this hierarchy best suited to the current need or mood. Factors which influence the position of caregivers on the hierarchy include the amount and quality of time spent together and the intensity of the caregiver's emotional investment in the infant.

Multiple caretaking across cultures

There are many examples of caregiving environments that deviate from the Western middle class ideal. For example, Meehan (2005) described the cooperative child-rearing practices amongst the Aka people living in the Congo Basin rainforest. Aka infants interact with approximately 20 caregivers on a daily basis, and whilst the mother is the primary caregiver for the first year, her role significantly reduces after this period. Observations of child-rearing practices amongst the Nso people of Cameroon raise questions about whether the mother necessarily has a special position amongst caregivers. By blowing in their infants' faces, the mothers force them to attend to other people, thus preventing infants from forming special bonds with them and making her one amongst many caregivers (Keller and Otto, 2011). As Keller (2013) points out, monotropy is the exception rather than the norm: '[monotropy] … can only be adaptive in contexts where material and social resources are plentiful so that families can afford the caregiver–child exclusivity without neglecting other tasks. It is obvious that this cannot apply to all humans' (p. 180).

Across all human cultures, mothers are the exclusive caregiver of their infants in only 3% of societies and the main caregiver in only 60% (Weisner and Gallimore, 1977). Indeed, from an evolutionary point of view, having lots of caregivers makes more sense in terms of infant survival and maximising the child-bearing opportunities for the mother. Indeed, Hrdy (1999) has argued that 'humankind would not have survived if solely mothers had been infants' caretakers'.

THE ROLE OF THE FATHER

Research shows that although fathers generally spend less time with infants than mothers, they are as caring as mothers and interact with infants in similar ways. Deater-Deckard et al. (1994) suggest that whilst there tends to be lower male involvement in child-rearing, this does not mean fathers are less caring. They showed that fathers were just as anxious as mothers about being separated from their infants when leaving them in day-care. Lewis and Lamb (2003) found no difference in the attentiveness and sensitivity of mothers and fathers towards their infants. Fathers responded to infant needs as effectively as mothers, and this included such things as feeding and soothing, adjusting speech during interaction and generally adapting to individual temperaments of children. Differences do emerge as infants grow older, with fathers becoming more boisterous in play and engaging in more games than mothers. Evidence consistently points to fathers being as competent as mothers in the care of a child. It is also the case that fathers and mothers show basically the same behaviours towards the child necessary for *secure attachment* – that is, sensitive responsiveness. Using the *Strange Situation*, Kotelchuck (1976) found that infants do indeed form attachments to fathers. Infants between 12 and 21 months showed separation anxiety at the absence of the father and sought contact at reunion. Infants also used the father as a secure base for exploration. These are all signs of a secure attachment, and a great deal of subsequent research supports this.

There is no sound evidence, biological or otherwise, that mothers are the 'natural' caregivers for children. This is not even supported by what we know of non-human animals where there are many examples of offspring being co-raised or even solely raised by males. Whilst women play the biggest role in child-rearing in most human societies, the fact that this is not a universal phenomenon suggests that sole maternal care is not an inevitability. Schaffer (1983) suggests that women play a bigger role in child-rearing because of social convention rather than biology. Hauari and Hollingworth (2009) point to powerful gender stereotypes that dictate social differences in roles between mothers and fathers. The Industrial Revolution changed the way that families were organised so that the roles became more differentiated, with fathers becoming 'breadwinners'. Full-time employment meant that fathers simply had less time and opportunity to engage with children. Whilst these social norms persist, they are changing. A 2011 report by the Organisation for Economic Cooperation and Development (OECD) based on data from 21 industrialised nations found that fathers, on average, spent 63 minutes a day looking after children – only 18 minutes less than mothers. It has been suggested that these differences may be due in part to the attitudes of the mothers themselves: they resist attempts by the father to assist in caregiving due to their strongly socialised role of caregiver.

ANIMAL STUDIES OF ATTACHMENT

The evolutionary approach sees humans as complex animals, so human behaviour is governed by the same principles of evolution that apply to other animal species. This means that findings from animal research might offer useful insights into the origins of some aspects of human behaviour. Studying animals in the wild and in captivity might deepen our understanding and help to develop theories and ideas of how attachments are developed and maintained.

THE WORK OF KONRAD LORENZ

Biologist Konrad Lorenz (1935) noted that the young of *precocial species* (i.e. animals that are mobile soon after birth) had a need to quickly recognise and follow a caregiver if they were to survive. For example, ducklings are mobile and able to feed themselves soon after hatching. This is not enough, however, and in order to help them survive a very vulnerable time in life they will need to stay close to an adult. The 'parent' will provide some direct protection from predators and the elements, and the ducklings will learn many skills necessary for later life, such as evading predators and interacting with other members of its species. An essential requirement for a duckling therefore is the ability, very early on in life, to recognise which particular object in its environment is its caregiver. This ability to develop this recognition is innate (inborn) and is called *imprinting*. As well as increasing the chances of the individual surviving, imprinting is important for the survival of the species. It enables animals to recognise members of their own species and to learn species-specific behaviours (e.g. how to be a duck). This ensures that when it comes to mating, sexual behaviour is directed towards other animals of the same species.

His studies indicated that young animals have a strong drive to imprint within the first 36 hours. He demonstrated this by presenting newly hatched goslings various objects for differing periods of time, and found that the goslings had a tendency to imprint on the first large moving object that they were allowed to follow for more than ten minutes. According to Lorenz, the effects of this critical period are irreversible – with appropriate imprinting the young would recognise and follow the parent, but outside of this critical period imprinting would not happen. If the young did not properly imprint, then they would be unlikely to survive for long by themselves without an adult to guide and protect them. Inappropriate imprinting would also have long-term consequences, even in circumstances where survival was not at risk. For example, Lorenz claimed that imprinting determines the choice of sexual partner in adulthood – he found that goslings which had imprinted on him showed a preference for humans over other geese when it came time to mate!

Evaluation of Lorenz's theory of imprinting

1. There is support for the idea that imprinting has a long-term persistent effect. Kendrick et al. (2001) demonstrated that if sheep and goats are cross-fostered at birth many of their behaviours grow to resemble those of their foster species. For example, if male goats are fostered (and thus imprinted) to sheep they show a strong preference later on for socialising and mating with sheep, even when kept in a mixed goat/sheep flock. However, their study also showed that the effects of imprinting can be different for males and females of a species. Males kept in mixed flocks for three years persisted with their preference, but females kept in mixed flocks tended to revert within a couple of years to preferring their own species. These sex differences are most evident in sexually dimorphic species (where male and females look different), where only male mating preference is influenced by the appearance of the 'mother'.

2. Research has shown that imprinting can occur outside of the critical period. For example, Sluckin (1965) showed that if young birds are hatched and reared in isolation, so that they are not exposed to a moving object, then the normal critical period can be extended. It seems that the critical period may not be so critical after all. Because of this, many researchers prefer to use the term 'sensitive period' to refer to a time when an animal will more readily imprint.

3. The process of imprinting is vulnerable to environmental factors. For example, Hess (1961) demonstrated that imprinting is affected by stress. He placed ducklings on a circular rotating runway and put in front of them, just out of reach, a dummy 'mother' duck so that the ducklings had to run to follow it. Hess made life difficult for some ducklings by placing obstacles on the runway which they had to clamber over to keep up with the 'mother'. He found that the ducklings who had to struggle hardest to follow the dummy mother developed the strongest bond with it. Likewise, he found imprinting strengthened in ducklings who experienced mild electric shocks whilst following the dummy mother.

4. Imprinting does not depend on visual stimulation only. Hess (1972) found that he could more readily make ducklings imprint on him by saying the words to newly hatched birds that he had been saying to them when they were still in the egg. It seems that the ducklings were more prone to attach to the object making the sound it had heard whilst in the shell. This reflects what happens in nature – chicks 'cheep' in the egg as hatching time approaches and parents make their own noises in return. This makes it more likely that young will imprint on the right object – one that is moving and makes the right sound.

THE WORK OF HARRY HARLOW

The importance of early attachment can be seen in studies of monkeys reared in isolation. Harlow and Harlow (1962) removed infant monkeys from their mothers soon after birth and kept them in cages with two artificial substitute 'mothers', one bare wire and the other cloth-covered. Given a choice between a bare wire mesh 'mother' with milk and a cloth covered one without, infant monkeys preferred to spend all their time clinging to the cuddly 'mother', only going to the wire one to feed. For infant monkeys, it seems that tactile comfort is more important than the comfort provided by food. Whilst the physical health of the monkeys was not obviously affected by their experience, they did show long-term social and emotional problems. The monkeys developed into timid, fearful adults with poor social skills, and they were clumsy and often unsuccessful during mating. They also seemed to lack normal monkey parenting skills, with females showing poor nurturing skills and often behaving very cruelly towards their offspring. Harlow concluded that these behaviours were due to the monkeys having been deprived of maternal care when they were young, which he called 'maternal deprivation'.

However, further studies by Harlow suggested that it wasn't necessarily maternal deprivation that the monkeys were suffering from but social deprivation (being deprived of the company of other members of the same species). He showed that monkeys given only 20 minutes a day to play with other monkeys developed into normal adults, unlike those raised in isolation and not given this opportunity to interact. It seems that monkeys need physical contact with a live, affectionate caregiver during a critical period in infancy (the first six months) in order to develop normal social and emotional skills, and that some contact with other monkeys helps to limit the negative effects of this deprivation.

If they did not attach during this period then there would be permanent social and emotional damage to the monkey.

Evaluation of Harlow's studies

1. It has been suggested that Harlow's monkeys did not really suffer maternal deprivation. Deprivation means that something you once had has been taken away. This is not what happened to the Harlow monkeys – they had absolutely no maternal care so strictly speaking experienced *privation* (never having had something) rather than deprivation (having something taken away).

2. The idea that contact comfort is important in attachment has been supported in some studies with humans. For example, Klaus and Kennell (1976) found that mothers in hospital given extra time for physical contact with their newborns showed stronger attachments later on than those who did not have this experience.

3. Monkeys are quite different from humans in evolutionary terms so it is debatable whether or not the findings of these studies could be directly applied to humans. Monkeys are much simpler animals and do not have the complex intellectual and emotional capacities that humans have.

Harlow used two 'mothers', a cloth-covered mother and a more basic wire mother. In this picture an infant monkey is seen clinging to the cloth mother.

EXPLANATIONS OF ATTACHMENT: BOWLBY'S MONOTROPIC THEORY

Influenced by the work of researchers like Lorenz and Harlow, John Bowlby (1958) applied the principles of imprinting to the human infant–caregiver relationship. According to Bowlby, an infant has a biological need to form an *attachment* to its main caregiver. (The term 'attachment' is used rather than 'imprinting' since attachment is a more complex social and emotional bond than that seen in the imprinting which occurs in other animals.) This attachment to one person is called *monotropy*, and although this person is usually the biological mother, it needn't be. This bond is a special one which is different from any other bond that the infant might develop, and the quality of it is important for healthy psychological development.

 Bowlby saw attachment as *reciprocal* (i.e. a two-way process). Babies are programmed to engage in behaviours that will encourage the main caregiver to stay close and provide protection and sustenance. These signalling behaviours are called *social releasers* and include such things as crying, smiling and gurgling. Because the infant is carrying half of her genetic material, the mother is motivated to look after this 'investment'. Consequently, the caregiver responds to these social releasers and behaves in ways that ensure the infant's survival. This proximity then leads to the development of strong emotional bonds between the two.

The kind of emotional relationship that an infant has with its mother provides it with a set of expectations about relationships which stays with the baby throughout life. This is called an *internal working model*. In effect, this is a kind of template or blueprint for all future relationships.

For Bowlby, attachments develop in a fixed sequence. For the first few months of life an infant engages in indiscriminate *signalling behaviours*. For example, it will smile and cry for the attention of whatever adult might be present. They develop a distinct preference for the company of people and can be easily comforted. By about 3 months the infants begin to demonstrate recognition of those who most often provide care. For example, the infant will direct signalling behaviours more at caregivers than they might at a complete stranger. By about 6 months signalling behaviours become increasingly directed towards the main caregiver (usually the mother). Infants will start to become visibly upset at the departure of the caregiver, a phenomenon called separation anxiety. An infant will also begin to show suspicion and sometimes fear at the approach of someone unfamiliar, a behaviour known as stranger anxiety. As an infant grows older and more mobile it will move about in order to stay close to the caregiver and avoid the proximity of the stranger. Attachment behaviours are harder to see after about 2 or 4 years of age, although the attachment to the main caregiver remains strong.

The critical period for this attachment to develop is the first three years of life, otherwise it may never do so, in which case there may be serious consequences for the child's social and emotional development. Consistent, responsive and sensitive care results in an attachment which has long-term benefits for the child (e.g. increases autonomy, independence and self-efficacy). These benefits of early attachment continue to show themselves in later life (the continuity hypothesis).

The quality of early attachment relationships, then, is largely due to the experience that the infant has with its primary caregivers. Especially important is the extent to which the infant feels that it can rely on the caregivers as sources of support and security; in other words, the extent to which the caregiver provides a safe haven. Infants that feel sufficiently comforted by the caregiver's presence are likely to explore their environments more, encouraging the development of, for example, autonomy and independence. This is called the *secure base hypothesis*.

Evaluation of Bowlby's theory

1. There is some doubt about the accuracy of the monotropy concept. Bowlby's theory is based on the observations of rhesus macaques made by ethologist Robert Hinde. Observations of other primates would more likely have shown that, like human societies, distributed caregiving is the norm. From an evolutionary point of view this makes complete sense. Cooperative care enhances the fitness of members to whom it gives increased maternal fertility and birth rates,

greater infant survival and freedom from child-care for other tasks. Moreover, shared parenting strategies are still very common in many cultures. Research suggests that, far from having a primary attachment figure, many infants form multiple attachments. For example, Schaffer and Emerson (1964) found that whilst many of the infants in their study did indeed form an attachment to one particular person, some had no obvious preferred attachment figure. Some of the infants showed clear signs of attachment to someone other than the mother – for example, to a father or sibling.

2. Bowlby underestimated the role of the father. Far from being mere supporters of maternal attachment by providing an appropriate environment for the mother and infant (e.g. through working and earning money), research suggests that fathers play an important and unique role. Grossmann et al. (2002), for example, showed that the sensitivity of the father's play in infancy was a predictor of security of attachment later in life.

3. Many of Bowlby's assumptions have been criticised for their cultural bias. Keller and Otto (2011) studied attachment behaviour in Nso children from Cameroon. No variation in the proximity of a female stranger could bring about anxiety in 1-year-old infants. It appears that whilst there might be a universal predisposition to stranger anxiety (it does, after all, have evolutionary benefits), it is the early socialisation of an infant which decides whether or not this behaviour becomes enacted. The Beng and the Nso people, for instance, place a great deal of emphasis in their cultures on friendliness towards strangers and multiple caretaking arrangements, so that children learn very early on to be indifferent about separation and strangers.

EXPLANATIONS OF ATTACHMENT: LEARNING THEORY

Learning theory recognises that humans have *drives*, such as hunger and thirst, which we are motivated to reduce. For example, when we feel hungry we will want to get rid of this feeling by finding food. Drives related to biological needs (like food) are called *primary drives*.

A baby has several primary drives, such as comfort and security, but the main one is hunger. Because the mother is most often the one providing food, she becomes associated with the satisfaction of this primary drive. This kind of association learning is called *classical conditioning*. Through the same conditioning processes the baby learns to enjoy other behaviours associated with the mother during feeding, such as physical contact and verbal communication. Basically, then, the mother becomes associated with providing food, satisfying hunger and providing other comforts, and this is the basis of attachment.

Once a baby has made the association between the mother and food it will engage in behaviours which encourage the presence of the mother. For example, babies who smile at their mothers are likely to get some kind of response from her. This is rewarding, or reinforcing, for the baby, who is now more likely to smile in the future in order to get the same reward – a response from the mother. This reinforcement process is reciprocal, meaning that the mother and child are, by their behaviours, reinforcing each other – for example, the mother finds the actions of the baby rewarding and so is more

likely to repeat whatever she did to get this response from the baby in order to get this reward again. This kind of learning through rewards is called *operant conditioning*.

Evaluation of learning theory

1. According to learning theory, whilst reinforcements increase the likelihood of behaviours occurring again, punishment will do the opposite and reduce the likelihood of behaviours reoccurring. However, this is contradicted by the observation that children continue to show strong attachment behaviours towards parents who have been very cruel to them – for instance, parents who have been punishing rather than reinforcing.

2. Learning theory predicts that in the absence of reinforcements, learned behaviours will eventually die away (the term for this is *extinction*). In this case, absence for a period of time from the caregivers who provide reinforcement should result in the strength of the attachment diminishing. Even everyday observations of children who have been separated from their parents for a length of time show this not to be the case.

3. Learning theory would predict that the infant's strongest attachments would be to the person who most often provides food, comfort, etc. – that is, the person who has the greatest impact on drive reduction. Schaffer and Emerson (1964), however, found that less than half of the children in their research had attachments to people with this kind of caregiving responsibility. Furthermore, research by Harlow on rhesus monkeys suggests that other factors, such as physical and social contact, are important in attachment formation.

4. For learning theory, feeding activity is crucial to the emergence of the infant–caregiver attachment. It also suggests that the infant is a passive participant in this process. Provided that it has an appropriate environment, the infant will learn to attach because of the rewarding activities of the caregiver. However, the findings of Harlow contradict this. Harlow's infant monkeys put contact comfort from a surrogate mother ahead of nourishment. Even when Harlow introduced a frightening stimulus into the cage, such as a toy spider, the infant monkey ran for security to the cloth-covered 'mother' rather than to the one providing food.

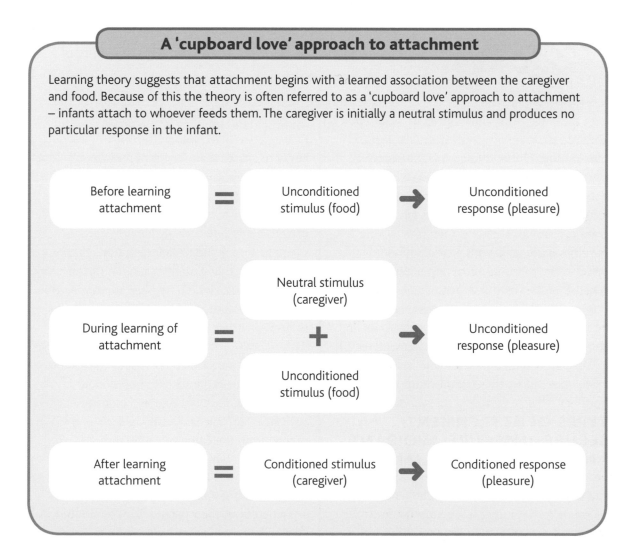

A 'cupboard love' approach to attachment

Learning theory suggests that attachment begins with a learned association between the caregiver and food. Because of this the theory is often referred to as a 'cupboard love' approach to attachment – infants attach to whoever feeds them. The caregiver is initially a neutral stimulus and produces no particular response in the infant.

| Before learning attachment | = | Unconditioned stimulus (food) | → | Unconditioned response (pleasure) |

| During learning of attachment | = | Neutral stimulus (caregiver) **+** Unconditioned stimulus (food) | → | Unconditioned response (pleasure) |

| After learning attachment | = | Conditioned stimulus (caregiver) | → | Conditioned response (pleasure) |

AINSWORTH'S 'STRANGE SITUATION'

According to Ainsworth's *caregiving hypothesis*, the quality of an infant's attachment depends largely on the kind of attention the infant has received from the primary caregiver (usually, but not exclusively, the mother). Based on her observations of infants, Ainsworth and Bell (1970) reworked some of Bowlby's ideas on attachment and developed a procedure for measuring it. For Ainsworth, the quality of a child's attachment to the caregiver could be seen in the use of the caregiver as a 'secure base' and the response of the child to both separation and reunion in the home.

The test that Ainsworth developed to assess attachment between an infant and caregiver is called the *Strange Situation* test. This is a standardised test which takes place in a laboratory setting. It involves a sequence of episodes, each a few minutes long, in which the mother and child and a stranger engage in a series of introductions, separations and reunions. Researchers discreetly observe the child's behaviour in response to the events. Two aspects of the infant's behaviour are observed in particular – namely, reactions to separation and reunion and the level of exploration throughout the procedure.

TYPES OF ATTACHMENT: SECURE, INSECURE-AVOIDANT AND INSECURE-RESISTANT

From studies using the Strange Situation, Ainsworth et al. (1978) categorised attachments into types and estimated the proportions of children showing each type of attachment. Most children show a secure attachment pattern. These children play happily in the presence of their caregiver and are unhappy when their caregiver leaves them. They readily seek out the caregiver for comfort when they return and are wary of strangers. Children use the caregiver as a safe base from which to explore the wider world. A secure attachment is associated with longer term resilience.

Insecurely attached children show one of a number of patterns of behaviour. Avoidant children show little distress on separation from the caregiver and tend to avoid contact when the caregiver returns. These children show little difference in behaviour towards the caregiver or a stranger. Ambivalent children tend to be anxious before being separated from their caregiver and get very upset when separated. When reunited they appear to want comfort but resist efforts by the caregiver to provide it.

The Strange Situation

The researchers wanted to see how a child behaved towards strangers and their caregiver under controlled conditions of stress, in which the infant might seek comfort, and also conditions of novelty, where the infant might be encouraged to explore his or her surroundings. From careful observation and measurement of child behaviour researchers are able to classify the type of attachment shown by the child.

A *controlled observation* procedure was used, whereby researchers control the activities of participants as much as possible in a laboratory setting. The participants are the principal caregiver (usually the mother) and their infants (aged between 9 and 18 months). The 'stranger' is a confederate of the researchers. The Strange Situation has eight episodes, each lasting about three minutes. The whole procedure lasts no more than half an hour.

During the procedure, observers note down how much the following behaviours are exhibited and rate them for intensity:

• The infant's unease when the caregiver leaves the room – *separation anxiety*.

• The infant's willingness to explore – *secure base behaviour*.

• The way the infant greets the caregiver on her return – *reunion behaviour*.

• The infant's response to a stranger – *stranger anxiety*.

EPISODE	BEHAVIOUR ASSESSED
1. Caregiver and child enter the room.	-
2. Whilst infant plays parent sits.	Secure base behaviour
3. Stranger enters the room and speaks to caregiver.	Stranger anxiety
4. Caregiver leaves the room; stranger remains, offers comfort if it is needed.	Separation anxiety
5. Caregiver returns, offers comfort if it is needed; stranger leaves.	Reunion behaviour
6. Caregiver leaves infant alone in room.	Separation anxiety
7. Stranger enters, offers comfort if it is needed.	Stranger anxiety
8. Caregiver returns, offers comfort if it is needed.	Reunion behaviour

Other types of *insecure attachment* have also been suggested. For example, Main and Solomon (1990) noticed that some children did not seem to fit the attachment categories identified by Ainsworth et al. (1978) and added an attachment type which they called insecure or disoriented attachment. Although

You are expected to know the Strange Situation. Make sure you learn the episodes and what is being measured in each episode. You can easily find videos of the Strange Situation on the internet – follow the events in the video with a checklist to hand. You will very soon understand what it is you are seeing, and the procedure will become clearer and easier to learn.

this category is estimated to account for 5–10% of babies, the percentage is greater in children who come from homes with parents who suffer mental illness or where the children are ill-treated. Downes (1992) suggested another type of insecure attachment called anxious preoccupation, which is most frequently seen in neglected and abused children.

Evaluation of the Strange Situation and types of attachment

1. The Strange Situation involves subjective evaluation. Because it is the same observer who both observes the mother's behaviour and classifies the infant's attachment, it has been suggested that perhaps there is

an element of observer bias. For example, if researchers are aware of the hypothesis and have a detailed knowledge of the research area (as they certainly would), they may be inclined to observe behaviours and record them in ways which support expectations. This is especially likely to happen where behaviours are unclear and require some judgement on the part of the observer – there could be slight misinterpretations of actual events.

2. If the Strange Situation is a reliable measure of attachment then children should be classified in the same way whenever they are tested and retested. However, studies which have retested children suggest that the second Strange Situation

TYPE OF ATTACHMENT	BEHAVIOUR OF THE CHILD IN THE STRANGE SITUATION	APPROX. % OF CHILDREN
Type B – secure attachment	Explores the environment Shows distress on separation Greets mother warmly When the mother is present the child is outgoing and friendly with strangers	60–65
Type C – insecure attachment (anxious-ambivalent, aka insecure-resistant)	Appears to be anxious Shows much distress when separated When mother returns the child shows ambivalence (no strong obvious feelings one way or the other) When the mother is present the child is nervous of strangers	12
Type A – insecure attachment (anxious-avoidant, aka insecure-avoidant)	Shows little or no interest in exploring When separated shows little distress When the mother returns the child avoids contact No nervousness around strangers	20
Type D – insecure attachment (disorganised/disorientated, Main and Solomon, 1990)	A mixture of the other two types of insecure attachment (types A and C) When the mother returns the child shows confusion over whether to approach or avoid her	5–10

Table 1.4: Attachment types as described by Ainsworth et al. (1978) and Main and Solomon (1990).

Factors influencing the development of attachments

Many factors have been suggested which contribute to the development of attachment – a number of influences consistently emerge as most important.

Maternal sensitivity

This refers to such things as caregiver's positive emotions, responsiveness to the child's needs and caregiver gentleness. The more sensitive the caregiver is to the needs of the child then the more likely it is that a secure attachment will develop.

Emotional availability

This refers to the quality of *emotional* interactions between caregivers and child. This is also about the parent's ability to *understand* the emotional experience of the child, to be sensitive to the emotional needs of the child and to respond appropriately.

Infant temperament

Temperament is an aspect of personality describing emotionality and sensitivity. Thomas and Chess (1977) argue that 'difficult babies' and 'slow-to-warm-up babies' are harder for parents to cope with than 'easy babies', and this might affect the emotional bond between them.

test is a different experience for the infant. For example, infants often behave in ways that suggest they remember the first experience and as a result alter their behaviour – for example, becoming upset more quickly. This casts doubt on the reliability of the Strange Situation test. Because of this problem it is recommended that the Strange Situation should not be re-administered to the same children within four to six weeks. Unfortunately, this may not be an effective solution. Four to six weeks is a considerable time in the life of a rapidly developing infant and there is a possibility that attachment could be affected by life changes occurring during this time. Even changes which might appear small to an adult can be big for a child, such as a change in child-minding. This could mean that the Strange Situation is not the best measure of the consistency of attachment over time.

3. Some researchers question the validity of the Strange Situation. For example, Lamb (1977) claims that the Strange Situation only assesses attachment to the person the child is with at the time (usually the mother). Evidence suggests that a child might have different attachment relationships with the father, and another again with the grandmother, etc. Main and Weston (1981) found that the behaviour of children varied in the Strange Situation depending on which parent they were with at the time. It seems that the Strange Situation might be assessing specific attachment patterns rather than an overall attachment type.

4. The Strange Situation is designed to see how infants react under conditions which are increasingly stressful. Many researchers argue that this is not an ethical practice and putting very young infants under enormous stress can never be justified. This concern has led some researchers to develop alternative methods of assessing attachment – for example, the Attachment Q Sort (AQS). Other researchers have used settings which are less artificial and more natural in order to assess attachment. For example, True et al. (2001) adapted the Strange Situation for use during a weigh-in at a baby clinic for infants in Mali.

CULTURAL VARIATIONS IN ATTACHMENT

Bowlby developed his theory of attachment on the basis that the features of attachment are *universal* – that is, they apply to all human beings in all cultures. However, the world is made up of many different cultures with many different ideas of ideal parent, child and caregiving behaviours. So, whilst all children might, according to Bowlby, need responsive and sensitive parenting, how children go about getting this through their attachment behaviours and how parents encourage attachment through their child-care practice is going to vary widely.

Although most research on attachment is North American or European in origin, the Strange Situation has been used to measure attachment across a range of cultures. Van Ijzendoorn and Kroonenberg (1988) conducted a meta-analysis, gathering together the results of 32 separate studies conducted in eight different countries, all of which used the Strange Situation to assess attachment.

COUNTRY	NUMBER OF STUDIES	SECURE (TYPE B)	AVOIDANT (TYPE A)	RESISTANT (TYPE C)
UK	1	75	22	3
USA	18	65	21	14
Netherlands	4	67	26	7
West Germany	3	57	35	8
Israel	2	64	7	29
Sweden	1	74	22	4
Japan	2	68	5	27
China	1	50	25	25
Average		65	21	14

Table 1.5: Results of Van Ijzendoorn and Kroonenberg (1988) showing the number of studies from each country and the proportions of children showing each type of attachment.

One of the most important findings to emerge from their analysis was the consistency of secure attachment – it appeared as the most common attachment type in all eight countries. Van Ijzendoorn and Kroonenberg suggest that this supports one of the most central ideas within attachment theory: that a secure attachment is best for healthy social and emotional development. It is the most common form of attachment across cultures because it is the norm.

One of the most significant cultural differences to emerge was the low occurrence of insecure-avoidant attachments in some cultures. Grossmann et al. (1985) suggest that high rates of insecure-avoidant attachments are due to the importance placed on independence and self-reliance in these cultures. In Germany for example it is seen as desirable that children do not get distressed at the absence of the mother (an indicator of insecure-avoidant attachment), whilst some of the behaviours that other cultures might see as acceptable as indicators of a secure attachment are not.

It is a normal part of Japanese child-rearing practice that mother and child are rarely apart for the first 12 months – dependency is highly valued. It is perhaps not surprising therefore that Japanese infants often show extreme distress when separated from the mother (an indicator of insecure-resistant attachment).

Another significant finding to emerge from the Van Ijzendoorn and Kroonenberg analysis was the one-and-a-half times greater variation within a culture than between cultures. This means that there were greater differences in attachment patterns in studies from the same culture than there were in the attachment patterns of studies from different cultures. One implication of this is that it may be wrong to use the term 'culture' to generalise and refer to all its members, as though they all act in the same way in some regard. Even within cultures there are important and identifiable subcultures and it is difficult to assess where the limits of cultural influence end.

Evaluation of the Van Ijzendoorn and Kroonenberg study

1. Care should be taken about drawing too many conclusions from the data because of the limited variety in the studies used. For example, whilst 18 studies are from the United States, there is only one study from China – a single study which involved observing the behaviour of only 36 infants. Many more studies need to be conducted in cultures other than the United States to allow meaningful comparisons.

2. Some researchers have questioned the use of the Strange Situation in different cultures. This test and its classifications were largely developed in the United States, based on observations of American infants, and therefore reflect the values and customs of this particular culture with regard to the forms of attachment and child-rearing practice considered best.

3. It is important to note that all 32 studies were either 'Western' or 'Westernised', and the parents would all have been exposed to similar messages in the mass media about child-rearing practices. What we might be seeing in these studies is the influence of the norms and values of Western industrialised cultures from which this media emerges. There have been relatively few studies of infant–caregiver attachments in cultures which have not been exposed to such influences.

BOWLBY'S THEORY OF MATERNAL DEPRIVATION

According to John Bowlby, an infant has to form an attachment to its mother, or a true mother substitute, during the critical period of 6 months to 2½ years. If this did not happen, or the infant experienced disruption to an existing attachment, then it would suffer both emotionally and socially in later life. This is called the *maternal deprivation hypothesis*. It was based partly on Bowlby's own insights into juveniles who had what he called 'affectionless psychopathy', which is basically an inability to have feelings for others. He noted that most of these affectionless psychopaths had experienced some kind of separation from their mothers in their early years of life – that is, they had experienced maternal deprivation.

Evaluation of Bowlby's maternal deprivation hypothesis

1. Bowlby's maternal deprivation hypothesis stimulated a great deal of research and attracted a lot of criticism. However, most of the subsequent research supporting the maternal deprivation hypothesis has been unconvincing, either because of flawed methodology (the studies were badly controlled with lots of confounding variables) or because the research wasn't necessarily focused on maternal deprivation as Bowlby described it.

2. There have been studies which appear to directly contradict this theory. Freud and Dann (1951) studied the development of a group of six children rescued from a Nazi concentration camp where they had spent their early life. In the absence of any adults to provide care, the six children became very close and developed attachments to one another. According to

Forty-four juvenile thieves

'Maternal care in infancy and early childhood is essential for mental health. This is a discovery comparable in magnitude to that of the role of vitamins in physical health, and of far-reaching significance for programmes of preventive mental hygiene.' Bowlby (1951)

Bowlby based his theory of maternal deprivation on a study he did in 1944 into the childhood experiences of boys who were attending his London clinic for disturbed adolescents. He compared 44 of these who were thieves with another group who were emotionally disturbed but did not steal. He discovered that 17 of the adolescent thieves had experienced 'early and prolonged separations from their mothers' compared to only two from the group who didn't steal. Bowlby concluded that there was a link between early separation and later emotional and social problems.

Bowlby's theory, these children all suffered maternal deprivation and as a result should have developed affectionless psychopathy. However, they showed no clear signs of this. This led some commentators to suggest that the inability to form any kind of attachment at all is the important factor, rather than the lack of an attachment to the mother.

 3. Rutter (1981) suggests that there should be a distinction drawn between the *distortion* of attachments (e.g. when the mother is present but the family relationships are affected by such things as illness and divorce) and the *disruption* of attachment (e.g. when the mother has died). The maternal deprivation hypothesis would predict that disruption would have a far greater impact on an infant than distortion. Rutter points out, however, that distortion can be more harmful to the child than disruption – the poor quality of family relationships can have a greater impact on a child than separation from an attachment figure.

4. It is far too simple to say that *separation* as such causes harm – the nature and consequences of separation need to be taken into account. There are many ways in which deprivation may occur – for example, death of a parent, hospitalisation or divorce – and each of these causes is likely to have its own particular effect on infants.

The effects of short-term deprivation

Whilst Bowlby was most interested in the long-term effects of maternal deprivation, he also considered the effects of the more common temporary deprivations caused by enforced separations of mother and child. Robertson and Bowlby (1952) investigated the behaviour of young children separated from their caregiver because of hospitalisation (it was normal in those days for parents to not visit their hospitalised children in order to allow them to 'settle in'). They found that there was a sequence in the child's response to separation:

1. Protest: The child is very upset, confused, appears grief-stricken and cries and screams in order to be re-united with the mother. This can last from a few hours to several days.

2. Despair: Gradually succeeding protest, the child feels progressively more hopeless. Crying becomes intermittent until the child becomes quiet and apparently withdrawn. They are uninterested in surroundings or attempts at reassurance.

3. Detachment: The child appears to be content and to have recovered. He/she no longer seeks the caregiver and seems to show little interest when the caregiver reappears. Emotional responses to future separations gradually diminish until there is hardly a response. This state of withdrawal whereby the child seeks no mothering at all was a sign of psychological trauma.

Whilst most children recover from this deprivation, not all that enter the detachment phase do. Bowlby likened the response of the child to the mourning process that adults go through when a loved one dies, and suggested that the loss of a secure base could have long-term consequences. Quinton and Rutter (1976) also studied children who were separated from parents by admission to hospital. Not only did they find that short separation caused few adverse effects but that there were important individual differences in how children responded: Poorer children and those with difficult family backgrounds coped less well than intelligent children and those with more stable families.

THE EFFECTS OF INSTITUTIONALISATION

According to Rutter, to use the term 'deprivation' suggests that there has been an attachment but that it has been broken. However, some children never have the opportunity to form a close attachment in the first place. He called this *privation*. This distinction is important, since privation and deprivation are likely to have different effects. Whilst privation is a lack of an attachment bond, deprivation can be graded – that is, it can be short term or long term with degrees of consequence. Most attachment research has focused on deprivation since instances of privation are actually quite unusual.

One possible source of information on the effects of privation are the rare cases of neglectful institutional care. There is a long history of such research. Goldfarb (1943), for example, compared one group of children who had experienced institutional care for the first three years of life before being fostered with another group of children who had been fostered straight away. He found that the early fostered group were much more socially skilled and scored higher on intelligence tests than the institutionalised children. Studies like Goldfarb's, however, were generally poorly controlled and conducted and were largely descriptive. We must therefore be very careful about any conclusions drawn from them.

ROMANIAN ORPHAN STUDIES

More recently, studies have been conducted using children adopted from Romanian institutions. In the 1990s, Romania was revealed to have severe problems in its treatment of institutionalised children. The children experienced a range of privations and conditions were generally very poor. They were rarely held and spent almost all their time in cribs in overcrowded rooms with drab walls and unsanitary conditions, and for most children the ratio of child to caregiver was as high as 20 to 1.

As part of the ERA study (see box 'The English and Romanian Adoptees (ERA) study'), O'Connor et al. (2000) reported the progress of 165 of these Romanian orphans who had experienced severe privation whilst in institutional care prior to adoption into UK families. At the time of adoption, most children were severely physically, behaviourally and cognitively delayed. A group of children from the UK adopted before 6 months of age, none of whom had experienced privation, were used as a comparison (control) group.

They found that, once placed in families, these children do remarkably well given their difficult start to life. Its seems that cognitive functioning can rapidly recover – many infants who were a year or more behind normal age levels at adoption were functioning at normal or superior levels within a few years. This is also the case for language, even though the Romanian children had the extra challenge of having to learn the language of their adoptive English families. In line with the findings of other studies of adopted Romanian infants, attachment disturbances were observed. There was a strong relationship between the presence and severity of problems and the duration of *institutionalisation* before adoption.

These findings are in line with other Romanian adoption studies. For example, Zeanah et al. (2003) reported on the Bucharest Early Intervention Project (BEIP). Half of 136 children were randomly selected for high quality foster care (average age 22 months), and their development was compared to the other half who remained in institutional care. Tested at 30, 42 and 54 months and again at 8 years, those children placed in foster care performed better than those in institutional care on every domain assessed. This included IQ, attachment, psychiatric problems and electrical brain activity. The researchers suggest that there is a 'sensitive period' for remediating the experience of institutional care. Although these sensitive periods vary for each domain, the removal from institutional care before 2 years of age is essential. Fundamentally, the earlier a child is placed in foster care, the better their recovery from the effects of institutionalisation will be.

Many children institutionalised in Romanian orphanages experienced severe privation.

Long-term effects of early institutional care

The first longitudinal study on the long-term effects of institutionalisation on children conducted as a natural experiment was by Tizard and Hodges (1978). Whilst in the institutions the children received good physical care and received a fair amount of attention from adults. However, they could not form lasting attachments to specific people because of high staff turnover – for example, the institutions were used to train student nurses. They compared the development of four groups of children: a group who remained in the institution; a group who were adopted between 2 and 4 years of age; a group who were returned to their biological families between 2 and 4 years of age; and a non-institutionalised comparison group. On measures of cognitive, behavioural and social development, the adopted group had the most favourable outcomes, with the institutionalised group faring least well. However, problems persisted in the institutionalised children's social relationships, such as an inability to form close relationships, indiscriminate friendliness towards strangers, attention-seeking behaviour, poor peer relationships, attention deficits and disciplinary problems. However, the Tizard and Hodges study does have its flaws – for example, it is not known whether or not those children who were adopted and those who stayed in institutional care differed in some important respects. Neither were there any independent checks on the reliability or validity of the interviews and questionnaires used by the researchers to gather information.

The English and Romanian Adoptees (ERA) study

The ERA study is an ongoing longitudinal study following the progress of a group of Romanian children adopted between February 1990 and September 1992, before they were 4 years of age. In 2007 Rutter et al. reported on the progress of 144 of these adopted Romanian children, now at 11 years of age. Results suggest that the effects of early institutional care continue to persist, especially in those children who had been adopted between the ages of 6 and 42 months (i.e. those who experienced the greatest amount of institutionalised care). This is despite having spent at least seven-and-a-half years with their adoptive families in caring and stimulating environments.

Cognitive impairments

Tested at adoption, the average IQ of Romanian orphans over 6 months of age was below average at 45 (someone with an average IQ would score between 90 and 109). Their physical development was also below average for age in terms of height and head circumference, with half in the bottom 3% of the population for weight. They were tested again at 4 years of age. Those adopted before 6 months showed an increase in IQ from 63 to 107. Those adopted after 6 months did less well in terms of IQ (increasing to an average of 90) and in physical development.

Attachment

Twenty-six per cent of Romanian infants tested at age 6 showed evidence of disinhibited reactive attachment disorder (a disorder characterised by indiscriminate over-friendliness and clinginess, attention-seeking behaviours and a lack of differentiation amongst adults, such as failing to seek security from a parent in anxiety-provoking situations and going off with strangers). This is compared to 3.8% of UK children. There was also a relationship between attachment quality and duration of care. It seems that the later the adoption (and hence the longer the institutional care), the greater the likelihood of attachment disorder. Rutter et al. found that disinhibited attachment persisted, with 54% of those assessed with this at age 6 still showing signs of the disorder at 11 years of age. Many of these children were receiving support for additional educational needs and/or mental health needs.

The researchers conclude that the effects of early privation are not necessarily permanent and can be overcome by subsequent good care. The early privations appear to have no lasting effects in children if they are removed from institutional care and adopted into good homes before 6 months of age, but problems may persist in children adopted after 6 months of age.

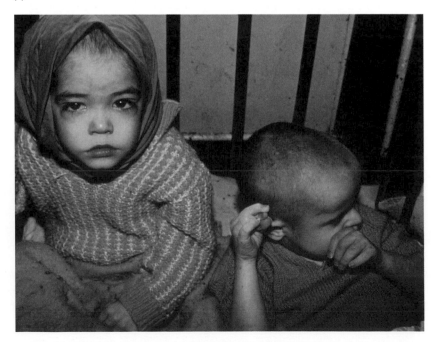

THE INFLUENCE OF EARLY ATTACHMENT ON CHILDHOOD AND ADULT RELATIONSHIPS

Bowlby suggested that the kinds of emotional bonds we have as infants with our caregivers creates an *internal working model*. This is a mental representation about our self, about others and how the world works. In essence, it is a blueprint for what we believe relationships are like. It influences our expectations of others and perceptions of ourselves. Whilst the *internal working model* becomes more complex as the individual develops, it is thought to remain relatively stable throughout life. This means that child, adolescent and adult relationships to some extent reflect early caregiving experiences.

THE INFLUENCE OF EARLY ATTACHMENT ON CHILDHOOD RELATIONSHIPS

A great deal of research has recognised a link between early attachment and later patterns of childhood behaviour. LaFreniere and Sroufe (1985), for example, found that securely attached pre-school (nursery aged) children showed a range of positive social behaviours, including empathy towards peers, greater curiosity, assertiveness, flexibility and self-reliance. In contrast, children with insecure attachments show fewer positive behaviours and fare less well during the pre-school years. These effects of early attachment also seem to persist throughout schooling (Kerns et al., 1996) and influence things such as play and relationships with teachers.

Relationships during play

Research suggests that because securely attached children have the necessary skills for higher levels of social play and positive peer interactions, they thus more readily attract other children to play with them (see box 'The play of securely attached children').

Research has also linked early attachment and the quality of later child–caregiver play. Slade (1987) used the Strange Situation to obtain her sample of seven secure and eight insecure attached children. These children were filmed during seven 30 minute periods of free play (children were allowed to play as they wished) over a 12 month period. Mothers were instructed to play with the infant but not influence how the child played. Slade found that children assessed earlier as securely attached played for longer and engaged in more symbolic (make-believe) play than those

The play of securely attached children

Rose-Krasnor et al. (1996) paired 4-year-old children who securely attached at 20 months with children of the same age assessed as insecurely attached. They then assessed their behaviour together during periods of social play. They found differences in the type of activities the children engaged in – for example, the play of securely attached children was more interesting and more cooperative in nature. They suggest that early attachments are related later on to greater social competence in play situations, increased confidence to explore, better social problem solving skills and more positive expectations of others. For Rose-Krasnor et al., these qualities underpin other important social behaviours, such as integrating into the play of others and forming friendships.

assessed as insecurely attached. They also engaged in a higher level of symbolic play at 26 and 28 months. Meins et al. (1998) found that 31–36 month old infants with early secure attachments were more likely to incorporate suggestions from adults into their symbolic play than insecurely attached children. They explain this by suggesting that the mothers of securely attached children are more sensitive to their children's needs and interests during play and have a more accurate understanding of their infants' mental states.

Relationships with teachers

The advantages gained from having an early secure attachment also mean that such

children are more likely to establish positive relationships with teachers. According to O'Connor and McCartney (2006), the internal working model of insecurely attached children impedes the development of such relationships with teachers. This is supported by Erickson et al. (1985) who found that insecurely attached children were more likely to show a range of undesirable behaviours, such as high dependency and non-compliance, leading teachers to describe such children as impulsive, withdrawn and hostile. As a result, teachers have greater difficulty building relationships with such children. O'Connor and McCartney (2006) suggest that a secure attachment relationship enables teachers to better understand and therefore respond to the students' learning needs. One consequence of this relationship with the teacher is that securely attached children are more likely to succeed academically. This is supported by West et al. (2013) who found that early secure attachment is related to better academic performance in middle childhood (around 9 years of age). It is important to note, however, that children can form attachments with teachers regardless of their attachment history. Indeed, teachers are often important members of a child's attachment hierarchy. Howes (1999) points out that a sensitive and responsive teacher can provide children with opportunities to form their only secure attachment.

THE INFLUENCE OF EARLY ATTACHMENT ON ADULT RELATIONSHIPS

Research suggests that attachment patterns that begin in infancy remain important and affect the quality of adult relationships. This demonstrates the continued influence of the internal working model. One of the first and most influential studies was conducted by Hazan and Shaver (1987). They suggested that there are similarities between infant and caregiver relationships and the relationships between adult romantic partners. For example, they share similar features such as feeling safe when the other is nearby, engaging in close contact and feeling insecure when the other is unavailable (see box 'Attachment and adult romantic relationships').

Whilst concerns have been expressed about the methodology adopted by Hazan and Shaver, their findings have received some support from other researchers. For example, it seems that those adults who were securely attached as children are more likely to have successful long-term relationships than adults who had early insecure attachments. Banse (2004) found that marital satisfaction was highest in those couples where both partners had a secure attachment history. Those with an anxious-ambivalent attachment as children had the most short-term romantic relationships, often entering into relationships quickly and becoming angry when their love was not reciprocated. This is supported by Senchak and Leonard (1992) who found that men with an anxious-ambivalent attachment history acquired their marriage licences after shorter courtships than those with a secure attachment history. Better marital adjustment was seen in relationships where both partners were securely attached than when one or both partners were insecurely attached.

Attachment and adult romantic relationships

Hazan and Shaver (1987) argued that the patterns of attachment described by Ainsworth were similar to what they called adult 'love styles'. They asked readers of the *Rocky Mountain News* (a newspaper in Denver, Colorado) to complete a questionnaire on their attitudes towards love. Participants were asked to complete a three-part questionnaire assessing love style, gathering details about their current and past relationships, and measuring attachment style and history.

Participants were required to read the three paragraphs and reflect on their history of romantic relationships to select which of the three best summed up their general experience of relationships:

The first described an avoidant attachment style, the second secure and the third an ambivalent one. After analysis of over 600 questionnaires, the researchers found that the distribution of categories was similar to that observed in infancy. In other words, about 56% of adults classified themselves as secure, about 24% described themselves as anxious-avoidant and about 20% described themselves as anxious-ambivalent. Participants with these different attachment styles differed in their experiences of romantic love. Securely attached adults readily trusted others and had satisfying romantic relationships. Anxious-avoidant style adults were uncomfortable being close to others and found them hard to trust; whilst adults with anxious-ambivalent styles were likely to be possessive and preoccupied about their relationships. These individuals want to be loved and needed, and Hazan and Shaver describe the relationships of these people as characterised by 'emotional extremes, jealousy, obsessive preoccupation, sexual attraction, desire for union, desire for reciprocation, and falling in love at first sight'. Basically, they are 'over-ready for love'.

KEY TERMS

Attachment An emotional bond between the child and the principal caregiver.

Classical conditioning Learning happens because we learn associations between things – for instance, an infant associates a caregiver with food.

Continuity hypothesis Consistent, responsive and sensitive care that results in a secure *attachment* which has longer term benefits for social competence, autonomy, independence and self-efficacy.

Critical period A period during which *attachments* must develop, otherwise they may never do so.

Deprivation Where there was once an *attachment* that has now been broken.

Imprinting According to Konrad Lorenz, *imprinting* is the act of *attachment* but applied to animals. Lorenz famously worked with *imprinting* in geese.

Insecure attachment There are two types: anxious-avoidant children explore less, show little distress on separation and are not very nervous around strangers. Also known as type A attachment. Anxious-ambivalent children show great distress when separated from the caregiver and ambivalence on reunion. Also known as type C attachment.

Institutionalisation Care that takes place in an institution, such as an orphanage.

Interactional synchrony A collection of behaviours, which include body orientation, movement, vocal exchanges and facial expression, that infants use in reciprocal turn-taking exchanges with caregivers.

Internal working model A set of expectations about relationships formed based on the kind of emotional relationship that an infant has with its primary caregiver which stay with the baby throughout life.

Learning theory An explanation of *attachment* based on the principles of *operant* and *classical conditioning* and social learning.

Monotropy *Attachment* to one person – although this person is usually the biological mother, it needn't be.

Operant conditioning Learning happens because we are rewarded (or reinforced) for our behaviour – for instance, a child learns that smiling is rewarded by loving, kind words so they may repeat the behaviour more often.

Privation The situation where a child has never had the opportunity to form a close *attachment*.

Reciprocity An understanding between infant and caregiver that interaction depends on the coordinated activities of both parties.

Secure attachment A secure attachment is one where a child in the *Strange Situation* explores their environment, shows distress when separated from the mother, greets their mother warmly on her return and is outgoing and friendly with strangers when the mother is present. It is the most common form of *attachment*. Also known as type B attachment.

Strange Situation A method of controlled observation developed to investigate *attachment* types in children.

Types of attachment The *attachments* formed between children and their caregivers can differ. They can be described as insecure or secure.

PAGE 60

Outline the stages of attachment as identified by Schaffer. (6 marks)

If this question was for 4 marks you might think it was one mark per stage, but this is a 6 mark question so clearly something more is required. For maximum marks you will need to provide a coherent answer – i.e. not just identifying the stages accurately but saying something about them too. Not a lot – just enough to give the impression that you know what you are talking about. This is only a 6 mark question after all.

PAGE 62

'Fathers are immensely important in bringing up balanced, well-adjusted and happy children.'

With reference to the quote, discuss the role of the father in caregiving. (8 marks)

The question is not asking you specifically to agree or disagree with the quote, but you *are* required to engage with it somehow. One approach to take would be to have an opinion (e.g. fathers are important) and then present a case for this, offering some evidence for and against. There are only 8 marks available so a big, complex response is not needed – but *organisation* is!

PAGE 68

Maria provides most of the care for her son, Ben – feeding, comforting and playing with him. She has noticed that, whilst he is happy to spend time with his father, Ben seems most content when he is with her.

Use your knowledge of the learning theory of attachment to explain Ben's behaviour. (4 marks)

You can use either or both classical or operant conditioning in your answer – do whatever you know best. Just remember that this is a 4 mark question, so watch the level of detail!

PAGE 70

Andrea has noticed that her two sons are quite different, even though they are the same age. When she gets home from work the first thing Sam does is run to her and give her a big hug, whilst Rob appears indifferent and she has to go and find him to say hello. When a plumber came to the house the other day Sam was fine with him, but Rob wouldn't stop crying and appeared scared of him.

a.(i) Identify the type of attachment shown by Rob. (1 mark)

a.(ii) Identify the type of attachment shown by Sam. (1 mark)

b. Explain how a psychologist might assess the type of attachment shown by each child. (4 marks)

The first two questions require the briefest of responses – think of the signs of attachment and just name the types. The third question is a little trickier. For only 4 marks you need to provide a summary of the Strange Situation. Rather than describe every step, consider what are the principal features.

PAGE 74

Research has shown that attachments vary considerably across cultures.

Outline two cultural variations in attachment. Refer to research in your answer. (4 marks)

You are expected to know the Van Ijzendoorn and Kroonenberg study, so use the findings here. Note the focus on *variations in attachment*, so make sure you emphasise this in your answer.

PAGE 83

Discuss research into the influence of early attachment on adult relationships. (12 marks)

Longer essay-style questions are nothing to worry about – they are an opportunity to gain lots of marks by talking about one topic rather than trying to gain the same marks by answering smaller questions on lots of different topics! It's all in the planning – you need to demonstrate two skills for 6 marks each. You are not expected to write much so be selective.

Psychopathology

WHAT YOU NEED TO KNOW ☑

Definitions of abnormality ☐

Deviation from social norms ☐

Failure to function adequately ☐

Statistical infrequency ☐

Deviation from ideal mental health ☐

Phobia ☐

The behavioural, emotional and cognitive characteristics ☐

The behavioural approach to explaining phobias: ☐

    The two-process model – classical and operant conditioning ☐

The behavioural approach to treating phobias: ☐

    Systematic desensitisation ☐

    Flooding ☐

Depression ☐

The behavioural, emotional and cognitive characteristics ☐

The cognitive approach to explaining depression: ☐

    Beck's negative triad ☐

    Ellis's ABC model ☐

The cognitive approach to treating depression: ☐

    Cognitive-behavioural therapy (CBT) ☐

    Challenging irrational thoughts (REBT) ☐

Obsessive-compulsive disorder (OCD) ☐

The behavioural, emotional and cognitive characteristics ☐

The biological approach to explaining OCD: ☐

    Genetic explanations ☐

    Neural explanations ☐

The biological approach to treating OCD: ☐

    Drug therapy ☐

Psychopathology

Psychopathology is the study of mental illness. This includes its classification, diagnosis, origins and treatments. Various terms are used to refer to mental illness, such as emotional disturbance, mental health problem, psychological disorder and psychological abnormality. 'Abnormal' is a term in widespread everyday use, and representations of 'abnormality' are common in all media – books, films, television, etc. It is, however, a term that psychologists approach with some caution. It is an elusive term, and it has such negative connotations that, once the label 'abnormal' is applied to someone, it has a tendency to stick like no other label. This is despite the fact that one in six people living in the UK will at some time in their lives seek help for a mental health problem. Sometimes, judging behaviour as abnormal is a relatively straightforward matter. Often, however, distinguishing between normal and abnormal is very difficult. This is because normality and abnormality are relative terms; they change according to such things as who is deciding what constitutes abnormality, what the cultural expectations are and when in history the decision is being made. We now have classification systems which are meant to make the process of diagnosis more objective and straightforward. The World Health Organization's *International Classification of Disorders* (ICD, 11th revision due in 2017) and the *Diagnostic and Statistical Manual of Mental Disorders* (DSM, now on version 5) are regularly revised to accommodate our changing appreciation and understanding of mental illness, suggesting that they have been at best only partly successful in this regard.

DEFINITIONS OF ABNORMALITY

In order to decide whether or not someone is behaving in a psychologically abnormal way we need a clear definition of what exactly we mean by 'abnormal'. The answer to this might be very simple, requiring no more than common sense: abnormality is the absence of normality. If we know what is 'normal' then anything outside this must therefore be abnormal. Unfortunately, defining normality presents us with much the same difficulty as defining abnormality. There is no clear agreement about what constitutes either abnormality or normality. Whilst it is likely that no single definition will be acceptable to everyone, taken together the various attempts at defining abnormality have helped to clarify what exactly we mean when we label behaviour as 'abnormal'.

DEVIATION FROM SOCIAL NORMS

'Norms' are unwritten rules, created by society to guide behaviour and usually learned through early socialisation. They tell us which behaviours are expected and acceptable, and they provide us with some sense of 'order' in society. There are norms for just about every kind of social behaviour. For example, age-based norms tell us about the kind of behaviour we can expect from people at different ages. For instance, although unwanted we might expect tantrums from a young child. If however we see an adult behaving in this way we might think the person is abnormal. Many mental health problems are considered to be abnormal because the behaviours associated with them break social norms.

Limitations
1. Societies change over time and so, therefore, do their norms. Consequently, we cannot use opinions held in the past to judge a behaviour as deviant – it must be based on present day thinking. For example, as recently as the 1970s homosexuality was listed as a mental disorder in DSM. Homosexuality between consenting adults over 18 years of age is now legal in the UK, it is now a behaviour falling within the social norms of most Western countries and therefore would not be considered abnormal.

2. Norms vary across cultures and so also therefore what is considered abnormal. For example, men of the Gururumba people of New Guinea occasionally enter into an emotional state known there as 'being a wild pig'. Men run wild, stealing, being aggressive and generally antisocial. The Gururumba people, however, are very tolerant of this behaviour – it is a cultural norm that 'being a wild pig' will occasionally happen to men aged between 25 and 35 and thus the behaviour, although unwelcome, is accepted.

3. Breaking social norms can be a good thing, and can even stimulate positive social change. For example, slavery was once considered 'normal' in this society. However, when some people broke norms and opposed slavery, the eventual result was its abolition. There are many other examples, such as voting rights for women and legal rights for children.

FAILURE TO FUNCTION ADEQUATELY

An individual who is failing to function adequately is engaging in behaviours that are somehow 'not good for them'. For example, there might be difficulties with maintaining close relationships, engaging in social activities, setting and achieving goals or living an independent and fulfilling life. Day-to-day living can be very difficult, and seemingly everyday behaviours can become challenging, such as going out to the shops or meeting up with friends. There is no one way of deciding whether or not someone is failing to function adequately. Rosenhan and Seligman (1989) suggest that there are seven features of failure to function. No single feature might by itself be enough to indicate abnormality, but the more indicators an individual has, the more likely they are to indicate the presence of abnormality (see Table 1.6).

Limitations

1. Rosenhan and Seligman's approach relies heavily on personal opinion about the presence or absence of features and then about the degree to which these are having an effect.

This subjectivity increases the likelihood of a person being incorrectly described as normal or abnormal. Things are complicated by many abnormal behaviours appearing to be exaggerations of normal behaviour. For example, it is normal to show grief at the loss of a loved one, but at what point does this distress become *abnormal* grief?

2. What is 'adequate' functioning in one culture might not be adequate in another. For example, someone brought up in a culture that values gentleness, cooperation and collective welfare could be seen as failing to function adequately when living in a culture that values assertiveness and personal success. Being somehow at odds with a dominant culture brings the risk of being labelled abnormal.

3. Abnormality does not necessarily mean dysfunction for the individual. For example, there are many instances of people who kill others and in all other respects lead normal lives. Whilst obviously one should not commit murder, for some the behaviour might be rational and fulfilling in the context of their own lives (e.g. contract killers, serial killers).

FEATURE	
Personal distress	The behaviour indicates that a person is suffering in some way.
Maladaptiveness	The behaviour prevents people from achieving major life goals (e.g. enjoying fulfilling relationships).
Vividness/unconventionality	The behaviour stands out as being different from usual observed behaviour.
Unpredictability/loss of control	The behaviour appears uncontrolled, inappropriate or random.
Irrationality/incomprehensibility	It is not easy to understand why anyone would behave in this way.
Observer discomfort	Observers of the behaviour are made uncomfortable by it.
Violation of moral/ideal standards	Behaviour is more likely to be judged 'abnormal' when it violates established moral standards.

Table 1.6: Seven indicators of failure to function according to Rosenhan and Seligman (1989).

STATISTICAL INFREQUENCY

A behaviour can be judged as abnormal depending on how common it is. The more statistically uncommon a behaviour or trait is (i.e. it doesn't happen very often), the more likely it is to be abnormal. In order to decide whether something is common or uncommon a normal distribution curve is used (sometimes referred to as a normal curve or Gaussian curve). The normal curve is an important statistical phenomenon in psychology that can be applied to many aspects of human behaviour. If, for example, intelligence is measured in many thousands of people and the scores plotted on a graph, the graph takes on a particular symmetrical bell-shape. This kind of graph has important mathematical properties that allow predictions to be made about the population from which the scores were gathered.

With two further pieces of information, the mean (i.e. the typical or average score) and the standard deviation (i.e. the average of how spread out the scores are), predictions can be made about how common or uncommon something is. As can be seen in Figure 1.11, 95% of people have an intelligence score within 2 standard deviations above and below the mean – something which is statistically common. Only 5% of people have intelligence scores outside of this range – this is considered statistically uncommon. Behaviour or traits that are this statistically uncommon could be considered abnormal.

Limitations

1. Some behaviours and traits that are uncommon are highly valued. People who are particularly brilliant at something are statistically rare but not considered abnormal. In fact, the rarity of what they are able to do often makes the individuals popular and desirable. This approach therefore fails to distinguish between behaviours that are statistically rare and undesirable and those that are statistically rare and desirable.

2. Statistical infrequency is not always a good indicator that behaviour is abnormal. For example, talking to oneself might be considered a clear sign of abnormality, yet it is something everyone does at some time. Clearly, context is as an important consideration as statistical infrequency.

3. Some behaviours which are clearly abnormal are not statistically uncommon. For example, it is estimated that over 20% of people will suffer some form of depression during their lifetime. Statistically, then, depression is relatively common – but is not considered 'normal'.

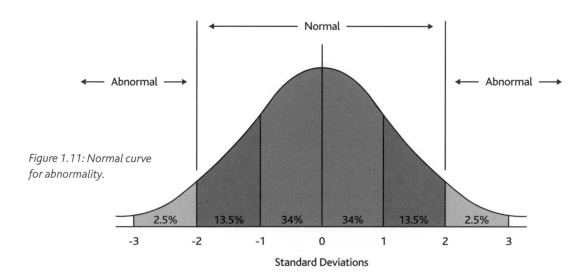

Figure 1.11: Normal curve for abnormality.

DEVIATION FROM IDEAL MENTAL HEALTH

An alternative approach to defining abnormality is to consider what is normal. If we can decide on what normality is, then anything not satisfying this condition must therefore represent abnormality. Jahoda (1958) talked about normality being a state of positive mental health. For Jahoda, several criteria have to be met in order to satisfy the conditions for what she called 'optimal living' (or living life to the full) (see Table 1.7). An absence of any one feature of ideal mental health implies that an individual is abnormal.

Limitations

1. A number of Jahoda's criteria are quite difficult to achieve, which increases the likelihood of an individual being incorrectly labelled as abnormal. Actualisation, in particular, is reached by few people in life, therefore, if this definition is taken literally most people would be classified as abnormal! In reality, the criteria should be considered as a set of ideal standards which, if attained, would suggest optimal living rather than an absence of any of the elements representing abnormality.

2. The emphasis on personal and individual fulfilment is a particularly Westernised view – some cultures place a greater emphasis on collective responsibility, where the welfare of the wider family is as important as that of the individual. The features are not necessarily shared by all cultures and are therefore culturally biased.

3. It is not always clear what some of the criteria actually mean in practice. For example, it is not certain what an 'accurate view of reality' is, given that 'reality' is a product of each individual's mind. Reality for a soldier on a battlefield is somewhat different from that of an accountant in an office, or for someone living on benefits with three small children to care for. The features are vague and difficult to measure, and that subjective judgement is needed.

FEATURE	
Positive view of self	The person must have a feeling of self-worth, with a reasonable level of self-esteem.
Actualisation	There must be personal growth so that a person can become the best that they possibly can be.
Autonomy	The person must not have to rely on others for everything. They must show a level of independence in their behaviour.
Accurate view of reality	The person's view of the world around them must not be distorted in any way. For instance, they must not think that everyone is untrustworthy or that everyone is watching their behaviour.
Environmental adaptability	The person must be able to change their behaviour to make it appropriate for different environments. For instance, a certain pattern of behaviour is expected at weddings, but not at funerals.
Resistance to stress	The person must be able to deal with the regular stresses and strains of life. They must be flexible in their ability to work through potentially difficult situations.

Table 1.7: The conditions for optimal living according to Jahoda (1958).

DEPRESSION

We all think we know what depression is, and the term is in such common use that maybe we even think we've suffered from it at some time. However, what most of us know about and have experienced is not depression in the clinical sense. Clinical depression is very unpleasant and seriously impairs everyday functioning. Depression is a complex disorder and a number of subtypes have been identified. Two key symptoms in the diagnosis of depression, however, are an increase in negative symptoms (persistent low mood) and a decrease in positive symptoms (loss of experience of pleasure) (Irons, 2014).

 Depression comes in many forms, and types vary according to the symptoms and their severity. Major depressive disorder (MDD) is often referred to as 'clinical depression' and is by far the most common mental health problem, thought to account for up to a third of all visits to the GP. It has been estimated that around 20% of all adults will experience some type of depression at some point in their lives. The rates of depression have been steadily increasing over many years, so that the World Health Organization now estimate that by 2030 depression will affect more people than any other health issue (Irons, 2014). At the same time, the average age for depression has been steadily dropping so that it is now 26 years. Women are twice as likely as men to suffer depression. It is also linked to income – the wealthier you are, the less likely you are to experience depression.

EMOTIONAL	BEHAVIOURAL	COGNITIVE
Sadness	Decrease in sexual activity	Low self-esteem
Irritability	Loss of appetite	Guilt
Apathy	Disturbed sleep patterns	Self-dislike
	Poor care of self and others	Negative thoughts
	Suicide attempts	Suicidal thoughts
	Loss of energy	Poor memory
		Lack of concentration

Table 1.8: The key characteristics of MDD.

THE COGNITIVE APPROACH TO EXPLAINING DEPRESSION

The cognitive approach to explaining depression assumes that people experience depression because of the negative ways in which they think about events that occur in their lives. The two most important and influential cognitive explanations in terms of their application to therapy are by Beck and Ellis.

Beck's negative triad

Aaron Beck (1967) believed that the symptoms of depression are the product of what he called a negative 'cognitive triad'. The triad consists of negative thoughts of the self, the present world and the future (see Figure 1.12). These three components interact to influence the normal cognitive processes that we all use to shape our understanding of the world and our reactions to it. According to Beck, depressed people tend to view themselves, their environment and the future in a negative, pessimistic light. As a result, there is a tendency to misinterpret facts and blame themselves for any misfortune that occurs. This cognitive triad interacts with *negative schemas* and *cognitive biases* to produce depressive thinking.

Negative thinking and judgement styles function as a *negative cognitive bias*: it makes it easy for depressed people to see situations as

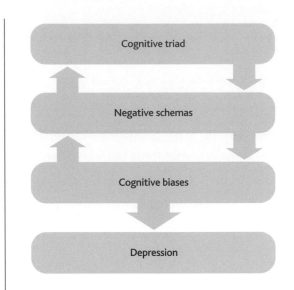

Figure 1.13: How the cognitive triad, negative schemas and cognitive biases interact to cause depression.

being much worse than they really are, and increases the risk of developing depressive responses to stressful situations. People who suffer depression will often focus on some negative aspect of a situation whilst ignoring other, more positive information, causing them to distort or exaggerate problems and the causes of those problems. The negative triad is also influenced by *negative schemas*. These are core negative beliefs, usually developed in early childhood, which are triggered when an individual encounters a situation which resembles that in which the schema was developed. So, for example, many adults respond to situations with 'I can't do that', not because they really can't, but because the situation activates a schema, developed as a consequence of failure much earlier in life, of being inept.

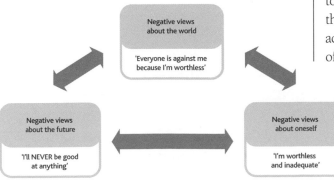

Figure 1.12: Beck's negative cognitive triad.

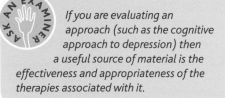

If you are evaluating an approach (such as the cognitive approach to depression) then a useful source of material is the effectiveness and appropriateness of the therapies associated with it.

COGNITIVE-BEHAVIOURAL THERAPY

 Developed by Aaron Beck, the main aim of cognitive-behavioural therapy (CBT) is to help an individual identify negative and irrational thoughts and replace these with more rational ways of thinking. Identifying and addressing the dysfunctional thinking that gives rise to depression should lead to more functional behaviour and positive emotional responses. Typically, CBT takes place over about 20 one hour sessions, but the duration of CBT is flexible and tailored to the needs of the client. Most therapists follow three distinct phases: case conceptualisation, skills acquisition and follow-up.

During the first phase of CBT it is common practice for a client to be asked to complete a self-report questionnaire as part of the initial assessment of their issues. Questionnaires such as the Beck Depression Inventory (BDI) can indicate how a client is feeling and allow them to express the extent to which their issues are affecting their day-to-day life. Completing the same questionnaire periodically throughout the course of the treatment can be useful to indicate the success of the treatment and monitor progress. Comparing the results of the questionnaire completed at the end of the treatment with those at the start will also help the client and therapist to see how much the client has improved. Part of the initial process of CBT also involves the client and therapist working collaboratively to identify the client's self-defeating beliefs (e.g. 'I must be excellent at absolutely everything, otherwise I am worthless'). Once these irrational beliefs have been uncovered they are challenged by the therapist by questioning the client as to why not excelling at everything makes them worthless. The client will also be required to practise certain optimistic statements which challenge their negative cognitions (e.g. 'I am a worthwhile person even though I am not excellent at everything'). Over time these challenges result in a person's cognition changing, leading to a change in their dysfunctional behaviour. During the skills acquisition phase, the therapist uses techniques such as questioning designed to challenge maladaptive thoughts and relaxation techniques such as breathing and guided imagery to relieve stress in anxious clients.

 You may be asked to describe CBT. Mention what the basic goal of the therapy is, and then say something about each of the three phases. Just vary the depth and detail according to the marks available.

PHASE	DESCRIPTION
Case conceptualisation	The client needs to understand the nature of CBT. A list of problems experienced by the client is created using self-report and questioning. Initial goals and a treatment plan are set.
Skills acquisition and application	The therapist works with the client on intervention techniques, including teaching new skills and ways of thinking about things. The success of this is evaluated, intervention techniques are refined and new goals and targets set as appropriate.
Ending and follow-up	Final assessment of progress using self-report and questioning. Ending treatment and maintaining change is discussed. Top-up sessions can take place three or six months after completion of treatment.

Table 1.9: The three phases of cognitive-behavioural therapy.

Evaluation: effectiveness and appropriateness of CBT

A study by DeRubeis et al. (2005) demonstrates the effectiveness of CBT in treating depression. The researchers studied three groups of depressed participants. Group 1 were treated using CBT, group 2 were given antidepressants and group 3 acted as the placebo (they were given a pill that had no effect). After eight weeks, 43% of the CBT group had improved compared with only 25% of the placebo group. The greatest improvement after an eight week period was for those participants taking the antidepressants: 50% showed signs of improvement. However, conclusions drawn from this study need to be viewed with caution since the study only shows what happened after eight weeks of treatment. For example, evidence suggests that relapse rate is greater for drug therapy than CBT, so therapy is better in the long term.

Hensley et al. (2004) found that the relapse rate for CBT is relatively low compared with that for antidepressants. It is estimated that 50% of those treated for depression with antidepressants will relapse within two years, whereas persevering with CBT offers the individual long-term benefits with little chance of relapse. Drugs therefore may only offer a 'quick fix' in terms of improving the symptoms of depression. Evans et al. (1992) found that CBT was at least as effective as antidepressant drugs in the treatment of depression and preventing relapse in sufferers over a two-year period. This is supported by Blackburn and Moorhead (2000) who found the effects of CBT for symptoms of depression to be significantly superior to antidepressant drug treatments over periods of more than one year. However, the most effective method according to Kupfer and Frank (2001) is a combination of CBT and antidepressants.

Whilst CBT has been found to be effective for treating depression, the active nature of

Beating the blues

In 2009 the Office for National Statistics estimated that just 2 in 100 people with a need are actually able to get CBT. Therapy has never been routinely available on the NHS, despite research showing overwhelmingly that a combined approach of CBT and drug therapy results in a much lower rate of relapse than antidepressants alone. In an attempt to meet the demand for CBT, computerised cognitive-behavioural therapy (CCBT) has been developed. There are a number of CCBT packages, but the NHS has adopted 'Beating the Blues', designed for mild and moderate depression. The course consists of 8 one hour weekly interactive online sessions with 'homework' projects to complete between sessions. CCBT appears to be an appropriate treatment option for those able to complete the programme, although there is considerable drop-out. It also seems to effectively reduce the symptoms of depression (Foroushani et al., 2011).

CBT means that it will not be an appropriate treatment for all people with depression. The time commitment required to attend weekly sessions and the energy and motivation needed to complete homework assignments may be daunting for some, especially since depression is characterised by a lack of motivation.

Unlike antidepressants, CBT doesn't just deal with the symptoms of depression but with the actual cause. It can make a real change in a person's outlook and behaviour and therefore helps them to deal with the problems they face every day, enabling them to adapt to stressful situations and problems in a way that drugs could never achieve.

ELLIS'S ABC MODEL

According to Ellis (1962), emotional problems arise from the way we think, feel and behave. As people consciously or unconsciously generate their own disturbed feelings they are 'largely responsible' for their own condition. It follows then that people also have it within themselves to create lasting and healthy change. Ellis's ABC model of personality and emotional disturbance explains the relationship between thinking, emotion and behaviour, and describes the sequence of events that leads to psychological problems. People begin with life goals that are constructive and positive. However, progress towards these goals is hampered by things which happen in life that cause us to think about what is occurring (A – activating events). For Ellis, these activating events are largely social in nature – for example, arising from relationships with family members, friends and peers. Such relationships are important and they give rise to expectations about ourselves and others. Whilst these relationships can make us feel positive and worthwhile, failing to meet these expectations can create negative feelings. How these activating events are interpreted result in beliefs about our role in the event and the world in general (B – beliefs). These beliefs lead to emotional and behavioural consequences (C – consequences). In many cases, the beliefs are irrational and negative and lead to psychological distress, and it is this that leads to symptoms of depression. Therapy involves disputing these beliefs in order to bring about (effect) change – the D and E of Ellis's rational-emotive behaviour therapy (REBT).

RATIONAL-EMOTIVE BEHAVIOUR THERAPY

According to Ellis, irrational thoughts lead to an irrational 'internal dialogue', and that this will go on to produce irrational behaviour. Therefore, these irrational thoughts should be challenged and replaced with more rational thoughts in order to bring about lasting change. The key idea underlying REBT is that people are not upset by an event as such but by their *perception* of it (i.e. the irrational ways they think about it). In order for their behaviour to change, therefore, their perception needs to change. From his work with depressed people Ellis identified a number of common irrational beliefs, often characterised by the words 'should' and 'must' (e.g. 'I should always be loved and approved of by everyone', 'I must be good at everything to be considered a worthwhile person'). As part of REBT, individuals are taught about the ABC model to help them understand patterns in their thinking and behaviour, and so are then better able to challenge their irrational beliefs. Clients are first of all helped to identify activating events (A) and how they felt as a consequence (C). They are then directed by the therapist to consider the beliefs (B) about the event that have triggered the negative feelings and actions. Next, they are encouraged to recognise and challenge (D – dispute) their 'should' and 'must' beliefs. If this is successful then there should be a new effect (E) or outcome to the client's feelings and actions as a result of changing irrational beliefs to rational ones.

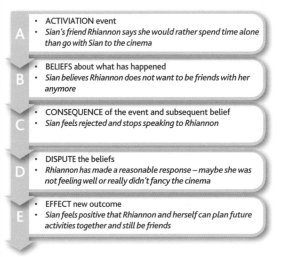

Figure 1.14: Ellis's ABC (and DE) model.

Evaluation: effectiveness and appropriateness of REBT

A study carried out in Romania by David et al. (2008) compared the effectiveness of REBT with other treatments for depression. Some 170 participants were randomly allocated to one of three conditions: REBT, cognitive therapy or antidepressant drugs. Each treatment was administered over a 14 week period with patients receiving up to 20 therapy sessions lasting around 50 minutes each. They also received three top-up sessions over a follow-up period of six months. After the initial 14 weeks of treatment, improvement rates were similar for REBT, cognitive therapy and drugs, with around 60% of patients in each condition making positive progress. However, assessment of patients after the six month follow-up period showed a significant difference between drugs and REBT, with a higher relapse rate for those taking the antidepressants. The researchers concluded that in the long term REBT was significantly better than drugs for treating depression.

REBT is appropriate for use in group therapy. The advantage of using REBT in a group is that each client can contribute to disputing other's irrational beliefs. The group can also support each other in learning the ABC model. The opportunity to take on the role of teacher in supporting others helps clients to feel more independent and in control – attributes which are often lacking in individuals suffering from depression or anxiety. Seeing change occurring in other group members is also encouraging. As REBT can be used in small or large group situations it could be used to treat a family or even a couple experiencing relationship difficulties.

Some therapists argue that REBT is not appropriate for use with all people. For example, empathy is considered a crucial component of therapy and is associated with improved outcomes for clients. However, empathy is

---

REBT in schools?

Not only can REBT be effective but it is also appropriate for use with a wide range of clients in varied settings. Gonzalez et al. (2004) carried out a meta-analysis of 19 studies of REBT conducted on children and adolescents. They found that all the studies in their analysis showed improved outcomes for those receiving REBT compared with control groups receiving no intervention. The biggest impact of REBT was seen with children who displayed disruptive behaviour in the classroom. They also found that REBT was equally effective for youngsters both with and without a specific identified problem, suggesting that REBT is also useful for problem prevention. The research found that the participants showed greater improvement when the REBT techniques were delivered by teachers and members of staff rather than health professionals. This has implications for practice in schools, with more children able to access the care they need within their school rather than seeking external support.

---

problematic in REBT since it is important for a therapist to remain detached enough from the client to be able to identify and challenge irrational beliefs. Also, some clients feel threatened by the active approach taken by REBT. If irrational beliefs are challenged by the therapist too vigorously too early in the therapeutic relationship then there is a risk that clients may drop out.

You need to be able to evaluate all the therapies and treatments in this chapter in terms of their appropriateness and effectiveness. Be warned, it is possible to be asked for one or the other, so make sure that you learn them as separate evaluative issues. If you are simply asked to evaluate a therapy then you can include whatever you like, including criticisms of the approach in general.

EVALUATION OF THE COGNITIVE APPROACH TO EXPLAINING DEPRESSION

There has been a huge amount of research surrounding cognitive theories of depression and, generally, they have arrived at quite a positive conclusion. For example, Reynolds and Salkovskis (1992) found that sufferers of depression do tend to indulge in a great deal more negative thinking than individuals who don't suffer from depression. They also experience a higher number and frequency of intrusive negative thoughts than individuals who don't suffer depression. Hammen and Krantz (1976) asked a group of depressed females and a group of females not suffering from depression to read paragraphs describing situations in which females were encountering certain difficult or stressful situations. The women suffering from depression made significantly more errors in logic in their interpretations of the situations than the women who were not suffering from depression. Evans et al. (2005) investigated the cognitions of sufferers of depression and found support for the cognitive explanation. Not only did depressed people tend to think more negatively, but the more of these maladaptive cognitions the sufferer holds, the more serious is their depression.

In a related line of research, it has been found that individuals who ruminate are more at risk of depression. Rumination refers to the tendency to mull over things and events. Ruminators contribute to their depression by negatively biasing their thinking so that it influences how they view their past, present and future. According to Kinderman et al. (2013), rumination is the most significant negative cognition influencing depression and is perhaps the biggest predictor of depression.

Whilst research has been generally supportive of the cognitive approach, critics argue that it isn't really a comprehensive explanation.

Biochemical factors in depression

The success of medical treatments indicates that depressed people may have chemical imbalances in the brain. The most widespread antidepressant drugs are selective serotonin reuptake inhibitors (SSRIs) of which there are several types (e.g. fluoxetine, also known by its brand name Prozac). SSRIs work by preventing the reabsorption (reuptake) of serotonin back into brain cells, so there is more of it available and its effects in the brain are prolonged. Another antidepressant in common use is serotonin-noradrenaline reuptake inhibitors (SNRIs). These work like SSRIs, but now concentrations in the brain of both serotonin and noradrenaline are increased. SNRIs work in a similar way to another common antidepressant, tricyclics, but without the negative side effects sometimes associated with tricyclics. Noradrenaline is also a target for monoamine oxidase inhibitors (MAOIs). Monoamine oxidase is an enzyme that breaks down noradrenaline, so blocking MAO means more noradrenaline is available. None of these drugs have proved to be entirely successful in treating depression, and some studies have shown drugs to be no more effective than a placebo. However, they remain the first course of treatment for most people diagnosed with depression.

Negative thinking and depression appear to be very closely linked, though it is not yet clear whether negative thinking precedes and thus causes depression or whether it is a symptom of another underlying cause. Depression is clearly linked to neurochemical imbalances (see box 'Biochemical factors in depression'), and it may be this that is responsible for the way that depressed people think.

PHOBIA

The term phobia comes from the ancient Greek *phobos*, meaning fear. It is 'an excessive, unreasonable, persistent fear triggered by a specific object or situation' (Davey, 2008).

The key characteristic of phobia is that the fear is irrational: the response far exceeds any real danger posed by the object of fear. The fear is accompanied by an excessive and unreasonable desire to avoid the thing that causes fear.

Phobias cause an intense fear response that is persistent and rarely disappears without treatment. It is estimated that about 10% of the population suffer from a specific phobia and between 4–14% a social phobia. Agoraphobia, at about 5%, is the least common phobia but the most frequent in terms of treatment. This is because it is particularly debilitating and its effects widespread. Whilst agoraphobia is very disabling, some phobias are not so disruptive that a person can't get on with life in a relatively normal way. For example, a person with a fear of horses might be able to cope with this fear (by avoiding horses wherever possible), but a teacher who develops a social phobia of public speaking is going to face major problems as a result. The emotional, behavioural and cognitive characteristics of a phobia will vary according to the type of phobia, but the common characteristics are listed in Table 1.11.

TYPE OF PHOBIA	DESCRIPTION
Specific phobias	Fears of particular objects or situations: natural environment type (e.g. fire or heights); animal type (e.g. the fear of spiders); situational type (e.g. fear of flying); medical type (fear of medical procedures and illnesses, e.g. fear of injection).
Social phobia	Fear of performing some kind of action in the presence of others (e.g. public speaking). Mostly related to specific situations, but can be a generalised social phobia where there is an irrational fear of most social encounters.
Agoraphobia	Fear of being incapacitated by a panic attack in a situation where escape would be difficult or embarrassing, or where help would be unavailable. This means that sufferers avoid public and unfamiliar places.

Table 1.10: The three main categories of phobia.

EMOTIONAL	BEHAVIOURAL	COGNITIVE
Fear	Escape from feared object or situation	Lack of self-confidence
Worry	Avoidance of feared object or situation	Mild depression
Anxiety		Self-doubt

Table 1.11: Common characteristics of phobias.

THE BEHAVIOURAL APPROACH TO EXPLAINING PHOBIAS

The behavioural approach explains the development and maintenance of phobia mainly using the theories of classical conditioning and operant conditioning. These were first combined as a single explanation for phobia by Mowrer (1960).

Mowrer's two-process model of phobia

Classical conditioning is learning by association. An individual experiences the pairing of a previously neutral object with a negative experience of fear and anxiety. For example, a child with no previous fear of dogs gets bitten by a dog and from then on associates dogs with fear and pain. Due to the process of generalisation, the child is not just afraid of the dog that bit her but shows a fear of all dogs (see Figure 1.15). Operant conditioning explains how phobia is maintained. The conditioned stimulus (in the dog example) evokes fear, and avoidance of the feared object or situation lessens this feeling, which is rewarding. This reward (negative reinforcement) increases the likelihood of engaging in this fear-reducing avoidance behaviour in the future. In the example of fear of dogs, the phobic feels better by avoiding any situation where there might be a dog. Unfortunately, because we are now less likely to learn that dogs are nice and very few bite, the phobia is not only maintained but probably worsens.

Social learning and phobia

It also a distinct possibility that social learning is involved in the development and maintenance of phobia. It is already well understood that behaviours can be acquired through vicarious learning (i.e. learning simply from watching others). This probably applies to phobias, too. For example, an infant that has never seen a snake before may look to its mother for

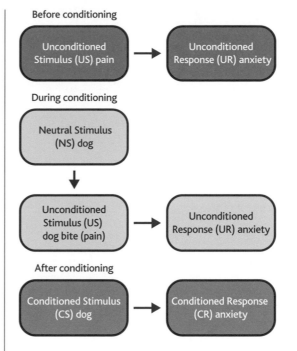

Figure 1.15: Classical conditioning of a phobia of dogs.

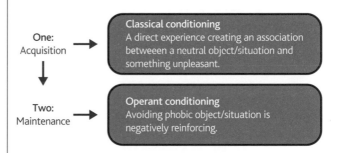

Figure 1.16: The two-process model of phobia.

information about how to respond to this novel object. If the mother's reaction is passive and neutral the baby will probably show a similar reaction. If, however, the mother displays anxiety and snatches the baby away the baby learns from this reaction that a snake is an object of danger, will not attempt to play with it, and may even display an aversion to snakes in the future. Alternatively, a child might observe a parent's fear reaction to a particular object and thus may learn, vicariously, to also show this fear this response.

BEHAVIOURAL APPROACH TO TREATMENT: SYSTEMATIC DESENSITISATION

The therapy begins with the client being given relaxation training. This step is very important because of *reciprocal inhibition* – this is where one response is inhibited because it is incompatible with another. In this case, fear involves tension and tension is incompatible with relaxation – one cannot be relaxed and fearful at the same time! A key component of desensitisation is the *anxiety hierarchy*. Developed in discussion between the therapist and the client, this is a list of specific situations and factors that influence anxiety level – for example, someone with a fear of spiders might list all the things about spiders they don't like and the situations in which they might encounter spiders. These are then ranked from the least to most frightening. This list is crucial as it provides a structure for the therapy. The therapist moves the client up the hierarchy, at each point associating relaxation rather than anxiety with the feared object or situation, until the highest point in the hierarchy can be reached in a state of relaxation. How long this takes before treatment is considered successful depends very much on the individual and the nature of the phobia. The therapy often involves imagining the phobic object or situation – known as *in vitro* desensitisation. It has been suggested, however, that the more realistic the situation, the more effective the therapy,

which has led some therapists to use *in vivo* desensitisation, where the feared object or situation is encountered from the very start.

Evaluation: effectiveness and appropriateness of systematic desensitisation

Paul (1966) compared the effectiveness of systematic desensitisation, insight therapy and an attention placebo (where participants took a harmless pill and listened to a 'stress tape') in reducing phobia of public speaking. He found that systematic desensitisation showed the greatest improvement, and also that this improvement was still evident two years later. Choy et al. (2007) carried out a meta-analysis of studies using systematic desensitisation *in vitro* (imagination based), *in vivo* (real life) and using virtual reality. They appeared to differ in effectiveness depending on what they were applied to – for example, using virtual reality for height or flying phobias is reasonably successful, but less so for specific animal phobias or social phobias.

Systematic desensitisation may be more appropriate for some types of phobia than others because of possibly different underlying causes. For example, if a fear of public speaking originates with poor social skills, then phobia reduction is more likely to occur in a treatment which includes learning new and more effective social skills rather than systematic desensitisation alone. Choy et al. (2007) also highlighted the issues surrounding the appropriateness of *in vivo* systematic desensitisation. It seems that using this type of therapy to treat phobias results in a very high level of drop-out due to the levels of stress involved. Discontinuation of a treatment part way through may actually do more harm than good – individuals have been exposed to the object of their phobia and experienced high levels of anxiety, thus their existing fear has been reinforced.

BEHAVIOURAL APPROACH TO TREATMENT: FLOODING

This type of exposure therapy is based on the classical conditioning premise that a phobia is a generalised conditioned response. This means that, in principle, if a phobic never again comes across the source of the fear then this conditioned response should extinguish. This rarely (if ever) happens, however, either because this is just not practical or because the phobic engages in avoidance behaviours which maintain the phobia – a phobic cannot learn that the thing they fear is not harmful or undeserving of a fearful response if they always avoid it. What flooding aims to do is expose the sufferer to the phobic object or situation for an extended period of time in a safe and controlled environment. Unlike other exposure therapies that might use *in vitro* or virtual exposure, flooding generally involves *in vivo* exposure. Before exposure the client might be trained in relaxation techniques so that they are best able to control their fearful response. Fear is a time-limited physical response – the initial strong bodily arousal caused by hormones such as adrenaline can only last so long before the body calms down. Prolonged intense exposure then eventually creates a new association between the feared object or situation and something positive (i.e. a sense of calm and a lack of anxiety). It also prevents reinforcement of phobia through escape/avoidance behaviours.

Evaluation: effectiveness and appropriateness of flooding

Flooding is not an appropriate treatment for every phobic. For reasons that are not clearly understood, some people actually increase their fear after therapy, and it is not possible to predict when or to whom this will occur. Wolpe (1969) reported the case of a client whose anxiety intensified to such a degree that flooding therapy resulted in her being hospitalised. A further problem is that flooding is successful only so far as the phobic is able to remain in the fearful situation until they are calm and relaxed. Exiting treatment before completion is likely to strengthen rather than weaken the phobia. For Wolpe, these unpredictable individual differences in responses to flooding means that it is a high risk therapy that cannot be justified except as a last resort. A survey of therapists by Shipley and Boudewyns (1980) however showed that very few negative side effects from flooding are reported, suggesting that for most people it is an appropriate and safe treatment.

The fact that flooding has been around since the 1950s, and is still in use today, suggests that it is an effective treatment for phobia. Some studies have shown it to be at least as effective as, and in some circumstances more effective than, systematic desensitisation (e.g. Marks et al., 1971). Other studies have found little or no advantage of flooding over other treatments (e.g. Shaw, 1979, with social phobia). It is not 100% effective, however, and factors that influence its effectiveness have been identified – for example, the initial level of anxiety, the degree of anxiety produced during treatment and whether the fear stimulus is imaginal or *in vivo*. Length of exposure seems to be particularly important – Marshall (1985), for example, found the greatest benefits of flooding with height phobics when there was prolonged exposure beyond the point at which anxiety levels fell back to baseline levels.

EVALUATION OF THE BEHAVIOURAL APPROACH TO EXPLAINING PHOBIA

Behavioural approaches take a limited view of the origins of phobia in that they overlook the role of cognition. This seems illogical, given that irrational thinking appears to be a key characteristic of phobia, as suggested by Tomarken et al. (1989). They presented a series of slides of snakes and neutral objects (e.g. trees) to phobics and non-phobics. Afterwards, all the participants were asked how many snakes, trees, etc. they had been shown. It was found that phobic people tended to overestimate the number of snakes.

An advantage of the behavioural approach is that it is open to scientific scrutiny. Indeed, the first controlled study demonstrating the role of classical conditioning in phobia was back in 1920 by Watson and Rayner (see box 'Little Albert's fear'). However, there are a number of aspects of the theory which are not supported scientifically:

» It should be possible to trace a phobia back to its original learning experience, but this is often not possible. Öst and Hugdahl (1981) claim that nearly half of all people with phobias have never had an anxious experience with the object of their fear, and some have had no experience whatsoever. For example, snake phobics have usually never encountered a snake.
» If the same learning principles underpin all phobias then it is not clear why only some people develop phobia following a similar trauma. Di Nardo et al. (1988) found that 50% of people with a fear of dogs had had some kind of negative experience with a dog in their childhood. However, 50% of participants who had no phobias at all reported that they had experienced a traumatic event involving a dog. Di Nardo et al. noted that those who had developed a phobia tended to have

focused more on the likelihood of that kind of event happening again, suggesting a role for cognition in the development of phobia.

In theory, a phobia to any potentially harmful object or situation could develop, however, this does not happen. Cars pose a very realistic threat to life, yet phobia of cars is virtually non-existent. This is despite almost every adult either having experienced, witnessed or heard about a car accident in which someone has been injured. Seligman (1970) suggested *preparedness theory* to explain why some phobias are more readily acquired than others. This theory proposes that humans have been 'prepared' by evolution to be fearful of things which in our distant past were a danger to survival. Our ancestors who quickly learned to avoid things like snakes, heights and spiders improved their chance of survival. We have not had enough time to evolve a tendency to fear cars and guns, even though they are far more dangerous to our survival in modern society than, say, spiders and snakes.

Little Albert's fear

Little Albert was a quiet 11-month-old child who showed no fear to any of the objects shown to him by Watson and Rayner (1920) (masks, animals, etc.). To condition Albert, Watson presented him with a white rat – an animal that Albert had previously felt no fear of. On presentation, Watson struck a metal bar with a hammer behind Albert's back, making a loud noise and upsetting Albert. After a few of these rat–hammer pairings, Albert became distressed when presented with the rat – he had been classically conditioned to fear the rat. Albert generalised his fear to other things, such as a Father Christmas beard and Watson's white hair.

OBSESSIVE-COMPULSIVE DISORDER

Many people have rituals and behaviours that they repeat (e.g. checking the door really is locked, stepping over cracks in the pavement). For someone with obsessive-compulsive disorder (OCD), however, these recurrent thoughts and behaviours are accompanied by intense feelings of anxiety which can be disabling.

Someone with OCD has obsessions or compulsions, or a combination of both. Obsessions are recurrent and persistent thoughts, impulses or images which are intrusive and cause significant anxiety or distress. Compulsions are repetitive behaviours or mental actions with rigidly applied rules, and often linked to obsessions (as an attempt to neutralise or abolish them). OCD is often co-morbid with other disorders, such as depression, panic and phobia. There can be a gradual build-up over several years to full-blown OCD, or it can develop quite quickly, at any time in life. There may be a 2.5% risk of OCD, but estimates vary because many suffers do not seek help and simply adjust their lives to adapt to their condition.

Kessler et al. (1999) estimate that as few as 40% of sufferers will actually seek help for their disorder. OCD differs in form across cultures. Fontenelle et al. (2004) found that not only were females more likely to develop OCD than males but that their obsessions and compulsions were different according to the countries in which they lived. Middle Eastern women for example were much more likely to have obsessions and compulsions involving religion than European and North American women.

EMOTIONAL	BEHAVIOURAL	COGNITIVE
Anxiety and distress	Impulsiveness	Intrusive thoughts
Worry	Compulsions	Repetitive thoughts
Fear	Rigid, habitual behaviour (e.g. double checking)	Irrational but irresistible thoughts
Mood problems and swings		Doubts
	Superstitious behaviour	

Table 1.12: Some characteristics of OCD.

THE BIOLOGICAL APPROACH TO EXPLAINING OCD: NEURAL EXPLANATIONS

Rauch et al. (1994) used positron emission tomography (PET) scans to study the brain activity of OCD sufferers. They found that when faced with the object of their obsessions and compulsions (e.g. a person with a cleaning obsession and compulsion was shown something unclean) PET scans revealed increased activity in the frontal lobes and another brain region called the basal ganglia. The basal ganglia comprise a series of interconnected brain structures running in a loop from the front of the brain (in particular, the orbital frontal cortex) through a series of structures deeper in the brain, which include the striatum, globus pallidus and thalamus, and back again to the cortex. The function of the basal ganglia is not fully understood, but they are thought to play a role in cognition, attention and movement.

Problems with the basal ganglia have been associated with compulsive-type behaviours in other disorders such as Tourette's syndrome, a disorder characterised by seemingly compulsive

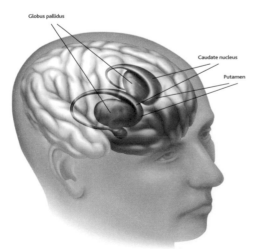

Figure 1.17: Some components of the basal ganglia. The striatum is made up of the caudate nucleus and putamen, which are separated by tracts of fibres called the internal capsules.

vocal and motor tics. Rauch and Jenike (1993) note that Tourette's syndrome and OCD are very often co-morbid, so it may be that the same brain dysfunction might be contributing to both OCD and Tourette's.

A possible link between OCD and the basal ganglia is the discovery that the basal ganglia are involved in the formation of habits, so dysfunctions in brain regions involving the basal ganglia could result in problems with the initiation and control of repetitive and habitual behaviours. Saxena et al. (1998), for instance, suggest that several basal ganglia structures together form a 'control system' that regulates something called the cortical-striatal-thalamic circuit (a loop of neurons which connect the prefrontal cortex, the basal ganglia and the thalamus). A failure in this basal ganglia control system means that habitual and routine-like motor responses originating in the cortical-striatal-thalamic circuit may not be inhibited. The result might thus be the uncontrollable compulsive habits seen in cases of OCD.

OCD is commonly co-morbid with depression, and it is often the case that when sufferers are given drug treatments for depression the symptoms of OCD also seem to ease. These drugs are typically SSRIs and work by increasing the amount of serotonin available in the brain. This has led many researchers to suggest that OCD is caused by a lack of serotonin. Research results, however, are quite varied. For example, many studies have found that drugs which increase the levels of serotonin in a person's system can actually make the symptoms of OCD worse (e.g. Hollander et al., 1992). This had led to the suggestion that OCD is related to an abnormality in neurotransmitter systems *linked* to the serotonin systems. Drugs which affect the serotonin system seem to be effective in treating OCD because they have a knock-on effect on the system that is linked to the serotonin levels, rather than because of direct effects on the serotonin system itself.

Evaluation of neural explanations

There have been numerous cases reported of OCD developing as a result of brain damage, supporting the notion that OCD may be associated with abnormal brain functioning. Rapoport (1990) for example, reports the case of an 8-year-old boy who, following treatment for a brain haemorrhage, developed OCD related to the number 7. Rapoport also reviewed the consequences of a widespread viral brain epidemic that occurred in Europe from 1916 to 1918 called 'the great sleeping sickness'. Records of the time indicate that there was also a significant rise in the number of cases of OCD. This might be because the viral infection caused some damage or dysfunction that contributed to the OCD.

McGuire et al. (1994) found that the cortical-striatal-thalamic circuit showed increased activity on PET scans when sufferers observed obsession-related images, suggesting that these brain structures do have some influence on the symptoms of OCD. Other studies however have reported a decrease in activity in this area. Pena-Garijo et al. (2011), for example, used fMRI to compare the brain activity of 13 OCD patients and found reduced activity compared to a healthy control group. It seems that whilst this brain area may be involved in OCD, its exact contribution remains uncertain.

Whilst SSRIs increase the amount of serotonin in the brain and can successfully treat the symptoms of OCD, the exact role of the neurotransmitter in OCD is far from clear. However, serotonin-based drugs are not helpful for all sufferers. Bastani et al. (1990), for example, found that increasing the amount of serotonin in the brain can actually make OCD symptoms worse. Other neurotransmitters have also been implicated, such as dopamine and glutamate. It is not clear whether OCD is caused by problems with particular neurotransmitters or by imbalances in how several interact. Symptoms can vary

Psychosurgery for OCD

A neural origin for OCD is supported by the treatment of OCD with psychosurgery (the destruction of a small part of the brain to bring about a change in behaviour). About 20-30% of sufferers do not respond to medication or psychological therapy, and for these psychosurgery may be an appropriate alternative treatment. D'Astous et al. (2013) evaluated an operation called bilateral anterior capsulotomy (surgical damage to a part of the basal ganglia called the internal capsules). In a seven-year follow-up, almost half of the 19 patients had responded well to surgery. Whilst two had permanent complications as a result of surgery, there were no deaths.

Deep brain stimulation (DBS) is an alternative procedure which carries low risk of permanent brain damage. A device is implanted that sends electrical impulses down thin wires (electrodes) into the brain. This moderates symptoms so that they are more manageable, e.g. making sufferers more responsive to psychological therapies. When the device is switched off or fails (e.g. the batteries run out), signs of OCD rapidly reappear, strongly indicating a neural origin for OCD. Various components of the basal ganglia have been targeted for stimulation, although the most effective targets have yet to be identified.

A new surgical procedure trialed by Jung et al. (2014) uses ultrasound to destroy the anterior internal capsules. Follow-up assessments of four patients showed gradual improvement in symptoms. As this is a non-invasive procedure there were none of the side-effects or complications associated with invasive surgeries.

considerably between sufferers so it may even be that OCD has a variety of neurochemical causes. Nor is it entirely certain whether changes in neurochemistry cause OCD or whether OCD causes changes in neurochemistry.

THE BIOLOGICAL APPROACH TO EXPLAINING OCD: GENETIC EXPLANATIONS

Some researchers have looked at rates of OCD within families, based on the premise that as genetic similarity increases between family members then so should rates of OCD. Shih et al. (2004) found that first-degree relatives (i.e. those with the closest genetic similarity – parent/child, brother/sister) have an 8% chance of both having OCD, much higher than second and third-degree relatives. A study of 46 children and adolescents with OCD revealed that 17% of the parents also suffered from the disorder (Lenane et al., 1990). In a later study, Leonard et al. (1992) found 13% of first-degree relatives of child and adolescent OCD sufferers also met the DSM criteria for OCD. Bellodi et al. (1992) noted that in children who suffered from OCD before the age of 14, the likelihood of relatives also having OCD was 8.8%. In children who were diagnosed with OCD at a later age,

the likelihood was lower at 3.2%. This suggests a greater prevalence of OCD in families when the onset of the disorder is early. These findings all show rates of OCD much higher than in the general population.

One way of separating out the effects of genes from those of the environment is to compare rates of OCD in identical (or monozygotic – MZ) twins. If OCD was entirely genetic then if one MZ twin develops OCD then we would expect the other to develop it too. The shared rates of OCD (or *concordance*) should be far greater in MZ twins than non-identical (dizygotic – DZ) twins, who only share 50% of their genes. One further advantage of such a comparison is that it clarifies the environmental contribution to OCD. MZ twins share very similar environments, as do DZ twins. This means that any differences in concordance rates between the two types of twin should be due to genetic similarity rather than environmental differences. Carey and Gottesman (1981) found that MZ twins were 87% concordant for OCD

Identical twins share the same genes. Research suggests that if one twin develops OCD then there is a high risk of the other developing it too.

compared with 47% for DZ twins. A meta-analysis of twin studies by Nestadt et al. (2010) found that 68% of MZ twins were concordant for OCD, compared to 31% of DZ twins. Whilst this clearly indicates a role for genes in OCD, it also shows that they do not fully explain the disorder, as otherwise the concordance rate for MZ twins would be 100%.

More recent research has discovered a particular gene that may play a significant role in OCD. This gene (called SLC1A1) in chromosome 9 helps regulate the flow of a substance called glutamate in and out of brain cells (Arnold et al., 2006). Research has established differences in the glutamate system between OCD and non-OCD individuals, indicating that this substance may play a role in OCD. It could be then that variations in the gene may lead to alterations in the flow of glutamate, thereby increasing the chances of an individual developing OCD. Since medication for OCD involves increasing serotonin levels in the brain, research has also focused on genes that play a role in the serotonin system. Wendland et al. (2007) found that gene SLC6A4 (in chromosome 17) may be responsible for creating too much of a protein that works to transport serotonin away for recycling, thus preventing its action in the synapse. Excessive activity of this gene will therefore result in too little serotonin available for important cell communication.

Evaluation of genetic explanations

Family and twin studies appear to support the idea that genes play a role in OCD. However, concordance rates are not 100%, which is what you would expect if the disorder was entirely genetic in origin. This indicates that genes are not the sole explanation and that there is an environmental contribution.

The findings of twin studies should be interpreted with care. For example, the assumption that the environmental effect can be eliminated when comparing DZ and MZ concordance rates because of shared environments is questionable. The environments of MZ twins are likely to be more similar than the environments of DZ twins, and MZ twins are more likely to be treated similarly (DZ twins may not even be the same gender). The similarity of MZ twin environments means that environmental risk factors for one twin are likely to be present for the other. It is very difficult, therefore, to separate gene/environment influences in order to conclude with confidence that concordance rates are solely due to the influence of one or the other. An added complication is that environmental factors can cause genes to be 'switched on' and 'switched off'. This means that MZ twins can have the same genes but have different genes functioning. This makes it difficult not only to compare MZ and DZ concordance rates but also to account for gene/environment effects.

OCD is a complex disorder where there may be a number of subtypes – for example, hoarding, primary obsessional, tic-related early onset (ages 10 to 12) and late onset (ages 18 to 23). It may be that different genetic factors contribute to these subtypes. Hemmings et al. (2004), for instance, found that a defect in a gene for dopamine (called DRD4) was much less common in people with early onset OCD than in those with late onset OCD.

A number of genes have been identified which might be related to OCD, involving neurotransmitter systems for serotonin, dopamine, monoamine oxidase and myelin oligodendrocyte glycoprotein (MOG-4). However, there is a lack of consistency in research findings which means we should be cautious about attributing the cause of OCD to one specific gene. It may well be that there are multiple genetic causes of OCD, including the possibility of an interacting network of genetic influences (some of which yet to be discovered).

THE BIOLOGICAL APPROACH TO TREATING OCD – DRUG THERAPY

The most common biological treatment for OCD is the use of tricyclic and SSRI drugs. These drugs increase the amount of serotonin available to the brain. Whilst they are usually prescribed to treat depression, they have been found to also effectively reduce the symptoms of OCD. (See earlier discussion of SSRIs and OCD on page 106.) Certain anxiolytic (anxiety-reducing) drugs are also used to treat the anxiety that accompanies OCD. In particular, clinicians employ a type of anxiolytic called benzodiazepines (BZ). These work by increasing the effectiveness of a neurochemical called gamma-aminobutyric acid (GABA). We produce this neurochemical naturally when we need to calm our physiological responses and brain activity. Benzodiazepines increase the effectiveness of GABA by mimicking its form and tricking brain cells into thinking important parts of the brain are indicating that their cells should be less active than they currently are. These drugs are very effective in reducing brain activity and consequently reducing the anxiety experienced by sufferers of OCD. Another drug occasionally prescribed to reduce the anxious side effects of OCD are beta blockers. Beta receptors are located in various parts of the body, such as the heart and blood vessels. When stimulated by the hormones adrenaline and noradrenaline these beta receptors increase blood pressure and cause the heart to beat harder. This is all part of the normal stress response. Beta blockers 'block'

Whilst drugs can effectively reduce the symptoms of OCD, they do not provide a cure.

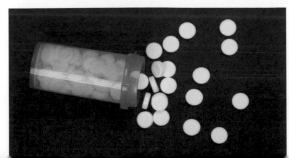

the effects of adrenaline and noradrenaline, thus preventing the stress reaction and reducing the physiological effects of anxiety caused by obsessions and compulsions.

Evaluation: effectiveness and appropriateness of drug therapy

Many psychologists argue that psychological treatments are more appropriate than drug treatments for OCD. Greist et al. (1998) compared the effectiveness of exposure and ritual prevention therapy (ERPT) to that of drug treatments. ERPT is a form of behaviour therapy, similar to systematic desensitisation, where sufferers are repeatedly exposed to objects or situations that produce anxiety, at the same time resisting their obsession and/or compulsions. Greist found that ERPT was just as effective a treatment for OCD as drugs were, and did not have the side effects and high relapse rates associated with drug treatment. This has led some to argue that ERPT should always be the preferred treatment for OCD.

Drugs are cheap, quick, easy and effective ways of managing the symptoms of anxiety associated with OCD. Whilst this is their greatest strength, it is also their greatest weakness. They treat the symptoms rather than the cause, so do not provide a 'cure' as such (there is no consensus about the *cause* of OCD). They are a cheap, quick and easy alternative to the lengthy and expensive process of psychological therapy, and this has led to their over-prescription. Whilst the risk of physiological dependency with OCD drug treatments is relatively low, there can be degrees of psychological dependency (i.e. the person thinks they need the drugs). There are also a great number of side effects from the medication, depending on the dosage and type of drug taken. On these grounds, many psychologists have questioned whether drugs by themselves are an appropriate therapy for most sufferers of OCD.

EVALUATION OF THE BIOLOGICAL APPROACH

One of the main issues with drugs as a treatment for OCD is that, whilst scientists have a good idea *how* they work, they don't really know *why* they work. Nor is it understood why they work in some people to some degree but offer no significant benefits to others. It has been argued that until the exact cause of OCD is known drugs will never be more than a 'preventative shot in the dark'. Delgado and Moreno (1998) state that as there is no consensus view on the function of serotonin and other neurotransmitters in the cause of OCD, drugs which increase these chemicals should be avoided when treating this disorder.

Whilst there is strong evidence to support a role for the basal ganglia in OCD, abnormalities in other brain regions have also been associated with the disorder. There are many different subtypes of OCD, characterised by their own set of symptoms. It seems likely that these subtypes have their own specific neural abnormalities. Furthermore, the differences in brain structure seen in OCD sufferers may be a consequence of the OCD symptoms rather than the cause of them. An unpicking of this cause and effect issue would require longitudinal studies beginning before the onset of OCD. These have not been conducted, and so 'a primary pathological process underlying core OCD symptoms has yet to be identified' (Zohar et al., 2012, cited in Davey et al., 2014). Clearly, the neural basis of OCD is very complex and understanding it will require much more research.

According to the diathesis stress model, OCD is a result of a combination of psychological and biological factors. Psychological stress is clearly linked to OCD, with sufferers often reporting increased stressors preceding the onset or worsening of symptoms. Furthermore, the importance of psychological factors in OCD can be seen in the greater long-term success of

An inflated sense of responsibility

A number of cognitive explanations have been proposed for OCD, but the most supported one is the inflated responsibility hypothesis (Salkovskis, 1985). Everybody has repetitive and intrusive thoughts, but most people dismiss these as trivial or emotionally neutral events. Some individuals, however, become disturbed by them. This is due to cognitive biases in how they are interpreted, specifically that they somehow represent a danger or threat and they are personally responsible for doing something about it. For example, a person has an anxiety that they may not have locked the front door. Most people will shrug this off but some can't do this since any consequences of not locking it would be theirs to bear. Such uncomfortable thoughts are *neutralised* by behaviours which reduce these intrusive thoughts, such as checking that the door is locked. As they are rewarding, anxiety neutralising behaviours are likely to be repeated when similar thoughts arise in future. Thus, obsessions develop (e.g. What if I haven't locked the door?) and individuals feel compelled to engage in neutralising behaviours with increasing frequency (e.g. I'd better go back to check that door!).

psychological therapies over biological ones. Also, some recent psychological theories have made major contributions to understanding OCD (for example, see box 'An inflated sense of responsibility'). All of this suggests that an explanation of OCD which does not take into account psychological factors is destined to be a less than comprehensive one.

Comments on the effectiveness of biological treatments can also be effective evaluation, as well as using alternative, contrasting explanations.

KEY TERMS

ABC model Ellis's model of personality and emotional disturbance explains the relationship between thinking, emotion and behaviour.

Anxiolytics Drugs used to treat the symptoms of anxiety.

Basal ganglia A system of structures found deep in the brain, problems with which are associated with the symptoms of OCD.

Cognitive bias People who suffer *depression* will often focus on some negative aspect of a situation whilst ignoring other more positive information, causing them to distort or exaggerate problems and the causes of these problems.

Cognitive-behavioural therapy (CBT) A therapy that aims to identify and address the negative thinking that gives rise to mental health problems.

Depression Negative triad – negative thoughts of the self, thoughts of the present world and thoughts of the future that can lead to depression.

Deviation from ideal mental health A person is regarded as 'abnormal' when he/she does not meet the criteria for optimal living.

Deviation from social norms A person is regard as 'abnormal' when he/she does not adhere to the norms laid down by the society in which they live.

Failure to function adequately People who are 'abnormal' engage in activities that are somehow 'not good for them' (i.e. maladaptive).

Flooding A type of exposure therapy where the phobic is exposed to the object of their fear for an extended period of time so that a new, more positive association is learned.

***In vitro* desensitisation** A form of *systematic desensitisation* where the phobic object or situation is imagined.

***In vivo* desensitisation** A form of *systematic desensitisation* where the feared object or situation is actually encountered.

Obsessive-compulsive disorder (OCD) A disorder where obsessions, compulsions or a combination of both create disabling anxiety.

Phobia An excessive, unreasonable, persistent fear triggered by a specific object or situation.

Rational-emotive behaviour therapy (REBT) Ellis's therapy whereby irrational thoughts are challenged and replaced with more rational thoughts in order to bring about lasting change.

Selective serotonin reuptake inhibitor (SSRI) Some drugs that treat *depression* and anxiety work by preventing the reabsorption (reuptake) of serotonin back into brain cells so there is more of it available and its effects in the brain are more prolonged.

Social phobia Fear of performing some kind of action in the presence of others.

Specific phobias Fears of particular objects or situations.

Statistical infrequency A behaviour is 'abnormal' due to its statistical rarity.

Systematic desensitisation A behavioural therapy based on classical conditioning where new learning is developed associating the feared object or situation with a feeling of relaxation.

Two-process model of phobia A behavioural explanation which explains how *phobia* begins with classical conditioning and is maintained due to operant conditioning.

PAGE 91

Abnormality can be defined as 'deviation from statistical norms'.

Outline and evaluate this definition of abnormality.

(6 marks)

This question illustrates the core skills needed for all four definitions of abnormality. You need to be able to outline in enough detail for 3 marks (don't be afraid to include an example to illustrate and clarify your outline). Knowing three evaluative points will give you plenty of scope for answering short questions like this, or longer ones where you might need more evaluative detail.

PAGE 99

Outline *and* evaluate the cognitive approach to explaining depression. *(12 marks)*

There are only 6 outline marks available here so don't go overboard with the detail. There are many ways of addressing the evaluative component. There is a section in this book specifically about this, but you could also add other relevant material – for example, to do with the effectiveness of cognitive therapies.

PAGE 100

Karl has a phobia of spiders. His fear completely dominates his life. Things have become so bad that he is now receiving systematic desensitisation therapy.

a. Outline one cognitive characteristic and one behavioural characteristic of phobia. *(2 marks)*

b. Outline a hierarchy that Karl and his therapist might use during systematic desensitisation. *(4 marks)*

The key thing here is to apply your knowledge to the context provided (i.e. Karl). Failure to do this will result in you losing lots of marks.

PAGE 101

Evaluate the behavioural approach to treating phobia. *(6 marks)*

The temptation with questions like this that only ask for evaluation is to describe – in this case the behavioural approach. You will get no marks for doing things not asked for by the question, so discipline yourself.

PAGE 108

'There is some evidence to suggest that a person with OCD is more likely to have another family member with the condition compared with someone who does not have OCD.'

Discuss research into biological explanations for obsessive-compulsive disorder. *(12 marks)*

Unless a question explicitly asks you to, you do not need to engage with quotes. Here, the quote is cueing you in to genetic research, but the question just asks for biological explanations so you can choose what it is you want to do. Also, the question says research – this is theory and/or studies. Again you are given a choice. This question illustrates well why you should not rush into answering a question – think and plan carefully first.

PAGE 110

'The aim of drug treatment is to effectively control the signs and symptoms of OCD.'

Evaluate drug therapy for obsessive-compulsive disorder (OCD). *(6 marks)*

Quotes can sometime cue you in to the kinds of things you should be talking about so remember to read them carefully. Here, the quote is giving a clear hint as to what you might mention in your evaluation!

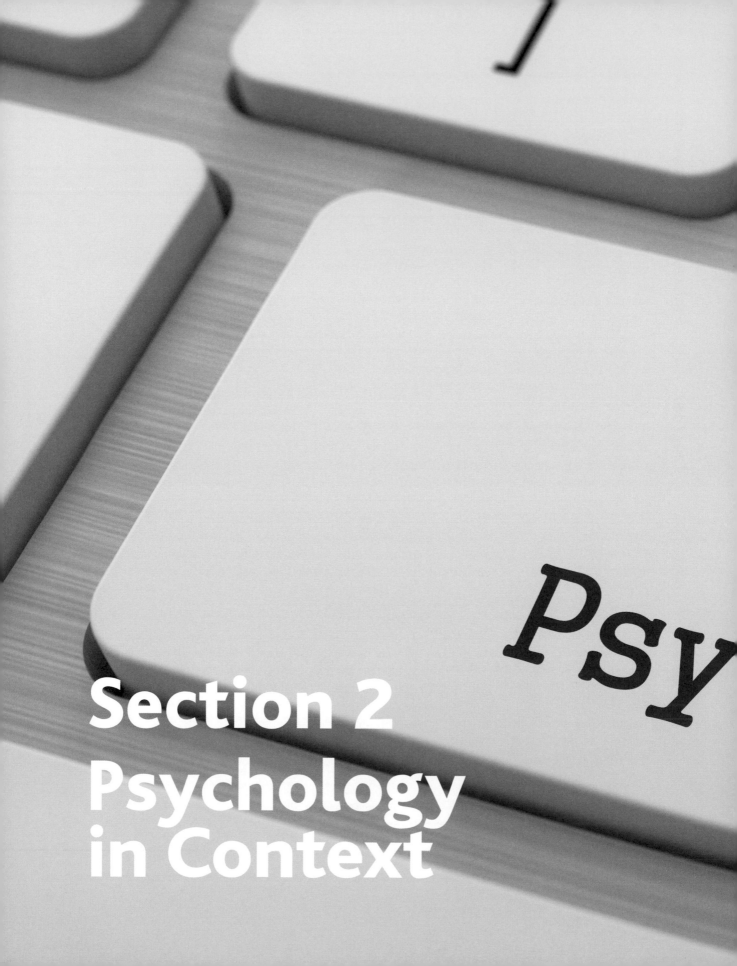

Section 2
Psychology
in Context

Approaches in Psychology

WHAT YOU NEED TO KNOW ☑

Origins of psychology ❑

Wundt ❑

Introspection ❑

The emergence of psychology as a science ❑

The basic assumptions of learning approaches ❑

The behaviourist approach: ❑

    Classical conditioning ❑

    Pavlov's research ❑

    Operant conditioning ❑

    Types of reinforcement ❑

    Skinner's research ❑

Social learning theory: ❑

    Imitation ❑

    Identification ❑

    Modelling ❑

    Vicarious reinforcement ❑

    Mediational processes ❑

    Bandura's research ❑

The basic assumptions of the cognitive approach ❑

The study of internal mental processes ❑

The role of schema ❑

The use of theoretical and computer models to explain and make inferences about mental processes ❑

The emergence of cognitive neuroscience ❑

The basic assumptions of the biological approach ❑

The influence of genes, biological structures and neurochemistry on behaviour ❑

Genetic basis of behaviour: genotype and phenotype ❑

Evolution and behaviour ❑

The basic assumptions of the psychodynamic approach ❑

The role of the unconscious ❑

The structure of personality (id, ego and superego) ❑

Defence mechanisms including repression, denial and displacement ❑

Psychosexual stages ❑

The basic assumptions of humanistic psychology ❑

Free will and self-actualisation ❑

Maslow's hierarchy of needs ❑

Focus on the self, congruence and the role of conditions of worth ❑

The influence on counselling psychology ❑

Comparison of approaches ❑

Approaches in Psychology

It is often said that psychology is a subject with a brief history but a long past. What this means is that although the origins of psychology as a separate discipline can be traced to the 19th century, thinkers have wrestled with questions about behaviour and human experience for thousands of years. Such considerations are ongoing and can still be seen in contemporary debates about what should (and shouldn't) be the goals of psychology. The way psychologists think about mind and behaviour is guided by their orientation – the approach they take. For example, one psychologist might lean towards thinking that behaviour is influenced by the way we think – irrational thoughts lead to irrational behaviours. Another might consider behaviours to be a result of our biology. Sometimes such orientations are directly at odds with one another, but at other times they are complementary. For example, a psychologist might be interested in the influence of mood on behaviour. Research has shown that the way we interpret (think about) events affects biological functioning (e.g. a negative interpretation can lead to the release of stress hormones which have a significant effect on the body and mind). Thus, psychology and biology are inextricably intertwined, so taking a biological or a cognitive approach to understanding the influence of mood makes much less sense than one which employs both approaches. One single approach rarely has all the answers to the complex problems posed by psychology. Each approach has its own place in the history and development of psychology. Psychologists might disagree on the merits of different approaches, but all would agree that each approach is able to make important and distinctive contributions to psychology and our understanding of mind and behaviour.

ORIGINS OF PSYCHOLOGY

Interest in the origins of behaviour can be traced back to the writings of the ancient Greek philosophers Aristotle and Plato. However, it wasn't until the mid-19th century that psychology emerged from philosophy as an identifiable discipline. The origin of modern scientific psychology is usually attributed to 1879 and the opening of the first psychology laboratory specifically with the aim of training students in the study of human behaviour. The pioneering scientist responsible for this was Wilhelm Wundt. Wundt was medically trained and this background was reflected in his goal of studying the conscious mind in much the same way as scientists at the time were studying natural behaviour.

Wundt's laboratory at the University of Leipzig, Germany attracted those with an interest in psychology from around the world. Many of these students went on to become important figures in psychology. One such person was Englishman Edward Titchener, who opened a psychology laboratory at Cornell University in the United States. Titchener became the founder of a school of thought in psychology called *structuralism*. Heavily influenced by Wundt, this emphasised that the analysis of the mind should be in terms of sensations, feelings and images, which are the basic elements of conscious experience. The principal technique for doing this should be *introspection*. This literally means 'look within', and involved a carefully trained observer analysing his own experience in terms of basic sensations and feelings. This was not an easy or straightforward thing to do, and those who could not master the technique were encouraged to pursue some other discipline. This method of studying the mind eventually died out in the face of much criticism, but it left its mark by introducing to psychology the scientific study of cognition, something which would undergo a resurgence in the 1960s and dominates psychology to the present day.

At about the time Wundt was opening a psychology laboratory in Leipzig, William James was doing the same at Harvard University. His biggest contribution to psychology was his two-volume book, *The Principles of Psychology*. Published in 1890, it contained chapters on topics which would be familiar to psychologists today, such as memory, emotion, perception and brain function. James considered the structuralist approach of Wundt and his followers as far too descriptive. Influenced by the research of Charles Darwin, James was much more interested in the 'how' and 'why' of behaviour. His approach to psychology inspired *functionalism*, a school of thought which emphasised the purpose of behaviour, especially in terms of how it helps an organism to adapt to its environment. Functionalism served to broaden the scope of psychology, had a major influence on the development of psychology as a science and could be said to live on today in the fields of cognitive psychology and evolutionary psychology.

THE LEARNING APPROACHES

The earliest learning approach was *behaviourism*, introduced by John Watson in 1913. He believed that psychology was a natural science that should only study observable events. 'Thinking', for example, was no more than talking to oneself, and could be observed by minute movements of the larynx. The strict early radical behaviourism of Watson later developed into other more moderate forms such as neo-behaviourism, which included elements of cognition in theories such as social learning theory. It was the most prominent approach in psychology from the 1920s to the 1950s, but waned in popularity with the rise of cognitive psychology.

BASIC ASSUMPTIONS

1. Behaviour is determined by the environment: All humans are born a 'blank slate', ready to be 'written on' by experience. Behaviour is learned from the environment, and the person we grow up to become is entirely the result of experience; genetics and other biological factors play little role in shaping who we are, so behaviourism takes an extreme nurture approach. Basically, within the constraints of our biology (e.g. someone 6 ft 7 is not going to become a jockey!), as long as we have the right environment, we could grow up to be anything. Since a person's behaviour is determined by their environment, people have no free will as such.

2. Only observable events are important: Behaviourists rejected the introspective method of the structuralists. It was the first approach that presented psychology as a science, emphasising the importance of empirical data obtained through careful and controlled observation and measurement of behaviour. Things like thoughts and unconscious motives were therefore rejected as unsuitable subject matter, at least by the early radical behaviourists.

3. Humans and animals learn in similar ways through conditioning: All behaviour, regardless of how complex it may seem, is the result of a *conditioning history*. Classical conditioning is where an animal learns a new association between two previously unrelated events. It is passive and reflexive learning in that it happens automatically beyond any conscious control. Operant conditioning is a more active learning where an animal has to do something first then learns as a consequence of this behaviour. Some animals also engage in observational learning, where learning occurs through observing behaviour of others (and its consequences).

You can read about examples of behaviours explained by the learning approaches in the Attachment and Psychopathology chapters.

THE BEHAVIOURIST APPROACH

Classical conditioning

The central tenets of *classical conditioning* were discovered by Russian physiologist Ivan Pavlov. Pavlov noticed that experimental dogs in his laboratory would become excited and begin to salivate at hearing the footsteps of the technician who normally brought their food. Recognising that this was not a natural response (since salivation is a reflexive response to food not to the researcher), he concluded that the dogs had made a link, or association, between the sound of the footsteps and the food. He then set about demonstrating how this new learning came about (see box 'Pavlov's research').

Pavlov further found that presenting the CS (the bell) repeatedly without any food made the link weaken and eventually disappear. He called this *extinction*. Another phenomenon associated with classical conditioning is *spontaneous recovery*. After extinction the new learning can appear to be lost. However, the CR may return spontaneously at some later time. However, the CR is weaker than it had been before extinction. This suggests that the relationship between the CR and the US is still present in the animal, even though the animal is not showing it. This means that the animal must have somehow suppressed the learning, which is called *inhibition*.

Pavlov's research

The first step involved presenting dogs with food, in response to which the dogs salivated. Pavlov called this natural reflexive behaviour the unconditioned response (UR). A UR is caused by a naturally occurring stimulus which he called an unconditioned stimulus (US). It is, for example, an automatic natural reflex (UR) for a dog to salivate to food. Each time, shortly before the food (US) was presented, Pavlov rang a bell. Dogs do not salivate to the sound of bells, so it is called the neutral stimulus (NS). After several pairings of the US and NS, conditioning was tested by presenting the sound of the bell (NS) alone. Pavlov found that the dogs would eventually salivate to the sound of the bell – they had learned a new association between the sound of a bell and food. The bell had become a conditioned stimulus (CS) and the salivation to its sound a conditioned response (CR). Pavlov called this learning process *conditioning*. He said that regularly experiencing one stimulus in the presence of another stimulus would eventually lead to the animal being conditioned to respond to both stimuli in the same way.

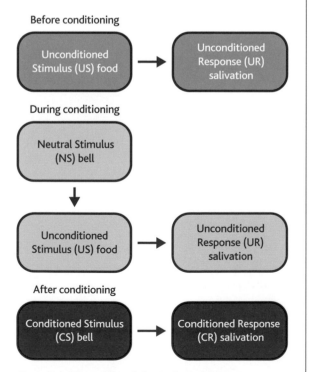

Figure 2.1: The process of classical conditioning.

Operant conditioning

Classical conditioning is essentially passive, involuntary learning – it happens *to* an animal. This clearly does not explain all animal learning – very often, an animal does something then learns from the consequences of its actions. The theory of *operant conditioning* was proposed by B. F. Skinner (1940) in order to explain this different type of learning.

A key concept in operant conditioning is *reinforcement*. A reinforcer is anything that increases the likelihood of a behaviour occurring again. In the case of the Skinner box, food is the reinforcer for lever pressing. There are different types of reinforcement (see Table 2.1).

There is a distinction in operant conditioning between primary and secondary reinforcers. Primary reinforcers satisfy basic needs, like water, comfort, warmth and food, and are particularly powerful reinforcers. A secondary reinforcer is something associated with a primary reinforcer. For example, if a clicking sound is heard by the rat in a Skinner box when it presses the lever, the rat will learn to start pressing the lever when it hears the clicking sound. In this example, the clicking sound is not directly related to a reward, but it is associated to a primary reinforcer by the lever pressing.

Many of the phenomena associated with classical conditioning also apply to operant

Skinner's research

To measure operant conditioning, Skinner developed a piece of apparatus called a conditioning chamber (or Skinner box). In effect, this is an easy to clean cage containing a feeding shoot, a lever and possibly a light and a buzzer. Hungry rats are placed in the chamber and their behaviour is observed and recorded. It is in the nature of a hungry rat to engage in exploration of the cage, and it will eventually accidentally press the lever. This lever press delivers a food pellet. The rat quickly associates the lever with food, and learns that as a consequence of its behaviour (lever press) something pleasant will happen (food will be dispensed). The rat will now happily press the lever whenever it wants food – it has been conditioned.

conditioning. Generalisation occurs when animals make responses which resemble the original reinforced response. For instance, a rat conditioned to push a lever every time it hears a buzzer will also lever press to a different sounding buzzer. Discrimination occurs when an animal is able to distinguish a behaviour that will bring about a reward from another behaviour that won't. If a response is never again reinforced then extinction will occur – that is, the learned response will gradually fade.

	DESCRIPTION	CONSEQUENCE
Positive reinforcement	Behaviour is followed by something pleasant, e.g. a rat presses a lever and receives a food pellet.	Increases the likelihood of a behaviour occurring again.
Negative reinforcement	Behaviour is followed by the removal of something unpleasant, e.g. a rat presses a lever and stops an electric shock.	Increases the likelihood of a behaviour occurring again.
Punishment	Behaviour is followed by something unpleasant, e.g. a rat presses a lever and receives an electric shock.	Reduces the likelihood of a behaviour occurring again.

Table 2.1: Reinforcement and punishment in operant conditioning.

SOCIAL LEARNING THEORY

Developed by Albert Bandura, social learning theory (SLT) shares the same basic rules and terminology as operant and classical conditioning, such as learning by association and reinforcement. Its focus, however, is on the type of learning that takes place without direct experience (i.e. observational learning). This is described through a process of *modelling*, *observation* and *imitation*. Social learning occurs when a model is observed engaging in a behaviour and, through reinforcement, imitates that behaviour. An important concept here is vicarious reinforcement. This means that *seeing* a model being reinforced for a behaviour can itself be reinforcing for the observer, making imitation of the behaviour more likely. If the outcome for the model is negative then the observer will be less likely to imitate the behaviour.

What sets SLT apart from the other learning theories is its focus on the role of *mediational processes*. The observer does not passively respond to the stimulus of the observation, but plays an active role in imitation. Internal mediating processes take place that affect the outcome of the observation:

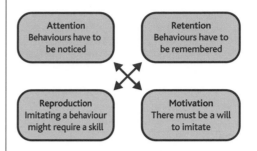

Attention
Behaviours have to be noticed

Retention
Behaviours have to be remembered

Reproduction
Imitating a behaviour might require a skill

Motivation
There must be a will to imitate

The extent to which an observer *identifies* with the model also affects the likelihood of imitation. Things that influence identification include the characteristics of the model (similarity in age, gender, status, etc.), perceived friendliness of the model and observer self-efficacy (the extent to which the observer believes they actually can imitate the behaviour and thus be like the model).

Bandura's research

The participants in Bandura et al.'s (1961) study were 36 boys and 36 girls with a mean age of 4 years and 4 months. A baseline test was conducted to assess existing levels of aggression in the children, and they were distributed across the groups using a matched pairs design to ensure that one group of children were not already more or less aggressive than another.

The participants were divided into three conditions. One group were exposed individually to an aggressive adult model who continuously hit, punched and kicked a 3 ft Bobo doll. A second group were exposed to a non-aggressive adult model who played quietly in the corner of the room with the children. A third group were used as a control and were not shown a model.

After exposure to the model, children were shown individually into a room for 10 minutes where they were presented with some toys but prevented from playing with them. Each child was then taken into another room containing a Bobo doll and mallet and a further choice of toys. The children were observed through a one-way mirror for 20 minutes and their behaviour was recorded.

It was found that the children who had been exposed to the aggressive model showed more imitation of the model's behaviour than the children in the other two groups, with some aggressive acts closely resembling those of the model. For Bandura, this was evidence of observational learning of aggression.

	STRENGTHS	WEAKNESSES
The learning approach is scientific	Its methods seek to be as objective as possible and so focus on behaviour that can be measured and observed, rather than internal 'mental' processes.	Many important behaviours, such as memory, are not observable or measurable in the way this approach expects so would not be a topic of investigation.
The learning approach is reductionist	Studies have demonstrated that humans can learn via conditioning and these principles have useful applications (e.g. developing effective therapies).	Behaviour is explained by reducing it to simple conditioning processes. It underestimates the complexity of behaviour (e.g. by ignoring important 'mediating' processes such as thinking) and social influences.
The learning approach often relies on research with animals	Research supports the idea that humans and animals learn by conditioning. This allows researchers to study animals when, ethically, they might not be able to study humans.	Humans have complex thoughts and feelings far beyond any other animal, and these have a major effect on behaviour. Assuming that humans only learn like other animals underestimates the complexity of human behaviour.

Table 2.2: Strengths and weaknesses of the learning approach.

1859	Charles Darwin publishes *On the Origin of Species*
1906	Ivan Pavlov publishes his first report on conditioning
1913	John Watson publishes *Psychology as a Behaviourist Views It*
1920	Watson and Rayner publish their Little Albert research
1938	B. F. Skinner introduces operant conditioning
1953	B. F. Skinner publishes *Science and Human Behaviour*
1958	Joseph Wolpe introduces systematic desensitisation
1961	Albert Bandura presents first bobo doll study findings on observational learning
1973	Albert Bandura publishes *Aggression: A Social Learning Analysis*

THE COGNITIVE APPROACH

When psychologists refer to 'cognition' they are referring to mental activities. It follows then that cognitive psychologists study internal mental processes – for example, the thought processes that help us understand and act in the world, such as consciousness, memory, perception and creativity. Whilst psychologists have always been interested in such topics, it wasn't until the development of computers in the 1950s that cognitive psychology really took off. The cognitive approach makes a number of assumptions when trying to interpret and understand human behaviour.

BASIC ASSUMPTIONS

1. The study of internal mental processes: In order to understand behaviour we have to understand the internal processes of our mind. According to cognitive psychologists, many processes work together to help us make sense of the world around us and to operate effectively within it. For example, imagine you are in a bakery solving the problem of trying to decide which cake to buy. You focus your attention on one cake in particular and perceive it as a round shape with a certain colour and texture. You use your memory to recall the name of the cake and your problem solving skills to consider the virtues of the doughnut over other cakes on display. You can then use language to ask to purchase the doughnut.

2. Abnormality is faulty thinking: Internal mental processes can sometimes go wrong and result in abnormal behaviour. For example, depression, phobia and eating disorders can all be explained by thought processes that have become irrational or distorted.

3. Information processing: An important goal of the cognitive psychology is to understand all the steps involved in the transformation of an experience into a cognition that influences behaviour. The technological developments of the 1940s and 50s, especially in computing, gave psychologists a framework to do this. Much like a computer, information is processed step-by-step in a sequence of simple operations. At each stage information is changed (encoded), it is held (stored), and is made available for later use (retrieval). Nowadays, models of human thinking are much more complex than this, but many psychologists still favour a computer metaphor.

You can read about examples of behaviours explained by the cognitive approach in the Memory and Psychopathology chapters.

THE ROLE OF SCHEMAS

A *schema* is best described as a collection of related ideas or concepts which we develop through experience. Stored in long-term memory, they make the cognitive system more efficient by providing a framework for thinking in a more organised way about the world. In effect, they provide a short-hand way of thinking – once a schema is triggered we don't have to rethink every detail, we can just do it. We have schemas for a vast number of people, places and activities. They usually start out as basic, simple structures that become more complex through experience. A schema can also help us to make sense of new experiences. For example, your first driving lesson will be a brand new experience, but existing schemas will help you to make sense of it – for example, you may be able to ride a bicycle and therefore understand something about gears, brakes and directions, the dangers of traffic and the likely behaviour of pedestrians. Your existing 'riding a bicycle' schema will help you to figure out the new 'driving a car' schema.

One type of schema is called a *script*. These are schemas for organised sequences of events. For example when we make a cup of tea we have a routine that we follow each time: filling the kettle with water, putting it on to boil, placing a tea bag in the cup and pouring on the boiling water. This would be our 'making a cup of tea' script. Scripts become more complex with experience, so that your 'making a cup of tea' script may become more complicated once you experience different types of tea and individual

preferences for the addition of milk, sugar or lemon. There are also social scripts, that we use to navigate social situations like using a cafe or catching a bus.

Whilst schemas are an important way of making our cognitive system more efficient, they come with costs. They can be rigid and inflexible and prevent us from learning new things and seeing the world accurately. For example, having schemas about certain groups of people may cause us to think about them in certain ways – as stereotypes – and such stereotyping can be interpreted as prejudice.

Relational schemas

The concept of schemas has been applied to many different situations. For example, *relational schema theory* focuses on the effects of schemas on relationships. The theory goes that we form self-schemas early in life through experiences with caregivers. These go on to affect the type of relationships individuals have with others later on in life. So, if someone has developed a negative schema of themselves, they are more likely to engage in a relationship with a partner who supports this schema. This explains why some people enter into relationships that, to outsiders, seem unusual – for example, one that is abusive or degrading. Cyranowski and Andersen (1998) found that women with positive self-schemas had more past romantic relationships, were more likely to be in one currently and reported being more passionate in relationships.

When a young child first encounters a dog she must create a schema for it. This will be very simple – for example, something which is hairy and has four legs. Anything she now encounters that fits this schema – four legs and hairy – will also be a 'dog'. The more she learns and grows, the more complex her schema becomes, so that she can soon tell the difference between dogs, sheep and cats – she has a separate schema for each one.

THE USE OF THEORETICAL AND COMPUTER MODELS TO EXPLAIN AND MAKE INFERENCES ABOUT MENTAL PROCESSES

A model is used by psychologists to help them think about hard-to-visualise phenomena. Simplifying something very complicated in this way is helpful because it provides psychologists with a framework for further investigations. Models have assumptions and rules, which can be tested by conducting experiments and by comparing the model with alternative ones. They can explain particular processes (e.g. how do we hold on to verbal material in working memory?) and how processes interact (e.g. how do verbal and visual memory operate together in working memory?). They might also be used to predict behaviour (e.g. what would happen to our memory for verbal material if another verbal task was undertaken at the same time?). Models are thus 'tools for exploring the implications of ideas' (McClelland, 2009) and are powerful ways of generating and testing hypotheses about mind and behaviour. Because of this they have thus been proven to be enormously important in cognitive psychology. One of the most influential models is the multi-store model of memory. This straightforward (and some would say over-simplistic) model of memory has given rise to an enormous quantity of research into the structure and function of memory.

The modern cognitive approach owes its dominant place in contemporary psychology largely to the development of computers. The computer provided a metaphor to understand

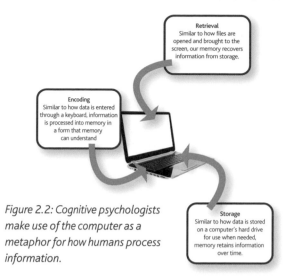

Figure 2.2: Cognitive psychologists make use of the computer as a metaphor for how humans process information.

and model the way the mind works. It allowed psychologists to think about processes they could not see, particularly the mind as an information processor – for example, like a computer, inputs are transformed (encoded), stored and retrieved (see Figure 2.2). Cognitive scientists make use of computing terminology for their models and many theories about cognition are tested using computer programs and simulations. The computer metaphor can also be seen in how cognitive psychologists view how the brain functions. Neurons (communicating cells in the brain) work on the all-or-nothing principle – they either fire or they don't. This is analogous to how information is used in a computer which uses binary – strings of 0 and 1 (off and on) signals. This kind of thinking has led to *neural network models* where, for example, a memory is represented as a unique pattern of interconnected nodes (the cognitive equivalent to a neuron).

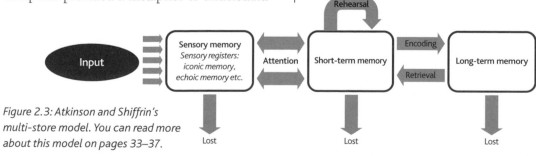

Figure 2.3: Atkinson and Shiffrin's multi-store model. You can read more about this model on pages 33–37.

THE EMERGENCE OF COGNITIVE NEUROSCIENCE

Whilst the cognitive approach uses the metaphor of a computer, cognitive neuroscience uses the brain as a metaphor for the mind. The brain processes and organises information in specific ways and this relates to identifiable patterns of neural activity. Research is beginning to reveal how particular neural activity is correlated with particular aspects of cognition. The assumption is that cognitive processes – like language, memory and thought – are a function of physiological processes in the brain, and not something distinct from the brain.

Cognitive neuroscience emerged as a separate area of study in psychology with the development of ever more advanced neuro-imaging technologies, enabling researchers to connect cognitive processes with brain activity. Functional neuro-imaging has been important in this regard, since it records brain activity whilst a participant is engaged in a specific task (see box 'The central executive and the frontal lobes' for an example of this type of research). The temporal resolution (i.e. when an event is occurring) of functional neuro-imaging is continuing to develop – already the activity of the brain can be recorded very close to when a task is being performed. McBride and Cutting (2015) argue that several key issues can be addressed by cognitive neuroscience, such as where activity occurs in the brain during specific cognitions, whether activity occurs in discrete areas or in networks across the brain, and whether brain activity is concurrent with or precedes cognition.

Whilst a great deal of progress is being made in cognitive neuroscience, it has its disadvantages. Some aspects of cognition are very difficult to record with neuro-imaging. For example, it is straightforward to record brain activity during linguistic tasks (you simply ask participants to speak or listen), but

The central executive and the frontal lobes

D'Esposito et al. (1995) used fMRI to record the brain activity of participants whilst engaged in tasks occupying their central executive (CE). They found that the prefrontal cortex was most active at this time. In addition, people with damage to the prefrontal lobes show problems with functions attributed to the CE, such as poor concentration, distractibility and disturbed attention. These symptoms are collectively known as dysexecutive syndrome (DES). Andrés (2003), however, suggests caution before concluding that the CE is specifically linked to the prefrontal cortex. She points out that other brain areas are also linked to CE functions. Some individuals showing DES have no damage to the prefrontal cortex and not all people with prefrontal cortex damage show DES.

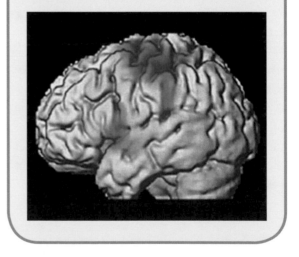

it is very difficult to record the many kinds of unpredictable and uncontrollable cognitions we have, such as impulsive thoughts and insights. Related to this is the criticism that the behaviours being examined by cognitive neuroscientists are too simple (e.g. listening, pressing a button) and do not reflect the much more typical (but also much more complex) behaviours seen in everyday life.

	STRENGTHS	WEAKNESSES
The cognitive approach lends itself to scientific testing under laboratory conditions	A high level of control can be achieved and the independent variable can be isolated so researchers can establish the cause and effect of a particular aspect of behaviour.	Studies of cognitive processes conducted in laboratories can lack ecological validity (e.g. it may be difficult to generalise results of a memory test to real-life experience of memory).
Laboratory testing of behaviour uses scientific equipment	Cognitive science uses brain scans to improve knowledge and understanding of information processing.	There is a danger of assuming all human behaviour is a result of information processing, which does not allow for the influence of social and cultural factors.
The cognitive approach is reductionist	The idea that complex behaviour such as depression can be explained through negative internal thought processes has led to the development of effective cognitive therapies.	The cognitive approach takes too narrow a focus on information processing and tends to overlook important social and cultural factors.

Table 2.3: Strengths and weaknesses of the cognitive approach.

1879	The first scientific psychology laboratory opened by Wilhelm Wundt
1890	William James publishes *The Principles of Psychology*
1950s	Post-war technological developments, e.g. telecoms and computing
1953	HM undergoes brain surgery, triggering 50 years of research into his cognitive abilities
1956	George Miller writes *The Magical Number Seven, Plus or Minus Two*
1967	Ulric Neisser publishes the first cognitive psychology textbook
1968	Atkinson and Shiffrin propose the multi-store model of memory
1974	Baddeley and Hitch propose the working memory model
1979	Michael Gazzaniga and George Miller introduce the term 'cognitive neuroscience'
1990	fMRI first used to measure brain activity in humans

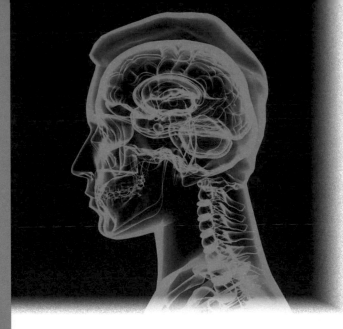

THE BIOLOGICAL APPROACH

Modern psychology has its roots in the natural science of biology. A biological approach did not emerge as a distinctive approach in psychology, however, until it could answer important questions about behaviour. A number of key events led to this. Darwin's theory of evolution proposed a continuity between humans and other animals, thus providing a rationale for the application of findings from animal research to humans. This led to important discoveries in the 19th century regarding electrical communication along nerve fibres and the localisation of function in the brain (see the discussion on Paul Broca and Tan on page 162). The biological approach really began to emerge, however, in the early 20th century following the work of Karl Lashley and Donald Hebb into the brain's role in learning. Lashley's systematic lesioning of rat brains led the way to later brain mapping, and it was Hebb who proposed that learning was due to changes in connections between neurons – something that ultimately led to the discovery of neurotransmitters.

BASIC ASSUMPTIONS

1. Behaviour is a result of the evolutionary processes: The biology and behaviour of a species evolves in response to environmental conditions. Therefore, in order to fully understand behaviour it must be viewed in its evolutionary context.

2. Genes influence behaviour: There is an important relationship between heredity and behaviour. Genes provide a flexible blueprint for psychological and physical development, and also provide the means by which characteristics are passed on to the next generation.

3. Behaviour is influenced by biological structures and neurochemistry: Behaviour is regulated by our biology. Neural circuits in the brain and their associated neurochemistries allow us to think and have sensations and emotions. The brain governs fundamental processes like sleeping, breathing and eating. The nervous system basically keeps us alive. The brain controls behaviour, but behaviour also 'controls' the brain, so that environment and behaviour work together to produce structural changes in the brain.

You can read about examples of behaviours explained by the biological approach in the Memory, Psychopathology and Attachment chapters.

THE INFLUENCE OF BIOLOGICAL STRUCTURES AND NEUROCHEMISTRY

The brain essentially consists of billions of neurons, each with many hundreds of connections for communicating electrochemical signals. However, about 90% of the cells in the brain are glial cells. Whilst these also communicate they are essentially support cells, doing things like supplying nutrients and insulation. Neural communication begins when a *neuron* receives electrical messages from others neurons. These stimulate the neuron into passing on a message to other neurons. Messages within neurons are electrical, but to other neurons it becomes chemical in nature. Neurons communicate with other neurons using chemicals called neurotransmitters. There are many different kinds of neurotransmitters, and research into these substances has told us a great deal about the origins of both normal and abnormal behaviour. For example, reduced levels of the neurotransmitter dopamine lies behind the symptoms of Parkinson's disease, and increasing levels of dopamine can help reduce these symptoms. Increased levels of dopamine are associated with schizophrenia, and antipsychotic drugs can help some individuals by reducing these levels.

What has become very clear from research is that the relationship between neurotransmitters and behaviour is a very complex one. Most neuroscientists now believe that behaviour is the result not of the action of single neurotransmitters, but the interactions and balances between many. The brain, with its vastly complex network of interacting neurons, is ultimately responsible for all aspects of behaviour. It appears possible to locate some discrete behaviours to particular parts of the brain – for example, receiving and interpreting senses, and initiating and controlling motor functions. Evidence now suggests, however, that most psychological functions are distributed across different areas. For example, specific aspects of language can be located in particular brain areas in most people, but language itself is distributed across the left hemisphere and also requires contributions from the right hemisphere.

The curious case of Phineas Gage

In 1848 Phineas Gage was working in a quarry when an accidental explosion drove an iron bar through his head – it entered his left jaw and exited the centre top of his skull, landing several yards away. Remarkably, he did not die from his wound. He did, however, experience a profound change in personality. Whilst previously he was well-liked and considered responsible and reliable, he now became obstinate, irresponsible and generally incapable of holding down a job. His intelligence, speech and motor skills seemed unchanged. We know now that frontal lobe injuries affect social behaviour, decision making and personality. The Gage case shows clearly that biology and behaviour are inextricably tied. It was one of the first examples for scientists of how behaviour can change as a result of damage to a specific part of the brain.

THE GENETIC BASIS OF BEHAVIOUR: GENOTYPES AND PHENOTYPES

Much of who we are and what we become is determined by what we inherit from our parents and their ancestors. The biological units of inheritance are the genes, carried in the DNA of chromosomes. Each human cell (with the exception of sperm cells and unfertilised egg cells) has within its nucleus 23 pairs of chromosomes – one half of each pair contributed by the father and mother respectively. One gene is *dominant* and the other *recessive* (i.e. non-dominant). It is the particular combination of dominant and recessive genes that determine inherited characteristics. Our actual genetic make-up is known as the *genotype* and the observable characteristic is the *phenotype*. Whilst mainly controlled by the genotype, the phenotype is strongly influenced by the environment. For example, we have all inherited genes for height – our genotype. It is the actual environment, however, that shapes this inheritance and gives us our phenotype

Genes provide a 'flexible plan' for physical and psychological development. Genetic material from parents can be combined in trillions of ways. The likelihood of gene mutation is thus quite high. These variations and gene mutations occasionally confer a survival advantage – the foundation of natural selection.

– our actual height. A person with 'tall' genes may have experienced illness or malnutrition at some point in their development meaning that their genetic potential has not been realised, so they are shorter than they could have been. This environmental impact may be coded within their own genes and now passed as part of the genotype of subsequent generations.

Genotype, phenotype and behaviour are all linked. For example, genes help to determine the structure and function of the brain but the environment plays a role in the final product, and hence how we behave. Psychologists have developed a number of methods for investigating the link between genes and behaviour. In *family studies*, the similarities and differences in blood relatives is investigated to see if traits run in families. If a trait is genetic then the closer the genetic similarity between family members, the greater the likelihood should be of them sharing that trait. Because family members are exposed to similar environments, however, family studies only give indications at best and can't establish true links between genes and behaviour. Twin studies involve comparing the traits of identical twins (who have the same genetic material) with fraternal twins or non-identical twins (who share 50% of their genetic material). This allows researchers to control for genetic factors, the assumption being that any difference between the twin pairs must be due to environmental factors. Studies of identical twins reared apart are also important since if they show strongly similar traits, having been raised in different environments, the similarity must be due to genetic factors. However, recent research has indicated that whilst twins are monozygotic, they are *not* necessarily genetically identical. Factors in the environment before and after birth can influence gene expression – they can be 'switched on' or 'turned off' by nutrients, toxins and other environmental factors. The accumulation of these effects means that, as they age, identical twins become more and more different.

EVOLUTION AND BEHAVIOUR

The basic premise of evolution theory is rather simple and elegant. Animals produce many more young than could possibly survive. Offspring are often very slightly different from either parent, and these variations (or mutations) sometimes enable animals to cope better with environmental demands and reach maturity. The ones that do reach adulthood are the strongest of their generation and when they breed they pass on to their young the characteristics that helped them survive. Those with traits that help them survive are more likely to reproduce themselves (i.e. they are selected by the process of evolution for their fitness), and so the cycle continues. As many generations go by, the traits (or *adaptations*) that have aided survival and reproductive fitness are passed on and become widespread in the population. Such a process involves changes to both physiology and behaviour, so that the end result can be an animal that bears little resemblance to its ancestors. This is the principle of *natural selection*. Characteristics that have aided reproduction are also passed on, thus increasing the chances of future mating success for the offspring. This is called *sexual selection*.

Evolution theory has had a profound influence on psychology. Darwin's notion that there is a *continuity* between humans and animals led to the increased popularity of comparative psychology (the study of animals to understand human behaviour). It has also given rise to the field of evolutionary psychology – the application of evolutionary theory to the understanding of human behaviour. The logic behind this is that the minds of our hunter-gatherer ancestors evolved to adapt to environmental challenges during the period of the EEA (the Environment of Evolutionary Adaptation refers to the period in which a species first evolved – for humans this was approximately 2 million years ago). Many of our behaviours now can be understood in this context (see Table 2.4).

THEORY	EXPLANATION
Attachment	Human infants are helpless and require adult assistance for a number of years in order to ensure survival. Creating an emotional bond to an adult who will subsequently care for it therefore confers a survival advantage.
Aggression	In males aggression can be seen as acquisition of status, with high status giving access to the resources necessary for survival and females for breeding. Lower levels of aggression in females reflects an adaptive behaviour motivated by the importance of the survival of her offspring.
Phobia	We have evolved a preparedness to learn to fear things which threatened the survival of our ancestors.
Food preference	Humans have evolved favourable attitudes to particular foods because they aid survival – for example, high calorie foods. By avoiding certain foods we are less likely to eat something that will harm us, thus increasing survival chances.
Sleep	Sleep patterns evolved to provide animals with the greatest chance of survival – for example, energy conservation (diurnal animals like humans would waste valuable energy being awake at night) and predator avoidance (it is useful to be out of sight and still during darkness).

Table 2.4: Some evolutionary explanations for human behaviour.

	STRENGTH	WEAKNESS
Scientific research methods can be used	A person's biology can be studied scientifically, so this approach is perhaps the most objective way to investigate human behaviour.	It is not always clear that behaviour is determined solely by a person's biology; it is not always clear whether biology influences psychology, or whether psychology influences biology.
The biological approach is reductionist	Lots of research indicates that behaviour can be explained in terms of altered neurochemistry, hormones and changes to brain structure.	Reducing behaviour to biological origins runs the risk of underestimating the importance of things like social and cultural influences on behaviour.
The use of animals in research	Using animals in research to test the effect of altering certain biological systems or processes means that we do not have to do this to humans. It protects individuals from harm, but also allows us to develop an understanding of our own biology and therefore further psychology and medicine.	Although other animals do share some similar body systems, it is not known if these systems always work in the same way as they do in humans. Therefore, the findings and conclusions from research on animals may not be generalisable to humans.

Table 2.5: Strengths and weaknesses of the biological approach.

1848	Phineas Gage's accident begins to help scientists understand the brain/behaviour connection
1849	Hermann Von Helmholtz demonstrates that nerve impulses travel at finite speeds
1859	Charles Darwin publishes *On the Origin of Species*
1861	Paul Broca performs autopsy on Tan
1870	Gustav Fritsch and Eduard Hitzig produce movement in dogs by electrically stimulating their exposed brain
1932	Charles Sherrington wins a Nobel Prize for his work on the synapse
1949	Donald Hebb proposed that the biological basis of learning lies in the connections between brain cells
1950s	The first drugs to treat mental illness are tested and approved
1954	Wilder Penfield publishes a functional map of the brain's cortex
1981	Roger Sperry wins a Nobel Prize for his work on the human split brain

THE PSYCHODYNAMIC APPROACH

The psychodynamic approach was developed by Sigmund Freud and others towards the end of the 19th century. The word 'psychodynamic' is used because this approach sees the mind (or *psyche*) as being influenced by powerful, active (*dynamic*) unconscious forces. Trained as a physician, Freud was confronted with patients who, whilst experiencing physical symptoms (e.g. loss of vision), showed no bodily symptoms. It was Freud's genius to reason that the causes of these illnesses must be hidden from sight in the unconscious. Whilst his theories were controversial, they were nonetheless very influential. Modern psychodynamic theories are very different from Freud's original theory which gave rise to them, tending now to focus on relationships and social factors and playing down unconscious sexual and aggressive motives.

BASIC ASSUMPTIONS

1. **Behaviour is influenced by unconscious forces:** Both normal and abnormal behaviours originate in the unconscious, particularly the dynamic conflict between id, ego and superego, but also as a result of experiences during psychosexual development.

2. **The importance of early childhood experience:** Experiences in childhood have

Sigmund Freud

life-long effects on a person. They can become repressed and locked into the unconscious, affecting behaviour in adulthood beyond conscious awareness.

3. **A focus on the whole person:** Rather than focusing on a particular aspect of behaviour, such as personality or aggression, the psychodynamic approach focuses on explaining the entire person. The behaviour of an individual is then understood within this context.

> **ASK AN EXAMINER**
>
> *Whilst Freud's ideas nowadays have little direct relevance to contemporary psychology, the psychodynamic approach has had a profound influence on psychology. It can be seen most clearly here in the Attachment, Social Influence and Memory chapters, but its influence can be seen anywhere where psychologists discuss unconscious forces and the impact of early childhood experience.*

THE ROLE OF THE UNCONSCIOUS

Freud likened the structure of our mind to an iceberg. The tip of the iceberg, which sits above the water, represents our conscious mind. Our conscious mind is the part of ourselves that we are aware of – the self we can describe. The unconscious part of the mind contains our deepest thoughts, feelings and desires of which we are unaware. It is constantly influencing our behaviour, particularly with urges to seek pleasure. Sometimes this unconscious pleasure seeking may manifest itself through our dreams or through 'slips of the tongue' which unconsciously reveal what we really think. The unconscious also contains repressed thoughts and emotions from our childhood which, if they became conscious, would be painful and unpleasant and disrupt our normal day-to-day functioning. For example, Freud believed that repressed memories of early traumatic events in our lives could appear later in adulthood as depression, phobia and obsession.

DEFENCE MECHANISMS

Unconscious conflict between the id, ego and superego lead to anxiety, so the ego prevents this becoming conscious using ego defences.

Freud compared the mind to an iceberg.

This is useful and normal, but overuse of defence mechanisms can lead to disturbed behaviour.

DEFENCE MECHANISM	DESCRIPTION	EXAMPLE
Repression	Pushing memories deep into the unconscious so that they appear 'forgotten'.	Being unable to consciously remember a traumatic event from your childhood. To reject the reality of this trauma is an example of *denial*.
Denial	Refusing or rejecting reality.	You deny being very mean despite the evidence (including the opinion of others!).
Displacement	Feelings are redirected to an alternate safer place.	You slam doors rather than take it out on the person causing you frustration.

Table 2.6: Some examples of defence mechanisms.

THE STRUCTURE OF PERSONALITY

Freud claimed that the adult personality has three components: the id, the ego and the superego. They appear at different points in our childhood and interact in dynamic ways to influence our thoughts and behaviour.

The id is present from birth. It is entirely unconscious and operates on the 'pleasure principle' (it is the source of our pleasure seeking drive). Freud described babies as 'bundles of id' as they seek satisfaction at any cost and are not capable of either logical or moral thinking.

The ego develops at around 2 years to meet the demands of the id in a socially acceptable way. It is the conscious part of our personality and operates on the 'reality principle'.

The tripartite personality – an example of how it works

As an adult your decisions about how to act in certain situations may be influenced by the three parts of your personality. For example if you found a purse lying in the street your id will drive you towards keeping it and any money it may contain for yourself. However, your superego acting on the morality principle will push you towards handing the purse into the nearest police station. If you satisfy the demands of the id and keep the purse, you risk feeling guilty and shameful as the conscience within the superego punishes you for acting immorally. The decision you make is down to the ego which tries to balance the demands of the selfish id and the moral superego. You may do the right thing by handing in the purse but selfishly hope to get praise or a reward for doing so thus satisfying both the moral and pleasure seeking sides of your personality.

All in the mind

There are three key ways in which the psychodynamic approach can explain abnormality:

Imbalance in the psyche: Freud considered it important for the id, ego and superego to be in balance. If one of these forces is dominant this will lead to problems in behaviour. For example, if the id is powerful and the superego is weak then anti-social behaviour may emerge. If on the other hand, the superego is strong and the id weak an individual may have unrealistic standards of behaviour and as a result feel intolerable guilt and shame.

Repression: Ego defence mechanisms protect us from anxiety. One of these defence mechanisms is known as repression which is the act of burying unwanted thoughts, desires and experiences into the unconscious part of the mind so that we are no longer aware or able to recall them. Traumatic childhood experiences may not be remembered because they are repressed and to recall them in the conscious part of the mind would cause extreme anxiety.

Unresolved conflict during psychosexual development: Our psyche develops through five psychosexual stages where we experience pleasure and gratification through different areas of our body. If too much or too little gratification is experienced we can develop fixations - an unconscious preoccupation with that particular psychosexual stage. These fixations are then expressed in our adult behaviour and personality.

The superego emerges at about 5 years, during the phallic stage of psychosexual development. It is unconscious and operates on the 'morality principle'. It acts as the individual's conscience, guiding behaviour with a sense of what is right and wrong, thus generating a sense of guilt or pride.

PSYCHOSEXUAL STAGES

For Freud, childhood experiences are a crucial element in the formation of our personality and the way we behave as adults. Especially important are our experiences during psychosexual development. Freud said we go through phases in our early development called psychosexual stages. At each stage we find pleasure and gratification from a different part of our body, called our erogenous areas. Each psychosexual stage must be successfully resolved or aspects of this stage will become fixated and form part of our adult personality.

PSYCHOSEXUAL STAGE	EROGENOUS AREA	HEALTHY RESOLUTION OF THE STAGE	PERSONALITY TRAITS	
Oral stage 0–1 year	Mouth: satisfaction gained from putting things in the mouth so feeding is very important.	Trusting, able to give and receive affection and form healthy relationships.	Under-gratified: aggressive and mistrustful, seeks oral gratification from smoking or eating when stressed.	Over-gratified: over-dependent on others, gullible and sycophantic.
Anal stage 1–3 years	Anus: pleasure gained from bowel movements. Conflict arises when parents demand child learns to use the potty.	Can deal with authority figures appropriately.	Under-gratified: potty training too strict – obsessed with cleanliness and order, difficulty expressing emotions.	Over-gratified: potty training too relaxed – messy and disorganised, lack of respect for authority figures.
Phallic stage 3–5 years	Genitals: child has unconscious sexual desires for the opposite-sex parent and fears punishment from the same-sex parent for the desires. This causes conflict.	The values and behaviour of the same-sex parent are internalised to resolve the conflict leading to the development of morals and gender identity.	If the conflict of unconscious sexual desires for the opposite-sex parent and fear of the same-sex parent is not resolved, the individual may have problems with sex and their sexual identity in the future. Freud believed that an unresolved conflict could lead to homosexuality.	
Latency stage 5–12 years	This is a period of consolidation and rest. Sexuality lies dormant and the child is busy learning their gender roles, social rules and developing self-confidence.			
Genital stage 12 years +	Genitals: the individual becomes interested in the opposite sex.	The individual becomes a well-adjusted adult.	If fixations have formed in the first five years they begin to emerge and exert their influence on personality.	

Table 2.7: An outline of psychosexual development.

	STRENGTH	WEAKNESS
Open to scientific testing	It has been argued that whilst Freud's theory as a whole cannot be tested, specific hypotheses can (e.g. research has indicated a correlation between adult personality and childhood experience).	Concepts such as the id, ego and superego are not tangible structures, therefore they cannot be tested scientifically to prove whether they exist or not.
Behaviour is determined by early experience and unconscious forces	Acknowledges the importance of forces guiding behaviour which we have no awareness of, and therefore helps us to understand behaviour which, on the face of it, appears unreasonable.	The approach underestimates the control we have over our own behaviour and portrays humans in a rather negative light.
Useful application to mental illness	The approach changed how mental illness is viewed and led to many psychodynamic therapies, some of which are still used today to treat a wide range of mental health problems.	There is relatively little evidence for psychodynamic therapies being more successful than other therapies. Freud himself developed psychoanalysis based on very little evidence.

Table 2.8: Some strengths and weaknesses of the psychodynamic approach.

1879	The first scientific psychology laboratory opened by Wilhelm Wundt
1886	Sigmund Freud begins practicing psychoanalytic therapy
1900	Freud publishes *The Interpretation of Dreams*
1923	Freud outlines his structural theory of personality in *The Ego and the Id*
1927	Freud's daughter Anna expands her father's ideas in her own book
1939	The death of Sigmund Freud
1950	Erik Erikson expands Freud's theory to include lifespan development
1951	John Bowlby publishes *Maternal Care and Mental Health*

HUMANISTIC PSYCHOLOGY

Psychodynamic and behavioural approaches dominated psychology up to the 1960s. In the 1950s, however, a third force in psychology emerged. It was largely in reaction to the rather negative view of human nature espoused by the dominating approaches. In contrast to the psychodynamic focus on destructive unconscious forces and the behavioural focus on mechanistic stimulus-response relationships, the humanists saw all individuals as naturally good, with a drive for betterment and personal fulfilment. This new approach was not interested in predicting behaviour, and nor was it concerned with the dominant nomothetic focus of psychology in general laws of behaviour. The most important thing was the uniqueness of each person's internal thoughts and feelings and sense of self-worth.

BASIC ASSUMPTIONS

1. The uniqueness of human beings: The dominant nomothetic approach in psychology (an approach which seeks to establish general laws) is rejected in favour of an idiographic one (which is concerned with the individual).

2. The importance of subjective experience: The focus of psychology should be human values and an individual's subjective experience. Human behaviour is best understood from the perspective of an individual's interpretation of events.

3. Humans have free will: Humanistic psychology emphasises an individual's free will – in other words, we all have the ability to make our own choices. These choices are driven by the need to self-actualise (i.e. develop potential to the fullest).

Like every sunflower, every individual, given a growth-promoting climate, has the potential to be the best that they can be.

Humanistic psychology offers an alternative view of human nature, and considers behaviour from the point of view of the behaving person. The best way to grasp the approach is to read about it and familiarise yourself with the language it uses so that you understand what it is really saying about the human condition. You will not be able to effectively demonstrate understanding by just trying to remember facts.

MASLOW: SELF-ACTUALISATION AND THE HIERARCHY OF NEEDS

Abraham Maslow believed that a fundamental human motive was to strive for personal growth. He proposed a *hierarchy of needs* to describe this. The satisfaction of the lowest need leads to another need, the second lowest on the hierarchy, the satisfaction of which leads to the third and so on. For example, before a person considers their love and belonging needs they must first satisfy their physiological needs and then their safety needs. Safety and security are a secondary consideration for a very hungry person! At the top of the hierarchy is self-actualisation. This relates to the realisation of personal talent and potential – when a person achieves all that they are capable of in life then they have self-actualised. This was the ultimate human motive, and as Maslow says, 'if you plan on being anything less than you are capable of being, you will probably be unhappy all the days of your life'.

The first four needs are often referred to as *deficiency needs*. These satisfy important physical and social needs, and arise from having a lack of something. It is this lack that drives a person to do something about it (e.g. if you lack food you will be preoccupied by the need to find it). Most people in society have their deficiency needs readily (and regularly) satisfied. Indeed, Maslow argued that people spend far too much time seeking satisfaction of these needs and too little time on their *growth needs*. These are at the top of the hierarchy and do not arise because of a lack of something, and nor are they quickly satisfied and go away like deficiency needs. Growth needs are much more difficult to satisfy and so many people never get to the highest level on the hierarchy. Maslow argued that this has serious implications for psychological development, growth and our sense of personal fulfilment.

Maslow's hierarchy of needs has had an enormous impact in a variety of settings. For example, in workplace settings it is now accepted that efficient workers are those that are having their needs satisfied by their work. In education, the well-being of students is now very high on the agenda – we recognise that learners will not be able to satisfy their growth needs when their basic deficiency needs are not being met.

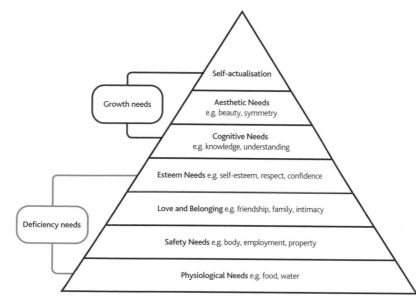

Figure 2.4: Maslow's hierarchy of needs.

ROGERS: FOCUS ON THE SELF, CONGRUENCE AND THE ROLE OF CONDITIONS OF WORTH

One of the leading figures in the development of the humanistic approach was Carl Rogers. Like Maslow, Rogers believed we have an *actualising tendency* – a drive towards personal growth. This can be seen in our attempts to master new skills, to seek out enriching experiences and in our efforts to work to the limits of our capabilities. Whether or not we become self-actualised depends on our childhood experiences. It is important that as children we receive *unconditional positive regard* – that is, affection and acceptance from significant others (especially parents) for who we really are. However, children often experience *conditional regard* – love and acceptance that comes with strings attached, such as being well-mannered or behaving as a boy or girl should. Rogers called these *conditions of worth*. Sometimes they are few and reasonable, but they may also be strict and punitive. For example, an expectation for a boy may be that he shouldn't cry, and if he does this is perceived as a sign of weakness and should be ridiculed or punished. Conditions of worth then begin to take control of our behaviour, become part of our 'self' and hamper the actualising tendency. A child who experiences only unconditional positive regard would not develop conditions of worth.

Rogers's humanistic theory has a particular focus on the self. A person's *self-concept* (or self-image) is all the information a person has about themselves, such as how we think we feel, look and behave. Rogers referred to this as the *real self*. It is a product of our development – it grows and develops from birth and is greatly influenced by childhood experiences, particularly conditions of worth. We also have an *ideal self*, separate from the real self. This is how we *want* to be, developed through experience – for example, what others (or society) expect of us or what we have been taught. When the real self and the ideal self are similar they are said to be congruent. *Congruence* is at the core of mental health and well-being. A healthy individual tends to see a congruence between their self (their sense of who they are) and their ideal self (who they think they should be). For Rogers, an incongruence (i.e. a mismatch) between real self and ideal self leads to unhappiness and poor mental health. The greater the difference between the real self and ideal self, the more likely the person is to suffer from poor mental health. For example, an individual suffering from an eating disorder such as anorexia nervosa may be experiencing incongruence between their real self and their ideal self (i.e. they see themselves as too fat and would like to be thin).

The influence on counselling psychology

Humanistic psychology has had a major influence on counselling psychology. In 1942 Carl Rogers described his person-centred approach as 'counselling and therapy'. This was the first time that counselling was used in a therapeutic context, putting him at odds with the medical profession which at the time considered that only someone medically trained could provide psychotherapy. One of Rogers's basic therapeutic principles can now be seen in most forms of counselling and psychotherapy: the importance of the *relationship* between client and practitioner. It is characterised by a high degree of respect, equality and authenticity (McLeod, 2009). This is demonstrated by the therapist showing the client genuineness (being open, honest and sincere), empathy (being able to understand the client's feelings) and unconditional positive regard (people need acceptance and respect from others so clients are valued for who they are without conditions being attached).

	STRENGTH	WEAKNESS
The scientific method	The humanistic approach provides an important antidote to the dominant scientific approach in psychology. The scientific approach, which does not recognise the uniqueness of individuals, is considered dehumanising.	The rejection of the scientific approach means that humanistic psychologists are unwilling to make testable hypotheses. As a result, the approach can be accused of being unscientific – a criticism humanists would reject as irrelevant.
Positive view of human nature	A positive focus on the fundamental goodness of people is an important antidote to the generally pessimistic view of humans seen in other areas of psychology.	A focus only on the positive, such as personal growth and human potential, seems at odds with the overwhelming evidence of human negativity, such as that seen in wars, murders, atrocities and other antisocial behaviours.
Individualistic	A focus on the individual's ability to satisfy their own growth needs is personally empowering, especially in a world where people are feeling ever more disempowered.	The values of the humanistic approach (and its overwhelming emphasis on the individual) reflects its cultural origins in middle class America. It fails to acknowledge other world views, such as those less individualistic ones held by collectivist cultures.

Table 2.9: Some strengths and weaknesses of the humanistic approach.

1942	Carl Rogers publishes *Counseling and Psychotherapy*
1943	Abraham Maslow introduces the hierarchy of needs
1954	Abraham Maslow publishes *Motivation and Personality*
1961	Carl Rogers publishes *On Becoming a Person*
1961	The Journal of Humanistic Psychology is launched
1964	The core principles of humanistic psychology are published
1980	Carl Rogers publishes *A Way of Being*
1998	Martin Seligman introduces positive psychology and in 2002 publishes *Authentic Happiness*

COMPARISON OF APPROACHES

An 'approach' in psychology refers to a view of how behaviour should be explained. Some of these views are fundamentally irreconcilable. For example, the humanistic assumption of human beings having free will is completely at odds with the psychodynamic assumption that behaviour is the result of unconscious forces beyond our control. However, whilst there may be areas of disagreement (or even contention) between approaches, they can also have things in common. They may even be complementary, so that ideas from two or more approaches combine to produce something new. For example, cognitive neuroscience is currently one of the most exciting areas in psychology, making great strides in our understanding of the

THEMES	BIOLOGICAL	BEHAVIOURAL
Interpretation of behaviour	Internal influences. Behaviour stems from physical elements that make up the human body. Behaviour evolves due to environmental demands and is passed on genetically.	External influences. We are born as a 'blank slate' and all behaviour is learned through a stimulus response process. Behaviour is learned through processes of classical and operant conditioning.
Assumption about abnormal behaviour	Behaviour is affected by damage to brain structures, genetic abnormalities and changes in levels of neurochemicals.	Abnormal behaviour occurs when learning is maladaptive (i.e. a person has associated fear with an object or situation). Undesirable behaviour has been associated with a positive response.
Therapeutic techniques	Drugs and psychosurgery are used to target physical abnormalities and rebalance neurotransmitters.	Aversion therapy and systematic desensitisation to 'unlearn' the association.
Methods of investigation	The biology of a person can be studied scientifically in a laboratory using scanning and other objective measures.	Laboratory experiments are carried out, particularly with non-human animals.

Table 2.10: Comparison of approaches.

origins of human behaviour. However, it came about because of the common interests and complementary perspectives of cognitive and biological psychologists.

Many psychologists now take an approach to human behaviour which could be described as 'eclectic'. Rather than rigidly adhering to one approach they combine ideas from several approaches and combine them to create what they consider to be a comprehensive explanation of behaviour. There are many advantages to such an eclectic approach. It also ensures that psychologists do not become insular and miss important ideas that are generated by other psychologists who take alternative approaches. This means that ideas are combined from across rather than within approaches, thus possibly producing a better and more holistic understanding of behaviour.

You need to be able to compare the approaches, that is, be able to explain ways in which they are similar and different. This table allows you to do that using four key themes.

COGNITIVE	PSYCHODYNAMIC	HUMANISTIC
Internal influences.	Internal influences.	Internal influences.
Behaviour is a result of internal processes of the mind.	Behaviour is affected by unconscious influences.	Humans have an inborn drive towards self-actualisation and fulfilling potential. Environments can frustrate this tendency for personal growth.
The mind processes information like a computer and develops schemas that help us to interpret our world.	Childhood experiences affect the development of the personality.	
Faulty cognition, negative thought processes and errors in logic lead to abnormal behaviour.	A lack of balance between id, ego and superego, unresolved conflicts during psychosexual development or repression of traumatic experiences into the unconscious can affect how we act and feel.	Mental health and happiness is affected when the actualising drive for personal growth and fulfilment is blocked.
An individual's perception of themselves is distorted.		
Therapy can be used to change negative irrational thoughts into positive rational thoughts that then lead to changes in behaviour.	Psychoanalysis can help to unlock and resolve unconscious conflicts.	Person-centred therapy is non-directive, it respects an individual's ability to solve their own problems and therefore aims to provide a supportive environment within which clients can discover their own solution.
Laboratory experiments are carried out mainly on humans.	Case studies of individuals or small groups of people such as a family.	Only accepts methods such as case studies which use qualitative data based on subjective experience.
Cognitive processes such as memory can be studied scientifically using brain scans.	Questionnaires to gather data on personality traits.	

KEY TERMS

Behaviourism A behavioural approach to psychology that emphasised the observable, measurable aspects of behaviour.

Classical conditioning Learning by association. For instance, Pavlov found that his laboratory dogs would learn a new association between the sound of a bell and food so that they salivated to the sound of a bell.

Cognition Refers to mental activities such as memory, problem solving, language and thought.

Conditions of worth Refers to the conditions in which love and affection is given, e.g. it is given only after certain demands are met.

Congruence According to Carl Rogers, there is congruence when there is a close match between the self (the sense of who you are) and the ideal self (who you think you should be).

Defence mechanism In psychodynamic theory, a tactic used by the ego to protect itself from anxiety.

Denial A defence mechanism where a person refuses to face reality or admit an obvious truth.

Displacement A defence mechanism where anger, frustration and other impulses are focused on objects or people that are less threatening.

Ego The rational part of the psyche that mediates between the unreasonable demands of the id and superego.

Evolution A theory that describes how species develop over generations to adapt to their environments. The mechanisms by which we do this include natural selection and sexual selection.

Genotype The genetic make-up of an organism.

Id The part of the psyche that is the unconscious source of sexual/aggressive impulses.

Operant conditioning Learning happens because we are rewarded (or *reinforced*) for our behaviour or because we are punished for it.

Phenotype The observable characteristics of an organism.

Psychosexual development In psychodynamic theory, the development of personality that occurs in stages during childhood.

Reinforcement In operant conditioning, anything which increases the likelihood of a behaviour occurring again is a reinforcer.

Repression In psychodynamic theory, it is the involuntary act of hiding uncomfortable thoughts, desires and memories in the unconscious.

Schema A 'collection of ideas', framework, that helps us to organise and interpret information about the world around us.

Self-actualisation The ongoing process of reaching ones full potential.

Social learning theory The theory that people learn through observing and imitating a model.

Superego The part of the psyche that is the source of moral standards, internalised from parents.

Unconscious In psychodynamic theory, where thoughts and desires reside which influence behaviour beyond awareness.

Vicarious reinforcement From social learning theory, refers to being reinforced by observing the reinforcement received by a model.

PAGE 121

Luke wanted to train his dog to do tricks, such as rolling over on command and fetching a thrown stick.

Use what you have learned from the behaviourist approach to explain how Luke could train his dog to do a trick. (*4 marks*)

This question is requiring you to apply your knowledge to a novel scenario. This shows that you can't simply rote learn material – you have to *understand* it to be able to *apply* it.

PAGE 123

'There is compelling evidence that early observation of aggression and violence in the child's environment or in the mass media contributes substantially to the development of aggressive habits ...' (Huesmann, 1997)

Outline evidence from research that could be used to support the view expressed in this quote. (*6 marks*)

The quote is clearly directing you towards a particular learning approach. The importance of careful thought and planning is obvious here. Think about your evidence and how you are going to present it to support the quote.

PAGE 125

Outline the basic assumptions of cognitive approach in psychology. (*6 marks*)

The number of basic assumptions you cover in questions like this should be dictated by the number of marks available – three for 2 marks each will probably give you better breadth than two for 3 marks each.

PAGE 132

Explain the difference between a genotype and a phenotype. Use an example of each to illustrate your answer. (*4 marks*)

Make sure you explain how they differ – the difference may not be clear if you simply describe them. Read the question carefully – use an example when explaining the difference. A good answer would probably do this anyway!

PAGE 136

(a) What is a 'defence mechanism'?

(b) Give one example of each of the following defence mechanisms:
(i) Displacement (ii) Denial (*6 marks*)

This question demonstrates why simply learning a definition of something will lead you into difficulties. Learn for understanding so that you can apply your knowledge. This is the only effective way of preparing yourself for these approaches questions.

PAGE 141

Maslow described a hierarchy of needs whereby people are motivated to reach the highest level.

Explain how knowledge of Maslow's hierarchy of needs might be useful in any one setting, education. (*8 marks*)

You must make a judgement about how much detail to put into a question based on the number of marks available. Clearly, you are expected to do more than offer a brief answer for 8 marks – some detail of the hierarchy is needed in a particular context of your choice.

PAGE 144

Outline one basic assumption of the learning approach and one assumption of the psychodynamic approach and explain how they differ. (*6 marks*)

Choose your two assumptions carefully before you begin to answer so that they nicely (and, for you, simply) contrast. This is a good example of why planning an answer before beginning it is a good idea.

A LEVEL ONLY

Biopsychology

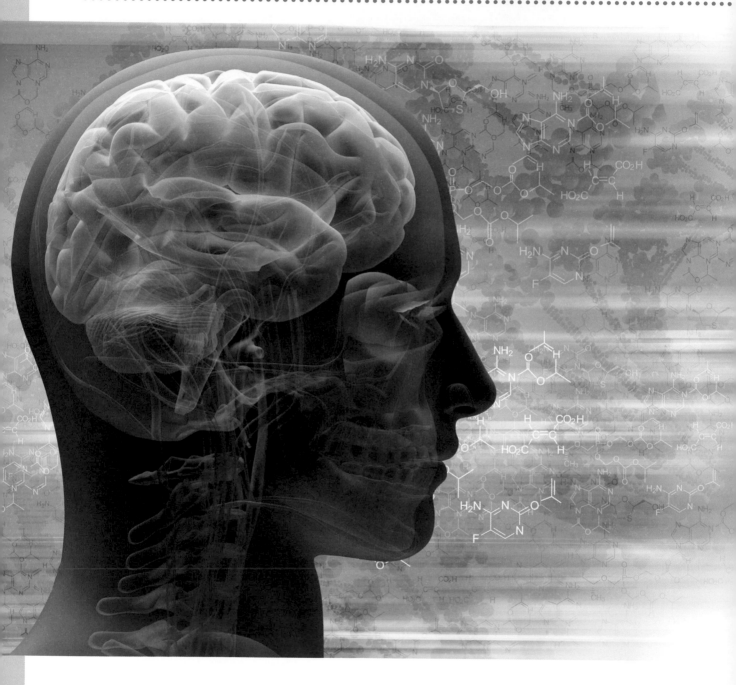

WHAT YOU NEED TO KNOW ☑

The neuron ☐

The structure and function of sensory, relay and motor neurons ☐

The process of synaptic transmission ☐

Neurotransmitters ☐

Excitation ☐

Inhibition ☐

The divisions of the nervous system ☐

Central and peripheral (somatic and autonomic) ☐

The function of the endocrine system ☐

Glands and hormones ☐

The fight-or-flight response including the role of adrenaline ☐

Localisation and lateralisation ☐

Motor ☐

Somatosensory ☐

Visual ☐

Auditory ☐

Language centres: Broca's and Wernicke's areas ☐

Split-brain research ☐

Plasticity and functional recovery of the brain after trauma ☐

Ways of studying the brain ☐

Post-mortem examinations ☐

Scanning techniques: ☐

    Functional magnetic resonance imaging (fMRI) ☐

    Electroencephalogram (EEG) ☐

Event-related potentials (ERP) ☐

Biological rhythms and the difference between them ☐

Circadian ☐

Infradian ☐

Ultradian ☐

The effect of endogenous pacemakers and exogenous zeitgebers on the sleep–wake cycle ☐

Biopsychology

Biology influences behaviour. We know this from the way that changes in brain chemicals affect moods and from how brain trauma can radically alter the ways that we think and act. Also, behaviour influences biology. This can be seen in the stressful effects of the environments we find ourselves in, the way that mood influences immune system functioning and the effects on our psychology and physiology of the recreational drugs that we choose to take, such as tobacco and alcohol. Biology and behaviour are clearly inextricably interwoven. Changes in one bring about changes in the other, and we cannot truly understand either without some understanding of both.

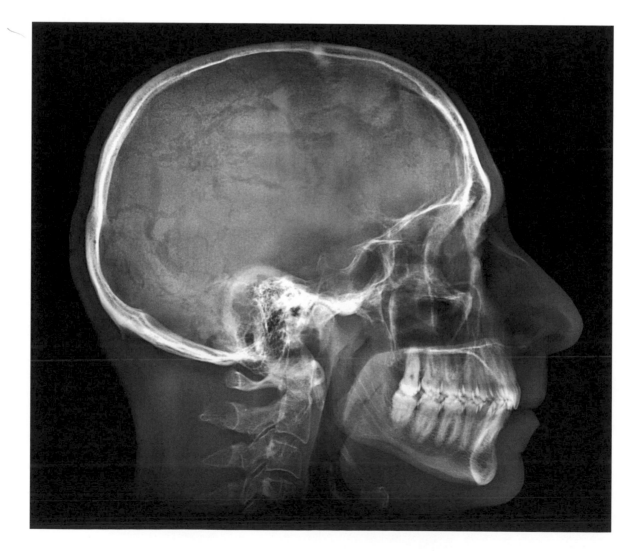

NEURONS AND SYNAPTIC TRANSMISSION

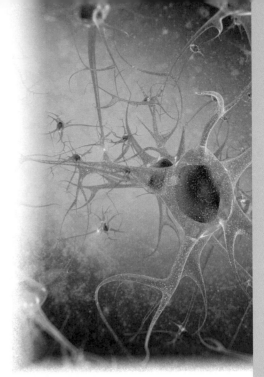

All living organisms are made up of cells. The more complex an organism is, the more cells it has, and the more these cells vary. For example, a simple organism like an amoeba has only one cell, whilst a complex organism like a human has an enormous number, organised into groups that perform specific functions.

The neuron is a specialist cell that makes up the nervous system – it processes information and carries it from one place in the body to another. A neuron has four main parts (see Figure 2.5). The *cell body* contains the nucleus, where all the genetic information is stored and all the structures that keep cells alive and functioning are normally found. *Dendrites* branch out from the cell body, sometimes in huge numbers. These appendages receive most of the input from other neurons. The *axon* is (usually) a longer projection, carrying information from the cell body along its length to other neurons. Axons are covered in a fatty substance called *myelin*. The signals travelling down the axon are electrical and chemical in nature, and the myelin provides insulation. There are breaks every so often in the myelin so that the axon comes into contact with the fluid surrounding the cell. These are called *nodes of Ranvier*. The end of an axon forms branches and at the tip of each is an *axon terminal*. These contain *neurotransmitters*, special chemicals that neurons use to communicate with one another.

THE STRUCTURE AND FUNCTION OF SENSORY, RELAY AND MOTOR NEURONS

The brain essentially consists of billions of neurons (how many is unclear and disputed but lowest estimates put the number at more than the number of stars in the galaxy!). Each one has up to 10,000 connections (synapses) for electrochemical communication with other neurons. As numerous as they are, neurons make up only about 10% of brain cells. The rest are *glial cells*, support cells that supply essential nutrients, clean up and separate and insulate neurons from one another (although tightly packed, neurons never directly touch). Neurons are responsible for everything we do – our thoughts, memories, emotions, and physical sensations, and coordination of all the functions of the body. The nervous system (of which the brain is a part) has three kinds of neurons: *sensory neurons*, *motor neurons* and *interneurons*. These have the same basic components and they operate in similar ways. They do however differ in their shape, which varies according to their specialised task.

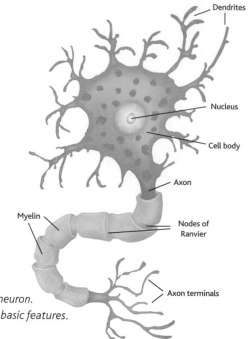

Figure 2.5: Key parts of a motor neuron.
Other neurons share these same basic features.

TYPE OF NEURON	DESCRIPTION
Motor neuron 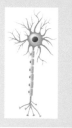	*The moving neuron*. These are the most identifiable neurons as they have the largest cell body with a single projecting axon. They are sometimes referred to as *efferent neurons* because they carry information away from the central nervous system. The axons exit in groups (or nerves) from the brain stem to the muscles of the face and head, or exit from the spinal cord as nerves to the muscles and glands of the body to do important things like cause muscles to contract or relax and keep the heart beating.
Sensory neuron 	*The sensing neuron*. They are sometimes referred to as *afferent neurons* because they carry information to the central nervous system. The cell bodies are gathered in groups called *ganglia*, lying just outside the spinal cord. These neurons carry sensory information from receptors (e.g. in the skin, tongue) and sensory organs (e.g. eyes, ears) to the brain. Pressure on the fingertip, for instance, causes a receptor to activate, sending signals along nerve fibres to the spinal cord and to the brain. If the sensation is 'hot' then this information would be conveyed to motor neurons by *relay neurons* which would cause muscles to contract – this is called a *reflex*.
Relay neuron	*The thinking, feeling and deciding neuron*. Also known as *interneurons*, they carry signals between other neurons – for example, between afferent (sensory) and efferent (motor) neurons, and between other relay neurons. The brain is entirely composed of types of relay neurons which are responsible for communication between different brain regions.

Table 2.11: Types of neurons.

THE PROCESS OF SYNAPTIC TRANSMISSION

Communication between neurons is a process of moving an electrical signal along the length of an axon to the axon terminals, and then sending a chemical signal across a very narrow gap (the synapse) to another neuron. The communication begins with an electrical signal called an *action potential*. This is created with an exchange of ions (electrically charged molecules) through gaps in the axon membrane called *ion channels*. When resting there are more negative ions in the cell fluid (intracellular fluid) than in the surrounding fluid (extracellular fluid). Ion channels suddenly but very briefly allow in sodium (Na+) ions. When these ion channels close, others immediately open allowing out potassium (K+) ions. The K+ ions are pushed out into the extracellular fluid by the Na+ ions because positive charges repel one another. The loss of K+ ions causes the axon to return to its original state of rest. However, the brief overabundance of positive ions inside the cell creates an electrical charge – this is the action potential. This action potential now travels down the axon (a process called *propagation*). Propagation occurs because an action potential in one part of the membrane causes another in an adjacent area. Because myelination prevents the exchange of ions, this can only then occur at a gap in the myelin – a node of Ranvier. In effect, the propagation pulses between nodes of Ranvier (this is called *saltatory conduction*), ensuring that the electrical signal maintains its starting strength until it reaches the axon terminals.

Axon terminals contain *vesicles* (small sacks) of neurotransmitter molecules. There are many different kinds of neurotransmitter but they all do the same thing – that is, transmit messages across a synapse. The action potential causes vesicles to move towards the presynaptic membrane and fuse with it, releasing molecules

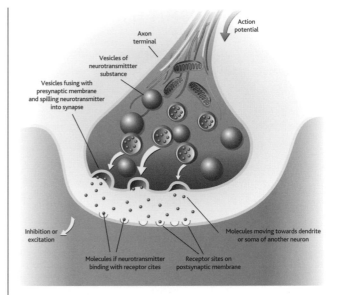

Figure 2.6: The process of synaptic transmission.

of neurotransmitter substance into the synapse. Within milliseconds these molecules reach the dendrite or soma of the next neuron and attach to *receptor sites* on the postsynaptic membrane in a 'lock and key' effect – receptor sites will accept only very specific neurotransmitter molecules. When there is a 'fit', ion channels open up causing an exchange of positive and negative ions, again creating an electrical charge – the signal which began in one neuron has now been transmitted to another.

Neurons can produce either *excitation* or *inhibition* in the receiving neuron. Excitation occurs when neurotransmitter messages make it more likely that receiving neurons will themselves 'fire' an action potential. As the name suggests, inhibition makes this firing less likely to happen. A neuron *integrates* all the excitatory or inhibitory inputs from thousands of other neurons at the *axon hillock*, and is continuously integrating thousands of signals from other neurons. The result is an all-or-nothing effect: if the sum of excitatory impulses is greater than inhibitory ones then the neuron will fire, and if there are more inhibitory impulses then it will not fire.

NEUROTRANSMITTERS

It is important that, after *synaptic transmission*, the neurotransmitter stops having a continuing effect on the receptor site – once it has completed its task the neurotransmitter must be *inactivated*. One way is that it can simply drift away so that it has no further effect; another is that it can be broken down at the receptor site by enzymes. Mostly it is transported away for *reuptake* (i.e. reabsorption back into the axon terminal). Whilst this is an efficient recycling mechanism, some neurotransmitter substance is always lost and new must be produced. Neurotransmitters are made up of quite simple chemicals and are readily manufactured. They derive from normal metabolic processes and from what we eat. For example, acetylcholine is produced from choline-rich foods such as egg yolks and vegetables, serotonin from tryptophan-containing foods like bananas and GABA from natural protein foods. Mechanisms in the brain ensure that the amount of neurotransmitter available for use is always limited to just the right amount. Too much or too little of a particular neurotransmitter can result in a brain disorder – for example, schizophrenia may be caused by an overabundance of the neurotransmitter dopamine and major depressive disorder by low levels of serotonin.

Lots of things that we eat and drink contain chemicals that affect neurotransmitters. Caffeine, for example, blocks the effects of adenosine, a neurotransmitter that not only makes us sleepy but also influences other major neurotransmitters, such as dopamine, serotonin and noradrenaline – three neurotransmitters closely associated with mood.

NEUROTRANSMITTER	FUNCTION
Dopamine	Increases addictive effects of reinforcement, contributes to control of movement; linked with schizophrenia, Parkinson's disease, addiction.
Serotonin	Associated with mood, eating, arousal (including sleep); linked with depression, aggression, OCD, eating disorders.
Noradrenaline	Increases arousal, attentiveness and sexual behaviour; released as a hormone during stress; linked with depression.
Adrenaline	Associated with lack of focus and fatigue, anxiety, attention deficit hyperactivity disorder (ADHD), sleep problems.
Acetylcholine	Involved in learning, memory, rapid eye movement (REM) sleep; linked with ADHD, Parkinson's disease.
Gamma-aminobutyric acid (GABA)	The main inhibitory neurotransmitter; linked with epilepsy.

Table 2.12: A selection of neurotransmitters and some of their functions.

THE DIVISIONS OF THE NERVOUS SYSTEM

A nerve is a bundle of axons. Together, the axons of billions of neurons in the body make up the nervous system. The nervous system is divided into two parts. The *central nervous system* (CNS) is made up of neurons in the brain and spinal cord. The *peripheral nervous system* (PNS) consists of all the nerves that lie outside of the brain and spinal cord – for example, those that carry sensory information from the arms, legs and torso to the brain.

The CNS does not have any direct communication with the outside world. It is the PNS that conveys information to and from the CNS. The PNS is further divided into the *autonomic nervous system* (ANS) and the *somatic nervous system* (SNS). The ANS is called 'autonomic' because it was once thought that it dealt with bodily functions that were beyond voluntary control. We now know this is not strictly the case, e.g. we have some control over our heart rate. One very important function of the ANS is to help the body prepare for and cope with emergencies and to calm the body

afterwards. The ANS has two parts to do this – the *sympathetic division* and the *parasympathetic division*. These are discussed further in the section on page 156, 'The fight-or-flight response'. The SNS connects the CNS to the body organs, such as lungs, intestines, bladder and heart.

THE FUNCTION OF THE ENDOCRINE SYSTEM

The *endocrine system* consists of a number of glands that control many biological functions and affect many behaviours. It does this by releasing chemicals called *hormones* into the bloodstream. Hormones are special chemical messengers that regulate a range of processes in the body. They travel rapidly in the bloodstream to all parts of the body where they can have either a very specific influence (e.g. on an organ or another gland) or a general effect on the body. There are a number of endocrine glands and they vary in terms of the hormones they produce and the function they serve. For example, part of the adrenal gland called the adrenal medulla is triggered by the sympathetic

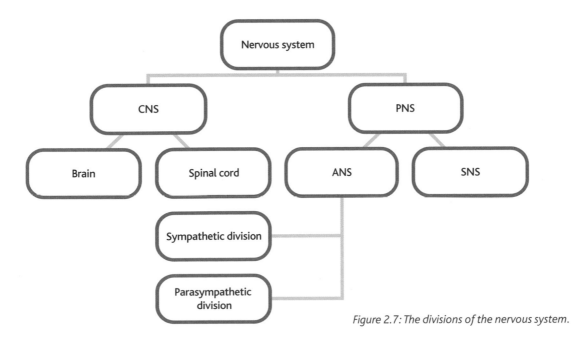

Figure 2.7: The divisions of the nervous system.

division of the ANS to produce adrenaline, a hormone which contributes to physiological arousal. Another part of the adrenal gland called the adrenal cortex is stimulated by a hormone from the pituitary gland to release a range of hormones called corticosteroids. These are essential for helping to regulate things such as sodium (salt) and glucose (sugar) levels in the body. One gland that exerts an influence over all others in the endocrine system is called the pituitary gland (because of its influence it is sometimes referred to as the 'master gland'). This is located at the base of the brain, just under the hypothalamus. It is this close association with the hypothalamus which connects the fast-acting nervous system to the slower-acting endocrine system.

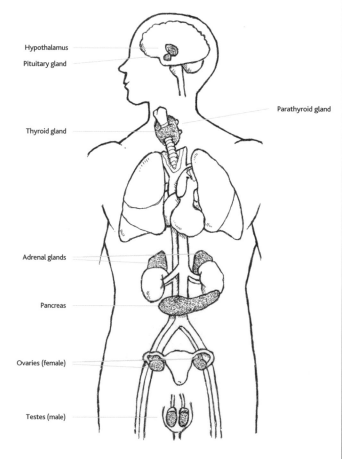

Figure 2.8: The major endocrine glands.

THE FIGHT-OR-FLIGHT RESPONSE AND THE ROLE OF ADRENALINE

Animals have evolved physiological mechanisms to deal with the very many potential threats in their environments. Basically, the physiological response to a threat prepares the animal to either confront it or run away from it – the so called *fight-or-flight response*. Either way, the body is better able to cope with the thing that has been appraised as a stressor. The fight-or-flight response begins with an appraisal of a situation as threatening in some way (i.e. stressful). A message is sent to the hypothalamus in the brain to begin a massive physiological change in the body by triggering two mechanisms: the *pituitary-adrenal system* and the *sympathomedullary pathway*.

The hypothalamus sets off the pituitary-adrenal system by releasing corticotropin releasing factor (CRF) which stimulates

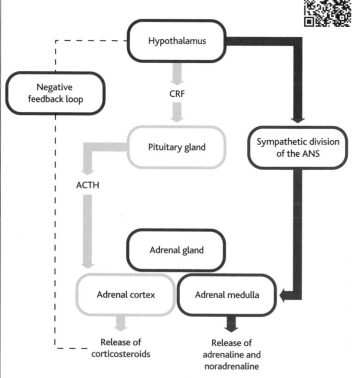

Figure 2.9: The fight-or-flight response.

The stress response is adaptive – it evolved and remained with us because it has survival value. However, it is now dealing with stressors that it was simply not designed for, such as exam stress. Prolonged stress is associated with suppression of the immune system, leading to increased risk of stress-related illness.

the pituitary gland, causing it to release adrenocorticotropic hormone (ACTH). ACTH is detected in the bloodstream by a gland called the adrenal cortex, and in response it releases further hormones into the bloodstream called corticosteroids. There are a number of corticosteroids, each having specific effects on the body. For example, one kind of corticosteroid causes the liver to release glucose, fatty acids and cholesterol for the extra energy needed at this time. Other kinds of corticosteroids change the water and salt balance of the body. Another still ensures faster coagulation (clotting) of the blood in case of injury. When corticosteroids are detected in the bloodstream by the hypothalamus it has the effect of switching off the pituitary-adrenal system. (That is, as long as the stressor has gone away. If it hasn't the hypothalamus will continue to stimulate the pituitary gland and thus prolong the stress response.)

At the same time as triggering the pituitary-adrenal system, the hypothalamus sets off the sympathomedullary pathway. It does this by activating the sympathetic division (a part of the autonomic nervous system involved in arousing the body). The sympathetic division stimulates a gland called the adrenal medulla to release hormones into the bloodstream, the major one being adrenaline. This is sometimes referred to as the fight-or-flight hormone, and it is easy to see why when you consider the effect it has on the body when released, which includes increased blood flow to the muscles, increased heart rate, increased glucose in the blood, accelerated lung action and blood redistribution (e.g. more to the brain). When released, hormones like adrenaline can take a little time to break down and their effects to disappear. This means that the after-effects of the fight-or-flight response can sometimes be felt for quite a while after the stressor has gone away.

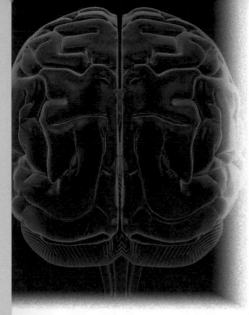

HEMISPHERIC LATERALISATION

The human brain is quite a large organ, scrunched up to fit into a small space – the skull. The thin outer layer of the brain, up to a few millimetres thick, is called the cerebral cortex. Unfolded, its surface area would be about 2.5 m² – much larger than in any other animal. The highly convoluted cerebral cortex makes up about 80% of the brain and is responsible for higher mental processes like thinking, planning and decision making. It is greyish in colour, reflecting the colour of the unmyelinated cell bodies from which it is largely composed, as opposed to the whiter myelinated axons which make up the underlying (subcortical) brain matter.

The brain is divided into two cerebral hemispheres. In the vast majority of people, the right hemisphere controls and receives information from the left side of the body, and the left does the same for the right side. The two hemispheres communicate with each other largely through a bundle of nerve fibres called the *corpus callosum*. It is common to consider the brain as highly lateralised (i.e. functions are located in one or other hemisphere). In fact, they are more similar than they are different. The real difference is in the dominance (i.e. control) that one hemisphere has over the other for some functions. This is perhaps most noticeable with language. Rasmussen and Milner (1977) estimate that 96% of right handers and 70% of left handers have left hemisphere dominance for language.

Split-brain research

In some very rare cases where drug treatments have failed, individuals have undergone *commissurotomy* to cure their epilepsy. This operation involves cutting the corpus callosum, thus preventing direct communication between the right and left hemispheres. The two halves of the brain still get sensory information and each continues to control muscles on the opposite side of the body. For the most part, individuals appear entirely normal following surgery. However, research begun by Roger Sperry and colleagues in the 1960s discovered some significant consequences of this surgery for our understanding of lateralisation.

If someone places a familiar object in your left hand whilst your eyes are closed, you would be able to say what it is because tactile messages would travel to the right hemisphere and pass from there via the corpus callosum to the left hemisphere, where the speech centres are located. A simple, almost mindless task. However, split-brain patients cannot do this. As the corpus callosum is no longer working, the left hemisphere receives no information about what the left hand is doing. This means that, whilst the right hemisphere understands what the object is, the split-brain person would not be able to name the object held in their left hand because speech is located in the now inaccessible left hemisphere. This is known as a *disconnection effect*. No such effect occurs when an object is placed in the right hand

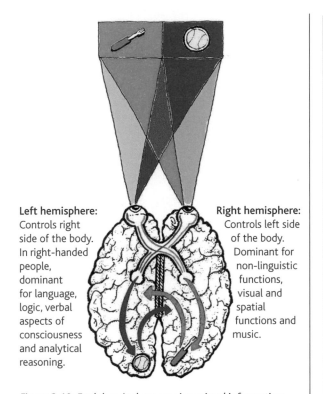

Left hemisphere: Controls right side of the body. In right-handed people, dominant for language, logic, verbal aspects of consciousness and analytical reasoning.

Right hemisphere: Controls left side of the body. Dominant for non-linguistic functions, visual and spatial functions and music.

Figure 2.10: Each hemisphere receives visual information from a visual field of each eye, and this information is then shared with the other hemisphere via the corpus callosum.

Split-brain research

A split-brain person is sat at a table with a dividing screen, preventing objects on it being seen but allowing the individual to reach under and feel them.

(a) The person is asked to fix their gaze on a dot in the centre of the screen.

(b) A word (e.g. 'fork') is then flashed very briefly (i.e. about 150 milliseconds – slow enough to be seen but too fast for the eyes to move towards it) to the far left side of the screen. When asked what they have seen, the split-brain person reports nothing because the word has gone only to the right hemisphere, which does not have speech so they cannot say the word.

(c) The person is then asked to use their left hand to select the object (that they have not been able to name) from a number of objects behind the screen. This is done successfully. The left hand is controlled by the right hemisphere which has seen the word 'fork'.

The right hemisphere clearly has some language ability (i.e. it has 'seen' and understood the word 'fork' since it controls the left hand which has correctly selected it), but it does not have the speech function with which to *express* this understanding.

of a split-brain person because of its direct connections to the left (linguistic) hemisphere – they can name the object as well as anyone else.

Each eye has a left and right visual field (left and right as you look in, not look out!). The left visual field of each eye sends information to the right hemisphere, and the right visual field to the left hemisphere. Normally, the two hemispheres would share their information via the corpus callosum so that both sides of the brain 'see' (see Figure 2.11). In everyday life, split-brain patients show no apparent problems because the eyes are constantly moving, meaning that both visual fields receive similar information. However, when visual fields are restricted so that visual information is sent very briefly to only one hemisphere, differences in the right and left hemispheres become apparent. The results of such tasks are described by Gazzaniga (1967) (see box 'Split-brain

research'). What these studies clearly reveal is that the right hemisphere is not a non-dominant hemisphere, and nor is it subordinate to the left. Whilst there is a 'division of labour' between the two hemispheres, they ultimately complement one another.

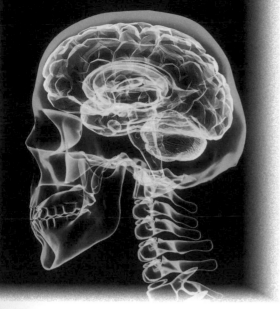

HEMISPHERIC LOCALISATION

Not only are there important differences between hemispheres but each hemisphere has regions specialised for particular things (i.e. they have *localised* functions). The cortex of each hemisphere consists of four areas called lobes.

The large *frontal lobes* are involved in higher functions (e.g. thinking), speech and motor control, and coordinating information from other lobes. Behind the frontal lobes sit the *parietal lobes* which receive and interpret sensory information. Visual information is received and processed at the back of the brain by the *occipital lobes*. Finally, at the sides of the brain are the *temporal lobes* which process auditory information and are also important for memory.

The areas of the cortex directly responsible for sensory information are called *primary areas*. All other cortical areas are collectively known as *association areas*. The neurons in the association cortex appear to be less specific in what they do, are more flexible in their functions and adapt to experience, much more so than neurons in the primary areas. This makes some sense in that they are involved in integrating and using information from the primary areas in high level functions such as perception, decision making and planning.

Motor cortex and somatosensory cortex

The primary motor cortex (PMC) is located in the frontal lobes and controls fine voluntary motor movements (e.g. dexterous tasks like picking up and holding a pen). The PMC on the left frontal lobe mostly controls movement on the right side of the body, and vice versa. Perhaps the most remarkable thing about the PMC is that it is *somatotopically organised*. This means that parts of the body are 'mapped' on

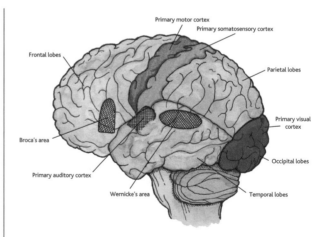

Figure 2.11: The left hemisphere of the brain showing the four lobes, the primary areas and the language centres (Broca's and Wernicke's areas).

to the PMC, and the more fine control the body part needs, the more cortical area is devoted to it (see Figure 2.12). For example, the hip needs much less voluntary control than the hand, so much less cortex is devoted to it.

The primary somatosensory cortex (PSC) is also somatotopically organised, and like the PMC mostly serves the opposite side of the body. The PSC receives and processes information from the skin's senses, such as touch, warmth, pain and sensations that tell us about movement. The mapping of the body on to the PSC is based on the amount of use and sensitivity of the body part (see Figure 2.12b).

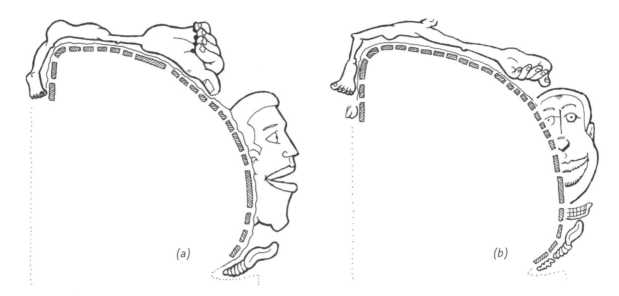

Figure 2.12: The amount of cortical area given to parts of the body proportional to the sensitivity of that area: (a) right primary motor cortex and (b) right primary somatosensory cortex.

The curious case of syndactyly

Syndactyly is one of the most common congenital limb malformations, where two or more fingers are joined together, usually by soft tissue. Magnetoencephalography (MEG) measures the minute magnetic field produced by the electrical activity of the groups of neurons. Mogilner et al. (1993) used MEG to assess the somatopic organisation of the hands of two people prior to surgery for their syndactyly.

For example, they would stimulate each finger to identify the location of the activity on the somatosensory cortex. They found that the fingers did not have the usual somatotopic representation. However, further assessments following surgery showed that within weeks there was significant reorganisation so that the fingers were appropriately represented. This is clear evidence not only of plasticity but also of the speed with which the adult brain is able to reorganise itself.

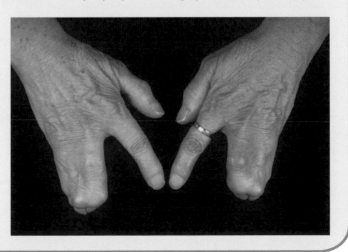

Visual cortex

The primary visual cortex (PVC) is on the occipital lobe, tucked inside the gap between the two hemispheres. The PVC displays a two-dimensional map of the visual world. This 'image' is a projection of the stimulation received by sensory receptors in the retina at the back of each eye. The left half of each retina projects to the right hemisphere PVC and the right half of each retina projects to the left hemisphere PVC. This means that the left hemisphere PVC only receives information from the right visual field and the right hemisphere PVC only from the left (see earlier discussion of split-brain research on page 158 and Figure 2.12a and b). Half of the cortical area of the PVC is taken up with information from the fovea. The fovea is a central area of the retina and, whilst small, it conveys a great deal of visual detail, thus requiring greater cortical area. Damage to the PVC can cause loss of vision (called *cortical blindness*) which varies in severity according to amount of cortical damage (e.g. from 'blind spots' (areas of no vision), to complete loss of visual fields, to complete blindness).

Auditory cortex

The primary auditory cortex (PAC) is located on the upper edge of the temporal lobe, largely tucked out of sight in the lateral fissure. Sound is processed on both sides of the brain. The PAC in each hemisphere receives information from both ears, though there are more connections to the PAC from the opposite side. Sound vibrations entering the ear activate hair-cell receptors on the cochlea in the inner ear. Sounds are converted to neural signals here, which then travel via several other brain structures to the PAC. The neurons in the PAC are arranged *tonotopically*. This means that they react to sounds of specific frequencies – neurons at one end of the PAC react to low frequencies and those closer to the other end respond to higher frequencies. The PAC is not completely responsible for hearing, so damage to this area produces difficulties in processing and understanding sounds rather than deafness (e.g. there might be an inability to perceive a certain pitch).

Language centres

In 1861 physician Paul Broca exhibited the brain of a patient who, before dying the year before, had lost the ability to say anything other than 'tan'. The brain showed clear damage to the left frontal cortex. This disorder has since become known as a type of expressive aphasia called production aphasia, where there is a loss of the articulation programmes that guide the PMC to move the right muscles to produce appropriate words. In 1874 Carl Wernicke described a patient who, following damage to the left temporal cortex, had great difficulty understanding speech. This disorder is a type of receptive aphasia now known as sensory aphasia, where there is damage to the brain area responsible for the comprehension of language. Since then a number of other locations have been discovered in the brain that are important for language. In 1970 Norman Geschwind developed a theory which suggests that language is a serial process involving seven brain components (see box 'The Wernicke–Geschwind model of language'). The Wernicke–Geschwind model has become an extremely influential model of language processing. It stimulated a great deal of research because it is a simple model which generates clear, testable hypotheses about language. For example, it helps us to understand that a particular type of receptive aphasia called conduction aphasia is due to damage to the arcuate fasciculus. Even though language comprehension and spontaneous speech are unaffected, these individuals have difficulty repeating words just heard because the communication pathway between Wernicke's and Broca's areas is damaged.

However, whilst many of its predications have been supported, the Wernicke–Geschwind model has been criticised on the grounds of it being neither sufficiently accurate nor comprehensive. Individuals with pure forms of aphasia (e.g. *only* expressive or *only* receptive) are extremely rare, with most aphasics presenting combinations of the two. A clear distinction between brain areas for language production and comprehension may therefore not be wholly justified. More recent developments in brain imaging technology have shown that many areas of the left hemisphere not identified by the model are involved in language, and, indeed, suggest that language functioning is scattered across all four lobes (see page 162). This fits in with the notion of *equipotentiality*, which is the view that the cortex functions as a whole and there is no functional specialisation.

The Wernicke–Geschwind model of language

Examples of how the various components of the Wernicke–Geschwind model coordinate in language comprehension and production:

Having a conversation: 3 ➜ 4 ➜ 5 ➜ 6 ➜ 7

Reading a book out loud: 1 ➜ 2 ➜ 4 ➜ 5 ➜ 6 ➜ 7

BRAIN COMPONENT	FUNCTION
1. Primary visual cortex (PVC)	Receives visual signals
2. Angular gyrus (left hemisphere)	Comprehends language-related visual signals (e.g. words on a page)
3. Primary auditory cortex (PAC)	Receives auditory signals (e.g. voice of another person)
4. Wernicke's area	Auditory inputs transformed into meaningful words (e.g. language comprehension)
5. Arcuate fasciculus	Communication pathway between Wernicke's and Broca's areas
6. Broca's area	Selects correct articulation programme for word sounds
7. Primary motor cortex (PMC)	Control of fine motor movements involved in speaking

PLASTICITY AND FUNCTIONAL RECOVERY OF THE BRAIN AFTER TRAUMA

 The term *plasticity* (sometimes called neuroplasticity) refers to how the brain reorganises itself due to experience. The brain becomes less plastic as it ages (Bedny et al., 2010). Much of the brain's plasticity is lost after 2 years of age, there is significant plasticity up until puberty, and relatively little in adulthood.

A number of processes are involved in plasticity, including synaptogenesis (creating new synapses), neurogenesis (growing new neurons) and synaptic pruning (eliminating unwanted or unused synapses). There are two types of plasticity. Experience-expectant plasticity refers to the normal neural development that takes place during critical periods early in life. For example, the brain expects certain kinds of sensory stimulation (e.g. vision) and if it is deprived of this stimulation during a critical period then the brain will reorganise itself and sensory functions will be lost. Gougoux et al. (2005) for example found that blind individuals who developed acute hearing had recruited to the task unused neurons in the visual part of the brain. It has also been noted that individuals who use Braille have increased development in the part of the somatosensory cortex corresponding to fingers on the left hand (which is mostly used for reading Braille).

The brain also has the ability to adapt and change in response to environmental experience across the lifespan. This is called experience-dependent plasticity. For example, when you learn a new motor skill (like driving) there is a great deal of synaptogenesis in several parts of the brain including the motor cortex and cerebellum. This is the crux of learning – it involves the creation of new synaptic networks.

Interest in plasticity (in particular, experience-dependent plasticity) has grown because of the

Some types of brain trauma

Tumour: a growth of new and abnormal tissue that damages surrounding brain structures.

Cerebrovascular accident (CVA or stroke): an interruption of blood supply, killing affected neurons.

Traumatic brain injury (TBI): damage caused by a blow to the head.

Infection: the brain is damaged by bacteria, parasites, viruses or fungi.

Neurotoxins: pesticides, solvents and heavy metals (e.g. mercury) destroy nervous system tissue.

hope it gives for repair of the nervous system following trauma. Neurorehabilitation is in part an attempt to take advantage of plasticity by training the undamaged parts of the brain to take over the functions of the damaged parts (a process requiring synaptogenesis). However, the outcome of brain trauma is uncertain and the prospects for recovery are extremely variable. Cells in the brain do not repair themselves like cells outside the nervous system. Kolb and Wishaw (2001) point out that the extent of recovery depends on the complex interrelationships of three factors:

1. The type, location and extent of the damage. For example, the more extensive the damage, the less likely is recovery. Also complex skills are more likely to recover than specific skills since loss of a component from a complex skill may be compensated for by other components.

2. The unique organisational features of an individual's brain.

3. The attitude of the person and those in support, including family, therapists and physicians.

WAYS OF STUDYING THE BRAIN

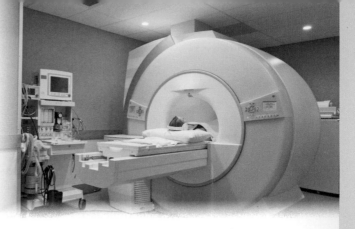

There are basically two ways of studying the nervous system: *in vitro* (which is to study it outside the living organism) and *in vivo* (which is to study it inside the living organism). The early days of brain research were characterised by *in vitro* studies involving dissecting the brains of the dead and using ever more powerful microscopes to study structures hidden to the naked eye. Many of the techniques developed by these pioneer neuroscientists are still being used today in post-mortem studies. Recent advances in technology have seen the development of brain scanning techniques enabling *in vivo* studies of the structure and function of living human brains.

POST-MORTEM EXAMINATIONS

Post-mortem literally means 'after death'. This was traditionally the main source of information about the brain and about the location of damage which leads to behavioural change.

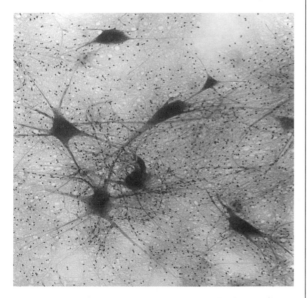

Neurons, revealed after staining. Post-mortem examinations enable investigations at the level of neurons, something that modern scanning methods cannot do.

Paul Broca, for example, noted the language problems of Tan whilst alive, but it was a post-mortem examination that told Broca where the damage was in Tan's brain (see page 162). The brain is an extremely difficult organ to investigate. Observations with the naked eye tell you very little about it, so it was only with the development of microscopes, and more recently electron microscopes, that the workings of the brain began to be uncovered. There are many types of post-mortem examination. The most common is called histology. Here, once removed from the body, parts of interest in the dead brain are cut into very thin slices (or *sections*) and attached to glass microscope slides. In order to reveal fine details the section is stained. There are various staining methods available, depending on what detail it is you want to reveal – for example, cell bodies or cell fibres.

Strengths and weaknesses

Whilst technological developments have reduced the use of data from post-mortem examinations, it is still an important research tool. The direct study of brain tissue allows detailed investigation at the level of neurons, synapses and neural circuits, and can complement neuro-imaging methods which shows activity in the brain whilst alive. However, research relies on the donation of brains for study. In the case of particular individuals with brain damage, researchers might have to wait many years before the brain becomes 'available' (even assuming the brain is ultimately bequeathed to science).

SCANNING TECHNIQUES: ELECTROENCEPHALOGRAMS AND EVENT-RELATED POTENTIALS

Communication between neurons is electrical in nature and with the right equipment this activity can be recorded. This recording is called electroencephalography (EEG) and the recording is called the electroencephalogram. Electrodes are attached to the scalp to pick up the electrical signals being produced by groups of active neurons in different areas of the cortex. An amplifier then magnifies these signals and displays it as a 'brain wave' (see Figure 2.13) showing the degree of activity of the brain. An event-related potential (ERP) is like an EEG except that there are many repeated trials of a specific cognitive stimulus (e.g. a sound or image). There is a lot of 'background noise' being picked up by the electrodes (many billions of neurons are firing and all beneath a bony skull surrounded by liquid). A computer program 'averages out' the responses so that the common responses

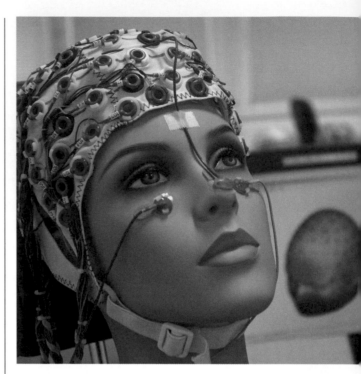

With EEG/ERP, electrodes are attached to the scalp with conducting gel and the electrical activity of the brain is recorded.

remain and this irrelevant noise is cancelled out, leaving a clearer signal.

Strengths and weaknesses

The temporal resolution of EEG and ERP is very good, being able to distinguish neural events one millisecond apart. Because of this they are particularly suited to research into the speed of brain responses. They are relatively easy to use and low cost and, as they are non-invasive, present no risk to participants. They have poor spatial resolution, however, and at best only allow estimates about location restricted to the cortex.

A

B

Figure 2.13: Brain waves recorded by EEG of (A) relaxed wakefulness and (B) rapid eye movement (dream) sleep.

SCANNING TECHNIQUES: FUNCTIONAL MAGNETIC RESONANCE IMAGING

The brain requires nutrients, including oxygen, and this is provided by the blood supply. The more active the brain (or a part of the brain) is, the more nutrients are needed, and thus the greater the blood flow. The functional magnetic resonance imaging (fMRI) scanner applies a very powerful magnetic field to the brain which causes a change to the oxygen atoms in the blood. Concentrations of oxygen are detected by the scanner: the greater the concentration, the greater the activity. The scanner basically takes a 'photo' of the areas of high oxygen use. The brain is scanned for activity before a cognitive task for a baseline measure and then again during a task. The difference between the two recordings is therefore only the activity associated with the task.

Strengths and weaknesses

Unlike other functional imaging techniques which require potentially harmful injections of radioactive material (i.e. PET scans), fMRI is non-invasive. This is one reason for it becoming the preferred scanning technique. It also provides good spatial resolution, although not good enough to pinpoint exactly what neural networks are active at particular times. The temporal resolution is about one second. However, whilst this appears quite rapid, it is a good deal slower than the speed at which the brain functions, so there is always a temporal 'lag' between the task and the recording of activity. Our cognitive functions in everyday life are very fast and do not usually resemble the slow, deliberate tasks that are usually required as part of an experiment.

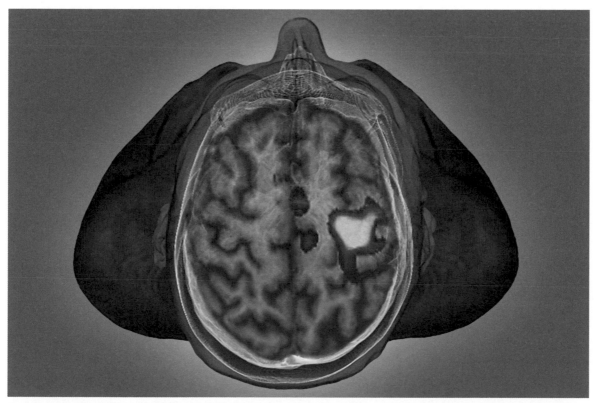

A computer analyses the scan results and presents them as images. The brighter colours represent areas of greatest activity.

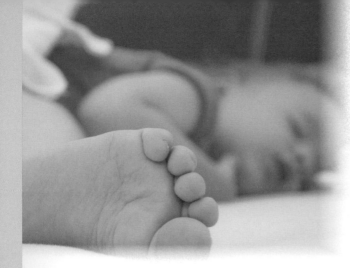

BIOLOGICAL RHYTHMS

The body has many different kinds of biological rhythms. Some may last only milliseconds, such as those found in individual nerve cells, whilst others may last minutes or hours, such as fluctuations in core body temperature. These biological rhythms that happen more than once every 24 hours are called *ultradian rhythms*. Many of the most observable rhythms are those that run to a 24 hour cycle, such as sleep and waking. These are called *circadian rhythms*.

When rhythms occur less than once in every 24 hours they are known as *infradian rhythms* – for example, the monthly menstrual cycle and the seasonal migration of some animals. Quite how these rhythms are controlled is still a matter of research and debate. The time-keeping is assumed to be controlled by endogenous (internal) pacemakers, which are in turn influenced to a greater or lesser degree by exogenous (external) cues, sometimes called zeitgebers (from the German 'time-giver'). *Endogenous pacemakers* and *exogenous zeitgebers* interact in often complex and obscure ways to synchronise the body's many biological rhythms.

CIRCADIAN RHYTHMS

There are many circadian rhythms in human behaviour, and whilst some, like the sleep and wake cycle, are obvious and unavoidable, others are subtle and go unnoticed (e.g. temperature, hormone secretion). These, like the rhythms in other organisms, have evolved to cope with the daily fluctuations in light and temperature due to the rotation of the Earth. Research has involved attempting to eliminate environmental

(exogenous) cues to time and observing the consequences for the circadian rhythm. One key finding is that in such conditions circadian rhythms become *free-running* (i.e. they are not aligned, or *entrained*, to external cues). They run to only an approximate 24 hour day and, because of this, require a daily adjustment to the light–dark cycle by a zeitgeber in order to entrain (reset) it to the natural environment (see box 'Aschoff's bunker study'). However, the fact that rhythms persist even under constant environmental conditions shows that there must be a biological clock. Even in free-running conditions these clocks are incredibly persistent and accurate. Richter (1968) blinded a squirrel monkey and recorded its rest–activity cycles for over three years. Whilst its cycles became free-running, the rest–activity cycles themselves varied by only a few minutes during this time.

The location of the biological clock was discovered in the early 1970s. Stephan and Zucker (1972) found that damage to a group of cells in the hypothalamus called the suprachiasmatic nucleus (SCN) affected a number of circadian rhythms in rats, including hormone secretion, drinking and wheel-running. Moore (1973) identified a neural

Aschoff's bunker study

Aschoff et al. (1967) had participants spend up to a month living in specially designed underground laboratories. These 'bunkers' were built to shield participants from any external influence which might affect their circadian rhythms. Participants were allowed to sleep or engage in any activity they wanted. It was noted that they kept a regular cycle of activity, confirming the idea of an internal biological clock. However, their cycles soon began to drift. After about two weeks, participants were found to be half a day out of synchrony with the outside world. It was suggested that this was because the body's natural circadian rhythm is closer to 25 hours, and without exogenous cues to constantly adjust it their internal clock became free-running – it was not bound to the 24 hour light–dark cycle or entrained by other environmental cues, like clocks.

pathway carrying light signals from the eyes to the SCN. It is this route that provides the light information which entrains the cells in the SCN to fluctuations of light and dark.

ULTRADIAN RHYTHMS

There are many ultradian cycles, the majority occurring without our awareness, such as temperature regulation, hormone secretion, urine flow and heart rate. Ultradian rhythms are largely under endogenous control. Probably the most obvious ultradian rhythm we have is the rhythm of sleep. Whilst part of a general circadian cycle, sleep has its own identifiable ultradian rhythm. The two basic phases of sleep which make up this rhythm are REM (rapid eye movement) and NREM (non-rapid eye movement). When we first go to sleep we progress through the first of four stages of NREM sleep. Stages 3 and 4 of NREM together are known as slow-wave sleep (SWS). After

about 20 minutes in SWS we enter REM sleep (see Figure 2.14). For the remainder of the night sleep alternates between SWS and REM sleep in an approximate 90 minute cycle, with periods of REM becoming longer throughout the night at the expense of time in SWS. By the morning awakening a typical night's sleep of eight hours might have contained five cycles of SWS and REM sleep. The REM/NREM ultradian cycle is thought to be generated by REM-on and REM-off cells in the brain stem (Hobson et al., 1975). REM-off cells are most active when we are awake and they inhibit the activity of REM-on cells. As we fall asleep (something under circadian control) the activity of REM-off cells declines, so allowing the REM-on cells to become more and more active, triggering REM sleep. The neurochemical activity of REM-on cells eventually triggers a switching on of REM-off cells, thus REM sleep ends, NREM sleep returns and the cycle begins again.

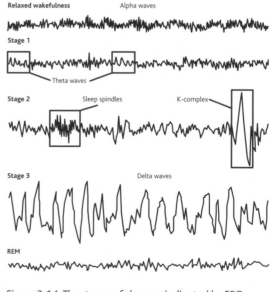

Figure 2.14: The stages of sleep as indicated by EEG.

INFRADIAN RHYTHMS

There are many variations in infradian rhythms. For example, some occur on a monthly cycle, whilst others are much longer, cycling on a seasonal or annual basis. Examples include skin shedding in snakes, antler shedding in deer and hibernation. A common infradian rhythm in humans is seasonal affective disorder (SAD), a kind of depression which seems to occur on a seasonal basis, with the problem worst in winter and lessening or disappearing entirely during the spring and summer. There are approximately 11 million sufferers in the United States, and its distribution seems to tell us something about its cause. Florida (in the far south) have rates estimated around 1.4% of the population, whilst in Maine (in the far north) the rates are as high as 10%. The important factor underlying this difference appears to be the decreased amount of daylight in northern latitudes during the winter months compared to the south. Perhaps the most obvious infradian rhythm in humans, however, is the monthly menstrual cycle. McClintock (1971) found that students who spent extended time together whilst living in university halls of residence tended to synchronise their menstrual cycles. She put

Something in the air

Russell et al. (1980) wanted to know if olfactory cues from one woman could influence the timing of menstrual onset of another. They collected odour by placing cotton pads in the armpits of donors for 24 hours. The donors were told not to use deodorants or wash their armpits during this time. This cotton pad was then rubbed on the upper lip of participants who were told not to wash their faces for six hours. This happened three times a week for six months. Russell et al. reported that participants shifted their menstrual cycles significantly to resemble the donor's monthly cycle. There have been many subsequent studies like this (e.g. Jacob et al., 2004, found that the menstrual cycle of participants could be influenced by exposure to pads odourised in the nursing brassieres of breastfeeding donors).

this synchrony down to an exogenous zeitgeber – pheromones. Whilst widespread in animals, there is considerable disagreement about whether human pheromones exist. Many studies directly contradict these findings, however, and other researchers have pointed to serious methodological flaws in McClintock's study.

Many animals engage in annual hibernation, an example of infradian rhythm.

THE EFFECT OF ENDOGENOUS PACEMAKERS AND EXOGENOUS ZEITGEBERS ON THE SLEEP–WAKE CYCLE

The sleep–wake cycle follows a regular 24 hour circadian rhythm. Endogenous control comes from the suprachiasmatic nucleus (SCN) which acts like a 'master body clock'. Cells in this brain region have 'clock proteins' which go through a 24 hour biochemical cycle, synchronising the rhythms of other body clocks such as those in individual cells. The SCN influences levels of the hormone melatonin. This substance has the effect of reducing alertness and increasing drowsiness. It is nearly absent in the body during the daytime, but concentrations begin to rise in the evening with dimming light. The SCN controls the release of melatonin by the pineal gland in response to light signals. The SCN also provides signals to other parts of the brain that influence sleep – for example, the lateral hypothalamus. Neurons here release hypocretin (sometimes called orexin), a neurotransmitter which directly influences arousal and plays an important role in wakefulness and sleep.

Light is clearly a key exogenous zeitgeber. The SCN is linked to the day–night cycle by fibres emanating from the retina, and it is this light signal that entrains the sleep–wake cycle. However, these light signals determine the timing of sleep rather than sleep itself. This has been shown in studies where individuals have spent extended periods of time in environments lacking exogenous cues like light and temperature. Possibly the most famous study of this kind was conducted by French cave explorer Michel Siffre (see box 'Life in a cave'). Studies like this (and the Aschoff study – see page 169) demonstrate that whilst the sleep–wake cycle is maintained by light, in the absence of this zeitgeber it becomes free-running (i.e. it is not bound to the 24 hour light–dark cycle). The vital

Life in a cave

In 1972 Michel Siffre spent 205 days isolated in Midnight Cave, Texas. Going deep into caves has the advantage of reducing influences on circadian rhythms such as light, temperature, geomagnetic and electromagnetic factors that also fluctuate on a daily basis. Whilst he could choose to illuminate his living quarters when he wanted, he had no way of knowing the time in the outside world. Researchers studying his progress found that at first, like other biological rhythms, his sleep pattern was erratic but soon settled into a regular free-running rhythm, whilst his day shifted to 25 hours in length.

importance of light as an exogenous zeitgeber can be seen in the circadian rhythms of totally blind individuals. Because light does not reach the biological clock in the brain, the pacemaker runs in and out of synchrony with the 24 hour day. Consequently, many behavioural rhythms, such as the sleep–wake cycle, temperature, hormonal rhythms and cycles of alertness, become desynchronised. The majority of blind people thus suffer from something called non-24 hour sleep–wake disorder, which is characterised by disrupted sleep cycles and excessive day naps (Skene et al., 1999).

A person's sleep–wake cycle is naturally synchronised to the light–dark cycle so that activity is largely diurnal (i.e. daytime). However, occasionally this synchrony is disrupted – for example, in order to accommodate night working and movement across time zones. Such disruption has potential negative consequences for our health and behaviour.

Disruption of the sleep–wake cycle: the effects of night shift work

Given the opportunity, our biological clocks will eventually adjust to altered sleep patterns of day–night activity associated with working through the night. However, this rarely happens, even in individuals on a permanent night shift. Life goes on as usual for everyone else, with more noise during daytime making sleep difficult, light-suppressing melatonin production (which is important for sleepiness) and social routines and responsibilities at odds with working hours. There is evidence to suggest that prolonged night shift work can be harmful to health, and it has been linked to a range of health problems including diabetes, cancer, stomach ulcers, hypertension and immune system problems. Schernhammer et al. (2001) used data gathered as part of a 10 year study following the health of 78,562 nurses in the United States. Accounting for potential confounding variables, like alcohol consumption, use of oral contraception, weight and post-menopausal hormone use, they found that the risk of breast cancer increased significantly with the number of years working night shifts.

There is a lack of agreement amongst researchers about why disruption to sleep–wake cycles should have such negative consequences, but they are likely due to a combination of factors to do with the stress caused by lost sleep and the disruption to underlying mechanisms of the sleep–wake cycle. Night work, for example, obviously requires artificial light, and we know that exposure to light, whether natural or artificial, alters the release of melatonin so that almost none is produced. Neither is melatonin secretion quick to recover after disruption. It has been found that it can take over two weeks for levels to get back to normal after night-time light exposure, and even then full recovery only occurs when there has been a period of constant day–night cycle (Zeitzer et al., 2000).

Reduction in melatonin leads to increases in levels of a range of hormones, particularly a type of oestrogen called oestradiol which is responsible for the growth of hormone-sensitive cells in the breast. Elevated levels of oestradiol have been associated with an increased risk of breast cancer (Swerdlow, 2003). Schernhammer and Hankinson (2003) point out that blind women, who do not have their melatonin levels suppressed by light, experience a lower incidence of breast cancer.

Disruption of the sleep–wake cycle: the effects of travelling across time zones

Jet lag occurs when normal circadian rhythms are disrupted by travelling across time zones. When crossing time zones there is a shift in zeitgebers, which causes a conflict between external cues (such as light and temperature) and the time kept by endogenous circadian clocks.

Basically, our body is telling us that it is one time and environmental cues are telling us that it is a different time, in other words there is a circadian misalignment. People with jet lag show a wide range of symptoms, including fatigue, poor concentration, reduced alertness, clumsiness, memory difficulties and lethargy. One of the main after-effects of jet lag however is disturbed sleep.

There are problems with falling asleep too early following eastward travel (there is a phase advance – early sleep-onset and early wake times). Westward travel causes problems with inability to sleep when you normally would (there is a phase delay – later sleep-onset and later waking times). Generally, phase advance (eastward travel) causes greater problems than phase delay (westward travel). Jet lag is less of a problem when travelling west because the body finds it less difficult adjusting to a slightly longer day than it does to a slightly shorter one. Even though the SCN can readjust and reset its clock within a day, the effects of jet lag can last

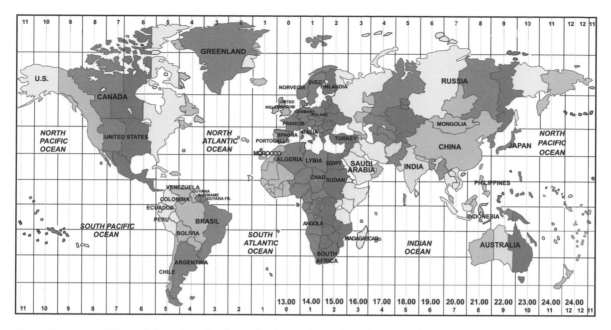

Generally, eastward flights (where there has been a backward shift in the 24 hour cycle) cause greater problems than travelling west (where there is a forward shift in the 24 hour cycle). Jet lag is less of a problem when travelling west because the body finds it less difficult adjusting to a slightly longer day than to a slightly shorter one.

up to a month because different internal clocks (for example in the lungs, liver and muscles) entrain at different speeds, so for a while remain uncoordinated.

Whilst there are obvious short-term consequences of jet lag (largely due to the effects of disturbed sleep), research also suggests that repeated jet lag may have more severe long-term effects. According to Cho (2001) constant travel across time zones has been found to increase the amount of the stress hormone cortisol in the body. He suggests that these increased cortisol levels caused by repeated jet lag have physical effects on the brain. Participants in his study were 20 healthy women aged 20–28 employed by international airline companies for five years. Half the women had a short jet lag recovery period of less than five days between transmeridian flights that crossed seven time zones. The other half were a long recovery group that had 14 days between transmeridian flights, during which time their flights were short and did not involve large time shifts. All the participants had MRI scans which were used to assess brain structure, and psychological tests of cognitive functioning. He found that the short recovery group had noticeably smaller temporal lobes and scored lower on visuo-spatial tests. One important implication of this research is that temporal lobe atrophy associated with prolonged jet lag might be reduced by introducing periods of jet lag recovery.

KEY TERMS

Adrenaline A hormone secreted by the adrenal glands that helps the body to meet physical or emotional demands of stress. It is also a *neurotransmitter*.

Autonomic nervous system Regulates the functions of internal organs – for example, heart and intestines.

Broca's area A region in the frontal lobe (usually left hemisphere) responsible for producing language.

Circadian rhythm A biological rhythm that follow a roughly 24 hour cycle.

Endocrine system A system of glands in the body that produce and secrete hormones (chemical substances that regulate the activity of cells or organs).

Endogenous pacemaker An internal (biological) body clock.

Excitation When *neurotransmitter* messages make it more likely that receiving *neurons* will themselves 'fire' an action potential.

Exogenous zeitgeber External cues from the environment that influence the timing of internal body clocks.

Fight-or-flight response A physiological reaction that either prepares the body to fight a stressor or flee the stressor.

Glial cell A support cell in the central nervous system. The most common brain cell, there are different types depending on the kind of support they provide.

Infradian A biological rhythm that occurs less than once in every 24 hours.

Inhibition When *neurotransmitter* messages make it less likely that receiving *neurons* will themselves 'fire' an action potential.

Motor neuron A cell that directly or indirectly controls the contraction or relaxation of muscles.

Neuron A brain cell that transmits information using electrical and chemical signals.

Neurotransmitter A neurochemical used to communicate across the synapse between *neurons*.

Phase advance A shift in the circadian rhythm caused by travelling east across time zones. One side effect is early sleep-onset and early wake times.

Phase delay A shift in the circadian rhythm caused by travelling west across time zones. One side effect is later sleep-onset and later waking times.

Plasticity How the brain reorganises itself due to experience.

Relay neuron Sometimes called interneurons, they carry information from one part of the central nervous system to another.

Sensory neuron Carry information from sensory receptors (e.g. touch) to the central nervous system.

Somatic nervous system Responsible for sensing external stimuli and for voluntary body movement.

Synaptic transmission The electrical and chemical communication that occurs between *neurons*.

Ultradian rhythm A biological rhythm that happens more than once every 24 hours.

Wernicke's area A region in the temporal lobe (usually left hemisphere) involved in the comprehension of speech.

PAGE 151

Outline the structure *and* function of a sensory neuron. *(4 marks)*

The question is asking you for structure *and* function. If you break it down you can see that you are not expected to write a great deal on either!

PAGE 153

Describe the processes of synaptic transmission. *(6 marks)*

Some questions lend themselves to diagrams very well, and this is an example of one of those. Learn about synaptic transmission using diagrams and reproduce the synapse here with an explanation of what is going on.

PAGE 155

Identify each division of the nervous system:

A..................

B..................

C..................

D..................

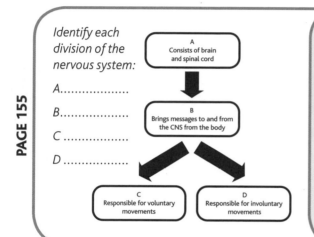

A
Consists of brain and spinal cord

B
Brings messages to and from the CNS from the body

C
Responsible for voluntary movements

D
Responsible for involuntary movements

This is typical of the kind of question you can expect in biopsychology at both AS and A level. The topic areas are quite technical and lend themselves to multi-choice and short answer questions. This doesn't necessarily make the questions easier – you have to know the detail to answer these questions!

PAGE 156

Outline the fight-or-flight response. *(3 marks)*

If you've done your learning then you definitely have too much material for a 3 mark question. Sometimes, questions are demanding because they require you to be selective and boil down what you know into core issues – and this is one of those! Remember – 3 marks only!

PAGE 159

'The great pleasure and feeling in my right brain is more than my left brain can find the words to tell you.' (Roger Sperry)

Discuss what split-brain research has told us about hemisphere lateralisation. *(12 marks)*

It's a 'discuss' question so you know you are going to have to show two skills (descriptive and evaluative). The question is about *research* so the descriptive bit will be about research. The rest of the marks will come from some evaluative commentary, possibly focusing on the complementary nature of the two hemispheres and reference to findings of research into language.

PAGE 166

Compare and contrast any two scanning techniques. *(6 marks)*

You have to know scanning techniques, so it is perfectly reasonable to be expected to know their relative strengths and weaknesses. Note here that you do not need to describe the technique – just compare the strengths of one against the weaknesses of the other. Think about your selection first so that you make the best choice.

A LEVEL ONLY

Section 3
Research
Methods

Research Methods

WHAT YOU NEED TO KNOW ☑

Experimental method ❑
Experimental design ❑
Variables ❑
Control ❑

Observational techniques ❑
Types of observation ❑
Observational design ❑

Self-report techniques ❑
Questionnaires and questionnaire ❑
construction
Interviews ❑

Correlations ❑
Analysis and interpretation of correlations ❑

Content analysis and thematic analysis ❑

Case studies ❑

Aims and hypotheses ❑

Sampling ❑

Pilot studies ❑

Demand characteristics and ❑
investigator effects

Reliability and validity ❑

Ethics ❑

The role of peer review ❑

The implications of psychological ❑
research for the economy

Features of science ❑

Reporting psychological investigations ❑

Quantitative and qualitative data ❑

Primary and secondary data ❑

Descriptive statistics ❑

Distributions ❑

Levels of measurement ❑

Statistical testing: The sign test ❑

Probability and significance ❑

Factors affecting the choice of ❑
statistical test

Research Methods

If you find this part of psychology tricky you are not alone, so don't think it means that psychology is not for you. Even at university many people find methods challenging, but don't worry – help is at hand. We believe that it all depends on how you think about it. Many students think that this section of the course is all about maths and statistics. They are partly right – there certainly is some maths here – but the best way to think about it is as the *art* of psychology, the *skills needed to do* psychology. The maths really comes last. This is all about how to find out things properly and how to choose the right ways to go about finding out what you want to know.

The other good thing about this section of the course is that you only really have to learn it once, and once you have done that you can apply it all over the place. For instance, being able to evaluate a particular method properly provides you with the skills to evaluate any study which uses that method. The very best way to learn how something works is to take it apart and put it back together again. If it's an engine, each part fits together neatly and in the right order to make the car work. Knowing how methods work and how choices have been made will allow you to see

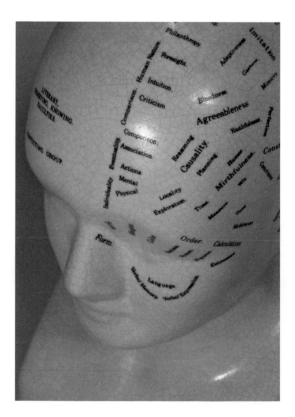

how studies you are reading about work in much more detail, and it will help your understanding of the points the authors are making.

Another problem people have is that they think that 'research methods' is just another separate area of psychology. That's partly the fault of textbook writers like us, and partly the fault of generations of psychologists. It just so happens that research methods tend to feature as a separate chapter and are therefore regarded as something you read about once, and forget about for the rest of the book. We would urge you to regard research methods as central to your study of psychology, with all the other bits (developmental, cognitive, social, etc.) as separate important extras. Without one you cannot have the other.

THE EXPERIMENTAL METHOD

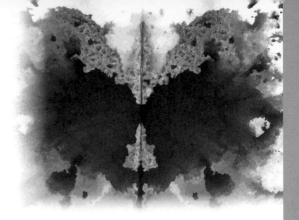

A great deal of psychological information has been acquired from experimental research – it is the prime method of enquiry in science. The experiment is a method of studying human behaviour that, through careful measurement, looks to uncover causal relationships – that is, factors that cause us to act in certain ways. It differs from other methods in that it involves the deliberate control and manipulation of variables.

LABORATORY EXPERIMENTS

Laboratory experiments, or 'lab' experiments for short, are those carried out in carefully controlled conditions. The logic of the experiment is straightforward: if we have two groups of people all doing the same task, except that one of the groups does *one* thing differently, then any change in behaviour between the two groups must be due to that *one thing*. For instance, if we had two identical tennis balls and dropped them using an identical dropping machine from an identical height, except that one ball was wet and one was dry, then if they hit the floor at different times, the thing that is different (the wetness) must have been the thing that caused the change in the speed at which they fell to the ground. See – simple!

» The thing that is different between the two groups is the *variable that we manipulate*, and this is called the *independent variable (IV)*. In the example we've just used, the independent variable is whether the tennis balls were wet or dry.
» What we *measure or record* as a change in behaviour is another variable, and we call this the *dependent variable (DV)* (because it 'depends' on the independent variable). In our tennis ball-dropping example, the dependent variable is 'how long it takes for the balls to fall to the ground'.

An *experiment* is perhaps best understood through looking in detail at an example. You may have noticed that some people have a strong preference to revise for exams with music playing in the background, whilst other people demand complete silence in order to concentrate. As a psychologist you might ask yourself which is best – music or silence? We can't just take a person's preference as evidence of what is best, since we know from other areas of life that what people prefer is not necessarily what is best for them! We need an *objective assessment* of which is best, and this is where an experiment is most useful. We need an *aim* for the study. An aim is a general idea of what the study is going to try to achieve. For example:

The aim: To investigate whether or not having some kind of noise in the background (e.g. music) affects the retention (memory) of something we have learnt.

We also need to formulate a *hypothesis*. The results of our experiment will either provide support for our hypothesis or they will lead us to the conclusion that our hypothesis must be rejected. A straightforward hypothesis might be something like: 'music affects memory'. This is not quite enough however. Whilst the hypothesis includes our independent variable and our dependent variable (the IV is the music, the DV is a measure of memory), it is not clear how the variables are being measured or *operationalised*. An example of a better hypothesis might be:

The hypothesis: Music played during learning will influence recall performance on a memory task.

 There are a couple of ways that we could conduct this experiment. One way would involve having two *conditions*, each containing a selection of *participants* chosen at *random* to be in one condition or another. Remembering the logic of the experiment, all participants would have the same experience except for one thing – the independent variable. The group in which the *IV* appears would be called the *experimental condition*. The other group would be in the

EXPERIMENTAL CONDITION (MUSIC)	CONTROL CONDITION (SILENCE)
P1	P6
P2	P7
P3	P8
P4	P9
P5	P10

Table 3.1: In research, P stands for 'participant'. In our experiment, participants 1 to 5 are in the experimental condition and participants 6 to 10 are in the control condition.

control condition, against which the scores of the experimental condition would be compared.

Assuming that all participants have the same experience except for one thing (the IV), then any difference in task performance between the two conditions could only be due to the one thing that varies whether or not participants listen to music whilst performing the memory task.

We now need to give our participants some kind of task to do. Since we are interested in memory, an important component of learning (which is what revision is all about!), we could give the participants something from a French textbook to learn, perhaps a list of verbs. How well the participants learn these verbs in a given time would be what we measure (this is the dependent variable).

Alas, things in psychology are rarely as simple as this. In order to ensure that the experience of participants differs *only* in terms of the IV, we must go to great lengths to ensure that we control the experience of the participants. For example, we have given a French verb learning task. Have we controlled for the linguistic ability of participants? Are some of the participants studying French? Indeed, are all the participants students? How do you know whether any of them are French? Have you checked?

What we need is a task which asks the same of all participants. In psychology, *word lists* are often used in these circumstances, consisting of words of equal length and matched for how often those words appear in the language in which you are testing; in most cases the language will be English. Music cannot be used either because of things like personal taste, types of music, etc. – one person's music is another person's noise! So, something a bit like music could be used. A steady rhythmic noise played through headphones perhaps.

These factors (things that you need to control for, such as ability in French or music preference) are the *extraneous variables*, things that *could* influence the dependent variable. For every factor that we fail to control, we become less confident that the IV alone has produced the DV (i.e. whether it was the presence of 'music' that really influenced their ability). There are many different sources of extraneous variables and as many as possible need to be eliminated during the design process. Extraneous variables that we fail to control become *confounding variables* (i.e. variables that *have* influenced the dependent variable).

In our experiment, then, we cannot use music as an IV and we cannot use verb learning as a DV. Our variables need to be somehow 'neutral'. This means that our hypothesis is going to need a slight change: 'rhythmic noise played during learning will have a significant effect on subsequent recall'. The IV is whether or not participants have noise played to them whilst learning, and the DV is performance on a word learning task.

Another essential control in an experiment is the use of *standardised procedures*. We must describe every step of our experimental procedure beforehand so that each participant gets an identical experience. This will also include *standardised instructions*, ensuring that participants have the same information. This standardisation will also reduce *researcher bias*, in that it ensures that we do not unconsciously influence the outcome by varying the procedure.

Hopefully it is becoming clear that whilst the logic of an experiment is straightforward enough, it takes a great deal of careful thought and planning to design a good experiment. We've got a bit more to do yet. Even though the question is a simple one, we must be really sure that the way we carry out the experiment will provide us with a useful answer.

QUASI-EXPERIMENTS

A quasi-experiment is one in which the researcher *cannot manipulate the independent variable*. Quasi-experiments lack the control of true experiments. Whilst experimental procedures are used, participants cannot be randomly allocated to conditions. For example, if an experiment is looking at sex difference in some ability or other, let's say creativity, then participants are allocated to each condition according to their sex – males in one condition, females in the other. In this example, the IV is the sex difference and it cannot be manipulated by the experimenter. This means that some studies which, on the face of it, appear to be laboratory studies are in fact quasi-experiments. This also means that natural experiments (see page 187) are quasi-experiments too, since the IV is naturally occurring and is not manipulated.

Strengths of laboratory and quasi-experiments
» Because of standardised procedures lab experiments allow for replication (i.e. other scientists can copy the experiment in order to support or refute its findings). This is an important feature of science.
» Extraneous variables are controlled, and because only the independent variable differs between experimental conditions, cause-and-effect relationships can be established.
» As an objective research method, the feelings and beliefs of the researcher should not affect the results.

Limitations of laboratory and quasi-experiments
» Experiments are not natural settings and the behaviour of participants often does not resemble their behaviour in real-life settings. This unnatural behaviour leads critics to argue that findings lack ecological validity and should not be generalised to settings outside the experiment.
» Some argue that experimenter objectivity is impossible and that results of experiments are always biased to some degree by experimenter effects.

» It is not possible to control all extraneous variables that might affect the dependent variable, so confounding variables are inevitable. The debate is really the extent to which confounding variables have an effect on the result, not whether they have an effect.

EXPERIMENTAL DESIGN

Experimental design refers to the process of allocating participants to experimental conditions. In the experiment on the influence of music on memory described on page 181, we randomly put five people in the experimental condition and five in the control condition (see Table 3.1). This is an example of an experimental design where different people are put in each condition of the experiment. Another option would be to put the same people in each condition. These are important design decisions, and it is important to be aware of the strengths and limitations of each type of design so that the most appropriate design is implemented.

Repeated measures design
In this type of design, each of our participants carries out the experiment twice – once in each of our groups. On one occasion they perform a task whilst listening to the sound, and on the other occasion they perform the memory task in silence.

Strengths of repeated measures design
» The two groups are made up of the same people, therefore all individual differences between the two groups are controlled for.
» Both groups are identical. There are no differences in age, gender, French-speaking ability, how good they are at hearing or whether or not they have beards and wear glasses. They're completely identical. In this type of design we often say that 'the participant acts as their own control'. One of your authors is fabulous looking, wealthy

The same people do the same task twice. On one occasion they perform in silence and on the other they listen over headphones.

and enormously intelligent. The other is old, overweight, short of cash and not very bright at all. If we both took part in the experiment, and it was designed with a repeated measures design, each of us would bring various problems to our performance on the experimental condition, but exactly the same issues would be a feature of our performance on the control condition.

Limitations of repeated measures design
» Repeated measures designs create *order effects*. For example, if participants recall more words on the second day (when they return to do the task again), can we be sure that this is due to the noise?
» It could be that this improvement is due to extra experience with the memory task. This kind of order effect is called a *practice effect*.
» On the other hand, the opposite could happen and performance on the second day is worse than the first. Again, we could not be sure that this was due to the noise – it could be due to tiredness or boredom with the task. This kind of order effect is sometimes called a *fatigue effect*.

Independent groups design
This is the design we originally decided on where we use *different people in each*

Counterbalancing and randomisation

There are two ways of dealing with order effects:

1. Counterbalancing: Half of the participants could do no noise followed the next day by noise (i.e. control condition followed by experimental condition). The other half could do noise on the first day and no noise on the next day (i.e. experimental condition followed by control condition). In this way, order effects would appear in both conditions and, in effect, balance themselves out.

2. Randomisation: The participants could be *randomly* allocated to do one or other condition first and second. Each participant would have an equal chance of appearing in a condition first or second. Because the researcher has not decided who goes where or who does what they cannot be accused of biasing the investigation.

The task is completed twice. On each occasion different people take part. One group complete the task in silence and one group wear headphones.

experimental condition. In this design, each participant is randomly allocated to one condition. In our experiment, one half of the sample would be allocated to the control condition and do the memory test in silence, whilst the other half of participants would be put into the experimental condition and do the test whilst listening to a noise.

Strengths of independent groups design
» There are no order effects with this design, so things like practice or fatigue will not confound the results.
» Because each person only provides data in one or other of the conditions, as long as it does not create an extraneous variable it doesn't matter when you carry out the task. You can just grab the person when you see them and ask them to carry out the task there and then.

Limitations of independent groups design
» Because the participants in each condition are *different* we cannot be sure that their *individual differences* are not influencing the results in some way. For example, whilst allocation to conditions is random, it could be by chance that more people with poor reading skills are in one condition than another (which might be important) or maybe a few people with extraordinary memories are allocated to one condition. In this case, the difference between the two conditions might not be due to the independent variable at all but to the contribution of several 'unusual' participants.

Matched pairs design

This design involves having two separate groups of participants but who are matched on some important variable in order to make them as similar as possible. The ideal participants in a matched pairs design would be identical twins, with one twin in each condition, as they are as matched as two individuals could ever be. If it was practical, this is the ideal compromise between the independent groups and repeated measures design, as it avoids most of the problems with both and has all their advantages. However, the problems associated with matching (or finding sufficient numbers of twins to participate!) means that this design is rarely used.

The task is completed twice, on each occasion by different but closely matched people. One group wear headphones and the other participate in silence. In this example we have two different vicars and two different sailors.

Strengths of matched pairs design

» Because the participants are matched there is less confounding caused by individual differences.

» The design is really an independent measures design with practically identical people in each group, so there are no order effects.

Limitations of matched pairs design

» Matching participants is very difficult and time consuming, and in any case, even with identical twins, individual difference is only reduced rather than eliminated. For example, twins may well share genes and look practically identical, but one twin may have engaged in activities which have developed skills over the other, such as writing or arithmetic. This could mean that, in some studies, they are not well-matched at all.

Experimental designs

Identify the type of designs used in experiments with the following hypotheses:

(i) Females are less likely to administer an electric shock to a woman than to a man.

(ii) The greatest attachment problems are experienced by children fostered after 12 months.

(iii) Leading questions have a greater influence on children's recall of a story than adults' recall.

(iv) Performance is better on memory tasks for those using mnemonics rather than those remembering by rote.

(v) Obedience increases according to the status of the authority figure.

(vi) Witnesses of violent crimes recall more details than witnesses of less violent crimes.

THE FIELD EXPERIMENT

A field experiment involves the direct manipulation of variables but, unlike the laboratory experiment, this is done in what the participant sees as a natural environment. This makes the study much more realistic and it is therefore argued that it produces data which are more valid. There is still an IV which is being manipulated and a DV which is being measured.

A field experiment would be used when it is considered that a natural setting is crucial to investigate a behaviour. Social psychology makes particular use of the field experiment as it is interested in the behaviour of people in social settings. Since participants should not be aware that they are taking part in a controlled study, their behaviour should be natural.

Strengths of field experiments

» Because of the natural setting there is much greater *ecological validity* with field than laboratory experiments.
» Because participants are supposed to be unaware that they are taking part in research, *demand characteristics* should be reduced or even eliminated.

Limitations of field experiments

» There is less control of *extraneous variables* in a field experiment than there is in a laboratory experiment, meaning that the results are more likely to be confounded in some way.
» Field experiments are generally more time consuming and expensive to design and run than laboratory experiments.

THE NATURAL EXPERIMENT

In a natural experiment, rather than direct manipulation, the researcher takes advantage of a *naturally occurring* change in an IV. There is no experimental control other than that which is already in place. Because participants are not randomly allocated, natural experiments are really a kind of quasi-experiment. However, the behaviour is genuine and the situations in which natural experiments arise are usually those in which a laboratory or field experiment would not be possible. For example, you might find that a local hospital has changed its policy on post-operative care for patients undergoing brain surgery. This might provide an opportunity to compare the effects of this post-operative care with another hospital that has a more traditional approach. The IV would be the kind of post-operative care offered – this has naturally arisen and is not something that you can possibly have manipulated.

Strengths of natural experiments

» Because it is a natural setting, with naturally occurring changes in the IV, there is high ecological validity.
» Because the researcher has little or no involvement with the situation, and participants would be unaware that they are taking part in a study, there are likely to be few demand characteristics and reduced researcher bias.

Limitations of natural experiments

» There is little or no control of variables in a natural experiment and there are likely to be extraneous variables that remain uncontrolled. At best, these can be identified and taken into consideration when causal relations are inferred from the findings.
» Opportunities for natural experiments occur rarely, and when they do they are generally unique events. This means that they are very difficult to replicate in order to check the reliability and validity of the findings.

You really need to understand the differences between these types of experiment. Simple rote learning will only get you so far.

THE OBSERVATIONAL METHOD

All research begins with some form of observation. Sometimes observations are used as a way of gathering data in other methods, such as experiments. These are *controlled observations*. However, observation is a research method in its own right. The observational method involves systematically watching and recording what people say and do. The behaviours observed are those that naturally occur, meaning that no attempt is made to manipulate variables. The main benefit of this is that we then get natural behaviour, unchanged by the presence of a researcher or research environment.

PARTICIPANT AND NON-PARTICIPANT OBSERVATION

In observational studies, a researcher can be either directly involved in the situation being observed (this is called *participant observation*) or remain outside and unobserved (called *non-participant observation*).

Both these methods are sometimes called *naturalistic observation*, since people are being observed in their own environment and will thus behave naturally. For example, a participant observation might be one where the experimenter is part of a sports team in which he is investigating group behaviour. A non-participant observation might be one where the experimenter is observing the play of children from behind a one-way mirror.

Whilst, on the face of it, observation seems to be a natural and straightforward method of gathering data, in reality it requires a great deal of thought and careful planning. Imagine that you are interested in whether or not boys are more physically aggressive than girls. You would need an environment in which to observe the natural behaviour of boys and girls, and an obvious choice for this would be the playground of a primary school. Aggression is quite a complex concept and in order to be able to observe it we must *operationalise* it. In this case, we are interested in physical aggression, so shouts and other verbal behaviours – which would otherwise be interpreted as aggressive – do not count. We must also use a psychological definition of aggression to clarify our observations further – other people must understand what is meant by aggression in this research. So, if we defined aggression as 'any behaviour in which one person is motivated to cause harm which the victim is motivated to avoid', this would exclude from our observation behaviours such as play fighting and other sorts of rough-and-tumble play.

Choosing the variables to operationalise creates *behavioural categories*. It is these that appear on the checklist that the researcher uses when observing the behaviour. A method of recording observations will need to be devised, probably involving producing an observational checklist.

Observation: method or technique?

An important distinction has to be made here between observation as a *research method* and observation as a data-gathering *technique*. Observations can be used as a technique to gather data in a range of research methods. For example, in an experiment on aggression, a researcher might show one group of participants a film containing only an aggressive scene. The researcher would then observe the participants some time later to see if their behaviour had changed as a result of the film, compared to the group of participants who did not see it. This is a laboratory experiment but the independent variable is derived through controlled observation.

Controlled observation is also often used in field experiments where the environment has been deliberately altered by the researcher in some way. Observations are then made of any changes in behaviour as a result of this manipulation. For example, drivers and other road users behave in a certain way when there are road signs present. Observing the behaviour and carefully noting down important aspects, such as overtaking frequency and speed, might be of importance to your study. Now, remove all the road signs and repeat the observation. You would look to see if the alteration of the environment had altered the behaviour of the road users.

Observation as a research method is different in that it involves no manipulation of variables by the researcher – the behaviour being observed is free and natural. The control here is the selection of the situation being observed and the manner in which observations are recorded.

BEHAVIOURAL CATEGORIES AND OBSERVATIONAL CHECKLISTS

A behavioural category is the behaviour that you are observing. It is important to clearly identify the behaviours that you wish to record in order to make data collection as straightforward and unbiased as possible. For instance, you might list all the types of physical aggression that you are likely to see on a school playground and create a checklist (see Table 3.2). This might be all you need if the only thing of interest is the frequency of types of aggression. The observational checklist would be more complex if you were also interested in the direction and duration of aggression. The key thing is that behavioural categories should be self-evident and require no further interpretation by the observers. The more complicated the observation checklist, the more likely there are to be errors in recording.

Unless we are able to film proceedings for later thorough analysis, it is impossible to record everything. In this case we have to be selective in what we observe. In other words, we have to take a *sample* of behaviours to observe. There are two basic sampling techniques we could use:

1. Event sampling: Event sampling is the act of ticking the behaviour checklist box every time it happens (e.g. the number of times kicking as a form of aggression was observed). However, it is easy to miss events with time sampling,

BEHAVIOURAL CATEGORY	Push	Kick	Throw object	Spit	Scram	Punch	Poke
FREQUENCY OF BEHAVIOUR							

Table 3.2: An example of an observational checklist containing behavioural categories.

especially with complex behaviours (e.g. Was that push a friendly one or an act of aggression? Whilst you are pondering this you just missed two kicks and a spit!).

2. Time sampling: Time sampling is just like event sampling, but a time limit is placed on the period over which the observation takes place. For instance, you may be interested in how many times in a period of two minutes children engage in aggressive behaviour. To do this, you start a stopwatch then observe for two minutes, and when the time period is over you stop and count up the frequency of the behaviour you have been observing. Whilst this reduces the amount of observing that needs to be made, there is a possibility of missing crucial events.

Awareness of the observer – covert and overt observation

Overt observation is when participants are aware that they are being observed. Knowing that you are being watched can however change the way you behave. For example, to have researchers suddenly turn up at the school playground is likely (understandably!) to change children's behaviour. This problem could be reduced by giving the researchers a rationale for being there (e.g. playground monitors or new teachers) and not recording observations until the children are used to these new people. This can take a lot of time and resources. A quicker solution would be to ensure that participants are unaware of the observation. This is covert observation. The children in the playground for example could be secretly filmed for later analysis. Covert observation however introduces ethical issues. To observe and record behaviour without participant knowledge could be unethical. There is no right to withdraw or chance to give informed consent. In a partial solution to this problem, it has been suggested that

only behaviours that occur in situations in which people could naturally be expected to be observed should be used in observational studies.

Strengths of observation

» Because observations occur in a natural setting the behaviours occur in their true form. This gives the method high ecological validity.

» The observational method allows behaviour to be investigated in situations where other methods would not be possible. For example, observing aggressive behaviour in children is possible in the laboratory if aggressive behaviour naturally arises, but encouraging a child to act aggressively would fall below the standards expected of ethical research.

» There are few demand characteristics in observational studies because people do not know they are being studied and are not put into a 'false' situation, as would happen in laboratory-based studies.

Limitations of observation

» There is a risk of observer bias as it is unlikely that researchers will be able to remain completely objective. This reduces the reliability of the data gathered.

» Unlike observational techniques used in experiments, the lack of control of variables in naturalistic observations means that confounding variables may be introduced. This makes causality difficult to establish and means that replication is going to be more difficult.

» Observations tend to be rather small scale so the group being studied may not be representative of the population.

Participant and non-participant observations can both be either overt or covert. It is easy to get muddled here. Remember, covert is undercover.

SELF-REPORT TECHNIQUES: QUESTIONNAIRES

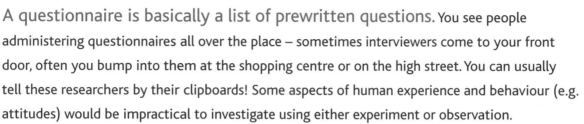

A questionnaire is basically a list of prewritten questions. You see people administering questionnaires all over the place – sometimes interviewers come to your front door, often you bump into them at the shopping centre or on the high street. You can usually tell these researchers by their clipboards! Some aspects of human experience and behaviour (e.g. attitudes) would be impractical to investigate using either experiment or observation.

A well-designed questionnaire can provide a wealth of useful information. Because people may feel reluctant to complete questionnaires, it is important to reduce the perceived cost of taking part (e.g. avoid asking for personal information, minimise embarrassment and inconvenience, make the questionnaire appear short and easy) and establish trust (e.g. make the questionnaire appear legitimate and important, inform about confidentiality, offer thanks for taking part).

There are two types of question to ask – closed and open.

Type 1: Closed questions

These allow limited responses from participants and may take a variety of forms. Whilst restricting the range of answers they have the advantage of providing quantitative data which are usually straightforward to analyse. There are a variety of closed question formats from which to choose:

a. Rank order questions

This is where participants are asked to rate or rank a range of options. This gives information about preferences, degrees of importance, etc. As ranking long lists is difficult, keep the list to about five items. For example:

» Please indicate, in rank order, your preferred drink, putting 1 next to your *favourite* through to 5 for your *least favourite*:
Coffee, tea, cola, water, hot chocolate.

b. Likert scale questions

These are statements to which participants are asked to indicate their strength of agreement or disagreement. For example:
» 'Psychology is so much better than mathematics.' Please indicate on the scale the extent to which you agree or disagree with this statement.

1	2	3	4	5	6	7	8

Disagree   Agree

c. Checklist questions

This is where a list of items is provided from which participants select those that apply. For example:
» Circle three of the following adjectives that most apply to your personality:

Happy   grumpy   friendly   miserable

sparkly   interesting   quiet   morose   sad.

d. Dichotomous questions

These are questions offering two choices. For example:

» Did you do any exercise last week? Yes/No.

e. Semantic differential questions

With this type of question two bipolar words are offered and participants are asked to respond by indicating a point between the two which represents their strength of feeling. For example:

» My home town is …

Interesting ____:____:____:____:____ Boring

Pretty ____:____:____:____:____ Ugly

Clean ____:____:____:____:____ Dirty

Type 2: Open questions

This is where participants are given space to respond more freely, for example by being given several lines to fill as they please. This can help the researcher to avoid accidentally biasing a closed question towards a particular point of view, and can provide a far richer source of qualitative information.

Strengths of questionnaire research

» Compared to other methods they can be a cheap and efficient way of collecting data.
» Because large numbers of questionnaires containing lots of questions can be distributed, they can be used to collect large amounts of information relatively easily.
» Because the participants can remain anonymous, and therefore perhaps be more willing to express themselves fully, questionnaires are a relatively reliable method of gathering data.

Limitations of questionnaire research

» Survey data are highly descriptive and as such it is difficult to establish causal relationships. The ability to infer causal relationships will be limited by the quality of the questionnaire

---

Questionnaires – things to avoid

Many of the problems of questionnaires come from poorly phrased open and closed questions. The following are some of the things that should be avoided:

1. Lack of clarity: Questions should be understandable and mean the same things to all participants. They should therefore be written in clear language, avoiding ambiguity and unnecessary jargon.

2. Embarrassing questions: Questions that focus on private matters should be avoided. As the questions become more personal, the likelihood of unanswered or wrongly answered questions increases.

3. Social desirability bias: Participants will often answer questions in a way that makes them feel better by giving the answers that they think they ought to give, showing them in a better light.

4. Leading questions: Leading questions encourage a certain response from participants.

– for example, it depends on having asked the right questions to start with.

» Whilst it is important to select a representative sample, it is very difficult to obtain one. Not only is it difficult to identify all members of a population, but even if you could there is no guarantee that they would agree to take part in the study. It might even be that those who do agree to complete the questionnaire make up a biased sample.
» There is no guarantee that people will respond truthfully to questions. There are many reasons for this. It might be social desirability, where participants say what it is they think should be said rather than give their own opinion. It might even be that some participants are bloody-minded and deliberately give wrong answers.

SELF-REPORT TECHNIQUES: INTERVIEWS

Interviews and questionnaires are similar in some ways in that they are both based around a set of questions. Unlike questionnaires, however, interviews are generally conducted face to face, and the way that information is acquired varies slightly depending on the type of interview. There are many different ways of conducting an interview but the methods are most simply categorised as either *structured*, *semi-structured* or *unstructured*.

The simplest kind of interview to conduct is the structured interview but, as with all forms of interview, the sex, personality and skills of the interviewer are extremely important variables that can have significant influences on the interviewee. Training is needed for effective interviewing, and the less structured the interview, the greater the skills and training needed by the interviewer. This means that, wherever possible, researchers lacking this training should opt for a questionnaire method of self-report.

1. Structured interview: This approach resembles the questionnaire except that rather than write their own responses, participants respond verbally to questions posed by the researcher. The same questions are presented to each participant in the same way and, because of this, it has been described as a 'verbal questionnaire'.

2. Semi-structured interview: Whilst there are no fixed questions, the interview is guided, perhaps, by a predetermined set of topics to be covered. The order in which these topics are covered, or the way in which they are addressed by the interviewer, can vary across participants.

3. Unstructured interview: With this method of interviewing the participant is free to talk about whatever they like. The interviewer may set the topic but the interviewee is free to dictate the content by taking the conversation in any direction they wish.

Strengths of interview research

» Semi-structured/unstructured interview data is often rich and varied. It is provided 'off the cuff', and is therefore spontaneous and often unexpected. The data are more realistic than you might get in a more formal structured interview.
» Structured interviews are relatively simple to administer and a lot of data can be collected relatively cheaply and quickly. A large sample can sometimes be obtained without much difficulty, depending on the subject of the questionnaire.
» When conducted by a skilled interviewer, the data can give insights into complicated and difficult issues which no other methods allow.

Limitations of interview research

» It might be difficult to find the right sample. Some people begin the interview and do not complete it because they find it too lengthy or possibly too difficult to sit through. In these cases the data may need to be rejected from the study.

» Sometimes people given the same interview provide such widely differing responses that you would think that they were given completely different interviews! In cases like this, the generalisability of the results is very low indeed.

» If the interviewer is not sufficiently skilled, the participant's responses may be guarded and the data will therefore be of little use.

Hypotheses

First (a) decide whether the following hypotheses are directional or non-directional, and then (b) identify the IV and the DV.

(i) The more stress a person experiences the more risk there is of a heart attack.

(ii) Stressful unemployment can influence the functioning of the immune system.

(iii) The risk of coronary heart disease (CHD) is affected by feelings of hostility.

(iv) Stress management techniques improve the functioning of the immune system.

(v) Stressful life events increase the likelihood of illness.

(vi) The more complex the question the more likely a child is to give an inaccurate response.

CORRELATIONS

Correlation is a statistical technique that shows whether or not two variables are associated.

Correlations are different from experiments because nothing is deliberately varied or changed. Rather than altering something and measuring what happens when the change is made, the researcher carrying out correlational work simply measures two things (variables) and looks at whether they are related (correlated).

 As well as being a research method in its own right, correlation can be used to analyse data gathered from any other research method. For example, data from observational studies and questionnaires might be analysed to see if there is a relationship between two or more observations or responses. There are basically three types of correlation:

1. Positive correlation: This means that as one variable increases, so too does the other. An example might be the relationship between how many hours you spend studying for an exam and how well you do in it. The more study you do (more minutes), the better your score in the exam. As one goes up, so too does the other.

2. Negative correlation: This is where one variable increases as another decreases. An

The more you study, the better you do in exams. The correlation between time spent studying and score on exams is 'positive'.

example might be the relationship between the speed at which a driver drives and the amount of petrol they use per mile (miles per gallon – mpg). As speed increases, more fuel is used so mpg decreases.

3. Zero correlation: This is where variables are not related at all.

Correlations and experiments

Correlation between two variables only indicates that there is some kind of relationship between them; it does not mean that one variable caused the other to change. Only an experiment reveals causal relationships between variables. However, *causality* is one of three possible explanations for a correlation:

1. The relationship is causal (one variable caused the other to change).

2. The relationship is chance (the two variables just happen to be statistically related).

3. There is a third factor involved (another variable is causing the relationship).

For example, let's say that in a questionnaire study on time management in students we are interested in whether or not time management habits are related to subsequent performance in assessments. We could analyse two pieces of information: how students manage their time and assessment performance (e.g. exam grades). Statistical analysis of the data will tell us whether we have a correlation and, if so, what type of correlation we have. We then have to interpret the correlation using existing theory and research (and a chunk of scientific common sense) to indicate the most likely explanation. Sometimes the answer is quite clear but often it is not, in which case it is up to the judgement of the researcher as to which explanation is most probable:

a. Did time management cause improved exam grades? (i.e. is the relationship causal)

b. Was the result a statistical fluke? (i.e. is the relationship just a chance one)

c. Is another variable operating in the background which makes the two factors appear causally related? (i.e. is there a third variable explanation)

In this example, it might be that time management *caused* improved exam grades, but students who are the best at managing their time are also the most motivated students. A third factor explanation might be the most likely explanation here: motivation is behind the relationship between time management and exam grades. However, if a causal explanation is considered the most likely one, an experiment can be designed to test this causal relationship.

Strengths of correlations
» Correlations allow researchers to measure relationships between naturally occurring variables (e.g. height and intelligence, weight and sleep duration) which would be difficult or impossible to create experimentally.
» Correlational studies can indicate trends which might then lead to further research using experimental means to establish any causal links. They are a really useful way of indicating directions for future research.

Limitations of correlations
» It is not possible to draw conclusions about cause and effect. Just because there is a positive correlation between the number of storks sighted and numbers of babies born, it does not mean that we can conclude that storks have caused babies to arrive!
» Extraneous variables which may influence the results are very hard to control. There may be a correlation between two variables but it might be that something else – something you do not know about and have not controlled for – has 'caused' or significantly influenced the relationship.

Exercise – correlation

The following are correlations. For each:

1. State the kind of correlation each represents (i.e. positive or negative).

2. Give an explanation for the correlations (i.e. causal, chance or third factor).

3. Rewrite the statement as the opposite correlation (e.g. if positive rewrite as negative).

(i) The more time spent studying for an exam, the better the grade.

(ii) There is increased conflict and stress at home when workers are overloaded at work.

(iii) The more quality day-care a child receives, the greater their social competence.

(iv) People who are good at managing time do better in assessments.

(v) The less control someone feels at work, the more stress they experience.

(vi) Children attending high quality day-care centres are more likely to interact positively with others.

ANALYSIS AND INTERPRETATION OF CORRELATION

Correlations can be represented mathematically as a *correlation coefficient*. This is the number arrived at by the statistical analysis of data (see page 196). This coefficient is a number somewhere between +1 and –1, and is represented by the letter r. For example, you may have coefficients that look like $r = +0.7$ or $r = –0.3$.

The strength of the correlation is given by how near to –1 or +1 the number (r) is. The sign only indicates the type of correlation; it says nothing about the number as such. So, $r = +0.7$ is actually the same strength correlation as $r = –0.7$ – the first is a positive correlation (as one variable increases so does another) and the second is a negative correlation (as one variable increases another decreases).

The *significance* of the correlation depends on a number of things including how many people have provided data for your experiment and the size of the coefficient. However, you can be pretty sure that if your correlation is close to +1 or –1 then it is going to be significant.

In addition to the coefficient, scattergrams (also known as scatterplots or scattergraphs) are used to depict correlation data. Scattergraphs are discussed in more detail on page 227. It is important to always plot a scattergram because sometimes a relationship between variables can give a coefficient of zero but still be important (see page 228 for a description of curvilinear correlations).

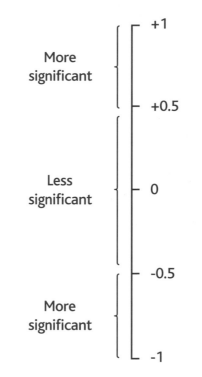

Figure 3.1: A correlation coefficient is a number on a scale from 0 to 1. The closer the number is to 1 (+ and – only signify whether it is positive or negative), the more significant the statistical relationship. A number of factors influence the point at which a coefficient becomes significant but a useful rule of thumb is that a coefficient greater than 0.5 is a significant one.

There is a lot to take in with correlations, and the information is in several different places in this chapter. Be sure to bring together general material on correlations, analysis/interpretation and scattergrams. This will give you the rounded knowledge necessary for both AS and A level.

Exercise – correlation coefficients

(a) Show what the following coefficients would look like on a graph by roughly sketching appropriate scattergrams.

(b) State the type of correlation each coefficient/scattergram represents.

(i) r = -0.35   (iv) r = -0.07

(ii) r = +0.78   (v) r = +0.91

(iii) r = +0.51   (vi) r = -0.42

CASE STUDIES

A case study is a careful and systematic investigation of a single individual. A researcher studies a single example either because they are rare or unique in some way, or because they are a typical example of a type of person. Case studies can take a long time to conduct and a variety of data collection methods can be used, therefore detailed in-depth information is obtained.

A researcher might use both primary and secondary data in the case study. *Primary data* are those that are gained directly by the researcher – for example, from interviews, assessments and observations of the individual or their family, or from information gathered from investigating the environment of the individual. *Secondary data* are those that have already been collected but which are reused by the researcher. Examples of secondary data might include school and medical records or initial studies of the individual that may have been carried out by other researchers. What information is collected will depend on what the researcher is trying to investigate – that is, on the *aims* of his or her investigation.

Strengths of case studies

» Case studies produce lots of detail and the depth of understanding acquired through this is useful for understanding the subtleties and complexities of individual behaviour.

» Although usually a detailed study of one person, the data from several people are often pooled and analysed to give insights into their similarities and differences. This is the case, for example, with neuropsychology where the symptoms of brain damage from a number of individual case studies might be compared in order to give a greater understanding of the causes of the symptoms they share.

» The case study is the only way to deal with rare and dramatic cases in psychology. For example, insights into the condition of someone who has had extremely harsh childhood experiences could only be gained through a detailed and careful study of his or her circumstances.

Limitations of case studies

» Because case studies relate to one individual the findings from them cannot easily be generalised to others. Even if generalisations are made they may lack credibility in the eyes of other researchers.

» Case studies rely on retrospective data – that is, information gathered about past events. This information might not be accurate. People have a habit of forgetting things and our memory for events, especially stressful ones, can be unreliable. Memory can also change over time so what really happened may never be known. Relying on this type of data can be very problematic.

» Because case studies can be very time consuming, involving a lot of time spent with the case, it has been suggested that the relationship that develops as a result, between the researchers and the individual, makes it difficult to rely on the objectivity of the data.

CONTENT ANALYSIS

Content analysis is an observational technique used to analyse the content of text. For example, it is used to assess the presence of meanings and concepts in written documents such as newspapers and books. However, it is not restricted to text – it can also be used to assess the content of interviews, film and television and is often used to analyse political speeches.

At its simplest level, a content analysis is conducted in much the same way as an observational study. The important difference is that in content analysis we produce a *record* of the behaviour, not just an *observation* of the behaviour. Once the aims of the research have been clarified a sample can be chosen, although, rather than participants, the sample will be of material. For example, if you are interested in how women are portrayed in tabloid newspapers you need to decide on the newspapers, their frequency and a time period. Then a checklist needs to be developed to record the content from this sample. This is often referred to as a *coding schedule*. Each item in the coding schedule is allocated a code and the material is analysed closely for the number of instances that each code appears. Reliability can be checked in the same way as observations by using more than one rater and investigating if their 'observations' are comparable (see page 211 for more on reliability). Content analysis generally produces data that is quantitative (i.e. expressed in numerical form). However, it is very similar to thematic analysis which focuses on the qualitative data in material.

Thematic analysis and coding

Thematic analysis is like content analysis but focuses more on the qualitative aspects of the material being analysed. It is a way of searching through material for themes which might help us to describe patterns of experience. For instance, consider a situation where you might want to look at how older people view a problem and compare that with how younger people view it, such as how secure each group feels in their community. The interviews carried out with individuals from each age group could be analysed for their feelings, attitudes and perceptions, and patterns of similarity and difference revealed. The analysis of interviews might take a similar form to the coding that took place in content analysis, with thematic coding identifying themes occurring across the data.

Strengths of content analysis

» A good coding schedule means the process is entirely clear and transparent, and all researchers engaged in the process and people reading the work are absolutely clear about what has been done.
» The process is a very useful way of looking at trends in data over time, so an analysis in 1995 can be compared with a similar analysis using the same coding in 2015, allowing us to comment on how attitudes etc. have changed over the years.

Limitations of content analysis

» The process does not look into the reasons for the attitudes or differences and so is very descriptive. It offers a useful and interesting snapshot but provides no insight into why the attitudes may be held.
» If the coding is inaccurate then the resulting analysis or conclusions based on the coding will be misleading.

SCIENTIFIC PROCESSES: CARRYING OUT RESEARCH

Psychologists get their ideas for research from either direct observation of behaviour or indirectly through background knowledge and theory. The best attribute you can have as a psychologist is curiosity and a real desire to seek out the origins and motives of human behaviour. The best research is very carefully planned, often taking many weeks or months before any data are gathered. The first two stages are to decide on the *aims* of the work and from this create *hypotheses* – something that can be tested in the research.

Aims

An aim is a reasonably precise idea about the area of the study and what the study is going to try to achieve. It is important that the aim clearly describes the purpose of the proposed research. This will help make clear very early on whether or not the proposed research is realistic and doable. An aim doesn't need to be detailed, it just needs to say very clearly what the focus of your research is all about. An example of an aim might be: 'To describe the effects of stress on memory' or 'To investigate whether listening to music whilst revising helps learning'.

Hypothesis

After the aim, the next step is to generate hypotheses. A hypothesis *predicts* what we expect to find, and the idea is to try to find evidence in the research that will 'support the hypothesis'. An example might be:

Aim: To describe the effects of stress on memory.

Hypothesis: The greater the stress, the poorer the recall on verbal memory tests.

The hypothesis takes the aim and makes a statement of it. The hypothesis predicts that people who are stressed will have a worse memory than people who are not stressed. The next step is to design a study to test this hypothesis. This involves selecting the most appropriate method (an experiment, observation, interview, etc.). The results of the study will either support the hypothesis or not. If the results do not support the hypothesis then it has to be rejected. In the current example, the method chosen to investigate the effects of stress on memory is the laboratory experiment. The hypothesis in this case is now called an *experimental hypothesis*. This is often written as H_1 or H_E. Using non-experimental methods the hypothesis is called an *alternative hypothesis* (or H_A).

To make the hypothesis complete a *null hypothesis* has to be written. A null hypothesis (written as H_0) predicts that what we find in our research just happened by chance. It looks like the opposite of the main hypothesis. For example:

Null hypothesis: Recall on memory tests will not become worse as stress increases; any change is due to chance.

The null hypothesis must be included in our research because psychologists can never rule out the possibility that the results gained in any investigation are due to chance. What this really means is that if the hypothesis is not supported by the research findings then the null hypothesis is probably true. Put another way, if you have to reject the hypothesis then you have to accept the null hypothesis, and if you accept the hypothesis because your research supports it then you must reject the null hypothesis.

Operationalising variables

A hypothesis will also express the things of interest to the researcher in the research. These are *variables*. They are called variables because they change or *vary* during the research. Some variables are changed by the researcher (the independent variable, or IV) and some change *because* the researcher has done something (the dependent variable, or DV). Operationalising variables means making them measurable. This is extremely important because we need to be clear about what it is we are studying and measuring in research and communicate this to others. In the example, 'The greater the stress, the poorer the recall on verbal memory tests', the dependent variable is operationalised – it is recall on verbal memory tests. An alternative non-operationalised version might be, 'Stress affects memory', but this is too brief and does not communicate clearly enough what is being measured.

Directional and non-directional hypotheses

Directional hypotheses are also known as one-tailed hypotheses and non-directional as two-tailed hypotheses. Look at the two hypotheses below. The type of research to which they relate is very similar indeed. In fact, the tasks you might decide on to investigate these two hypotheses could be identical, but the predictions they make are different:

Hypothesis 1: Eating chocolate for dinner makes you sleep more.

Hypothesis 2: Eating chocolate for dinner alters the amount you sleep.

Hypothesis 1 predicts a direction for the results, so is called *directional*: chocolate eating will *increase* the amount of sleep we have. Hypothesis 2 does *not* predict a direction, it is *non-directional*. It simply states that chocolate eating will alter the amount we sleep. It does not predict an increase or a decrease; either may happen.

So, which is best, directional or non-directional? The answer is, it depends. A non-directional hypothesis might be chosen if the researcher is not terribly clear what will happen – perhaps when carrying out a study that has not been done before. Eating chocolate may keep people awake or it may help them go to sleep – for instance, there is no previous research to indicate what might happen one way or another – so choose a non-directional hypothesis. That way, if *anything* happens to your dependent variable (the amount we sleep), then you are bound to find it. In your next piece of research, once you have an idea of what might happen, your hypothesis may change to a directional prediction.

A directional hypothesis is generally used when a researcher is confident enough to make a clear prediction. Previous research may suggest that something quite specific will be found, or a quick study the researcher has tried out (often called a *pilot* study) may have suggested a direction for the findings. If a directional hypothesis is selected, then results have to be even more convincing for it to be supported; in other words, a directional hypothesis is easier to reject than a non-directional one. The benefit of choosing a directional hypothesis, however, is that because they are harder to support, research that *does* support a directional hypothesis is more convincing.

SAMPLING

The people who take part in research are termed *participants*. Researchers get their participants from a *population*. A population is defined as all the members of a particular group from which the participants are selected. For example, if you were interested in investigating attitudes to bullying in 14 to 16-year-olds, your target population would be 14 to 16-year-olds. You might want to make the population more specific – for example, 14 to 16-year-olds in a geographical area or even 14 to 16-year-olds from a particular school within that area. You might want to see whether there is a bullying problem amongst 14 to 16-year-olds in South London amongst people of a particular ethnic group. Your population in this case would be 14 to 16-year-olds from a particular ethnic group who live in South London. These kinds of decisions are all part of the design process. Because it is usually impractical for everyone to take part in a study, researchers need to *select* from the population. This selection is called the *sampling*. The main aim of sampling is to select a number of people who are typical, or representative, of the rest of the population from which they were chosen – the *sample*. Because the sample is a typical cross section of people, the findings can be safely *generalised* to everyone else in the target population. If the sample is not *representative* then it is *biased*, and *sample bias* is something to avoid if we want to be able to generalise the findings.

The choice of the number of participants used in the study will be influenced by a number of factors. The larger the population,

the larger the sample size should be in order for it to be representative; for a smaller population you might choose a smaller sample. For instance, if you are interested in investigating a possible difference in intelligence between men and women then you might choose a quite large sample to be representative, since the number of individuals in each population investigated (males and females) is very large indeed. However, if you were investigating whether actors suffer with an unusually large incidence of depression then the sample might be smaller, actors making up only a relatively small part of the community. Whilst the rule is that the sample must be representative of the population, like many other areas of research design, the size of the sample is often down to good judgement and common sense.

Random sampling

In a *random sample*, every member of the target population has exactly the same chance of being selected to participate. There are several ways of doing this. The most straightforward is the 'names from a hat' method, whereby all members of the target population are identified

Names from a hat – not to be taken literally! Not the most practical method of selecting a random sample, especially when you have lots of names from which to draw, or a small hat.

on slips of paper. These are then shuffled in a container and the desired number are selected. Whilst this appears simple, names from a hat is not practical with anything other than a small population, such as the members of an A level class. Fortunately, there are computer programs which can select a random sample from even very large populations, so there is no need to spend hours writing names on hundreds of bits of paper! The simplest program requires each member of a population to be given a unique number. The program randomly generates a series of numbers within the limits set. All we need to do then is match the numbers produced by the computer to the names on the list.

Implications

» One problem is that random sampling relies on all the target population being available to take part if chosen. If you select someone using your clever random number generating program, and one of those people cannot take part, you will need to replace them – and your random sample is no longer as random as you might have liked it to be.

» Another possibility is that, by chance, the randomly selected sample might end up being biased anyway! If you shuffle a pack of cards and drop them all into a hat, you could pull out 10 red cards one after the other, weighting your sample in favour of red cards. In the same way, a psychology study into the effects of alcohol on reaction time might, by chance alone, end up with a group of participants with unusually high or low tolerances to alcohol, or very fast or very slow reaction times or reflexes. The results these people provide may not give you a true picture of what is happening and your investigation may thus be flawed.

Opportunity sampling

A very common method of sampling is to use anyone you can get hold of. This is very straightforward and little planning is needed, since the sample selection is based on whoever is willing and available to take part at the time.

Implications

» Some students of psychology think that just picking people to take part, without any obvious selection criteria, makes it a random sample, but this is not the case at all. Remember, a random sample gives *everyone* in a population an equal chance of being chosen, which will clearly not happen here. If you decide that your target population is a sixth form department and then you set about waiting at a doorway for someone to pass, although you are selecting from your population, you are not doing it randomly. Not only is most of the population excluded because they are unlikely to all come marching past you, but all sorts of unconscious biases are going to be at work guiding who it is you approach. For example, is the participant the same or different sex from you? Are you attracted to this person? Do they owe you a favour? Some people rather like helping others, so these individuals are more likely to help you collect your data.

» Whilst this method can lead to sample bias, the extent to which this matters varies according to the topic of the research you are doing. For example, it is likely to be much less important in studies of physiological responses to stress than it is in social psychological studies of friendship patterns and helping behaviour!

Volunteer sampling

It is not uncommon to find appeals for people to take part in psychological research pinned on university notice boards. Here, either through goodwill, curiosity or financial encouragement (some researchers may pay a small fee to those taking part!), people are asked to volunteer themselves as participants.

Implications

» It is possible that individuals who volunteer are not typical of members of a population. In fact, it has been suggested that people who volunteer in this way have particular personality types which make them different from the rest of the population. Just as in an opportunity sample, some individuals are more likely than others to help out. Similarly, the placing of the poster for volunteers to sign up might influence the type of people volunteering.

» If the poster is situated in a psychology department, then you'll get mainly psychology students signing up. The problem here is that psychology students may have a good idea of what you are looking for and their responses might be biased. Similarly, placing a poster in the sports department may provide you with volunteers of higher fitness than those provided by a poster placed elsewhere. If your research is concerned with the relationship between attention and tiredness, a higher level of fitness in the participants may influence your results, so the sample collected from this poster may not be ideal.

Systematic sampling

A systematic approach is one which is logical and with a rule, or rules, carefully applied. So a systematic sample is one where people from the population are chosen for a study in a careful and logical way. For instance, you may choose every tenth person in the phone book or every third person from an alphabetical class list. One way of choosing which participant to select is by dividing the population size by the sample size – so, for example, if the population is 100 and the sample size is 10, 100 divided by 10 is 10, so every tenth name is selected for participation.

Implications

» Given a large enough population it should be possible to achieve a sample that is representative of the population itself.

» There is no guarantee that all the people chosen to participate will want to or be able to participate.

Stratified sampling

The researcher constructing a stratified sample must first work out the proportions (or *strata*) of different people within that population. For instance, if the population contains 25% men and 75% women, then a stratified sample should contain the same proportions of each randomly selected, so a sample of 40 participants would contain 10 men and 30 women. Populations vary in very many ways and a true stratified sample involves identifying all the factors considered important in a population and ensuring that these are proportionately represented in the sample.

Implications

» Because the sample is so representative of the population a stratified sample can be smaller than other sampling techniques. There is greater control in stratified sampling – for instance, control over which subgroups are included.

» It can be very difficult to identify the relevant strata for a study. Also, organising a sample from each strata significantly increases the workload and complexity of sampling.

Populations and samples

(a) Identify the target population in the following studies and (b) suggest an appropriate technique for selecting a sample.

(i) Whether there are gender differences in conformity amongst participants under 19 years of age.

(ii) Whether the cognitive interview is more effective in stimulating recall than a standard interview in elderly eye-witnesses.

(iii) Whether children brought up with nurses show weaker attachments to their mothers.

DEMAND CHARACTERISTICS

Psychological research often involves a direct interaction of researcher and participant – it is a social situation. Since people generally alter their behaviour when around others, it is reasonable to assume that behaviour will change in a research situation. Participants may be aware that they are being observed, or may think that they are being personally assessed or evaluated in some way. This might motivate them to attempt to find clues in the research environment or procedure as to what the study is about and to alter their behaviour accordingly. These features of research, which participants use to change their behaviour, are called *demand characteristics*.

Demand characteristics can seriously affect the findings of research. The extent to which this is a factor, however, varies according to the research method used and the way the study is designed and conducted. For example, demand characteristics are going to be much more of an issue when people know that they are taking part in a study, such as is the case with a laboratory experiment. Although often impossible to eliminate entirely, well-designed research will try as much as possible to minimise demand characteristics.

INVESTIGATOR EFFECTS

As well as the participants reacting to the research setting, the researchers too might behave in ways that influence the investigation. For example, the researcher might have expectations about the study and unintentionally influence the behaviour of participants. The age, gender or ethnicity of the researcher may also affect the behaviour of participants. It should also be remembered that researchers will have put a great deal of time and effort into their research and may unconsciously interpret ambiguous situations in ways which are favourable to their point of view. The amount of influence that a researcher has on the research will vary according to the research method used – for example, the age, gender or ethnicity of a researcher is likely to have a much greater effect in an interview than an observation – but *investigator effects* are an issue in all types of research. They have to be identified early in the research design and, as far as possible, be eliminated.

Be prepared not only to define these two terms but also to explain how you would reduce demand characteristics and investigator effects in practical situations.

REDUCING DEMAND CHARACTERISTICS AND INVESTIGATOR EFFECTS

If there is to be communication between the researcher and the participant then the verbal and non-verbal content of this communication needs to be controlled using standard instructions.

The setting of the study will need to be carefully considered, especially since some participants may be familiar with the research area and others may feel highly intimidated.

The researcher needs to be the right type of person to interact with participants (e.g. the right sex, age, attitude, communication skills).

A single-blind control (keeping participants unaware of the research aims) can reduce demand characteristics. A double-blind control (where both the participants and the researchers involved in gathering data are kept unaware of the research aims) can reduce investigator effects.

Table 3.3: How to reduce demand characteristics and investigator effects.

ETHICAL ISSUES IN PSYCHOLOGICAL RESEARCH

The breadth of the subject matter studied within psychology makes it unique amongst the sciences. Psychology might be described as the study of the experiences of living, feeling organisms and, as such, special care must be taken. There is the potential for participants to be affected by their experiences of taking part in psychological research.

When engaging in research, psychologists have to remember that it is considered both morally wrong and professionally unethical to do anything which in any way violates the rights and dignity of participants. Researchers in psychology are guided by a set of ethical principles designed to prevent research from infringing the rights of participants. Drawn up by the British Psychological Society (BPS), these guidelines must be adhered to and the failure of psychologists to maintain such professional standards can lead to serious reprisals.

Dealing with informed consent

The researcher has to plan very carefully what the participant is to be told. Revealing too much, or revealing information in the wrong way, may influence the participant's behaviour during the study, which has the potential to invalidate the research. If the participant has an idea of how the researcher wants them to respond then demand characteristics may emerge. In these instances a case can be made to withhold information from participants.

If anyone below the legal age of consent is to be used in research, then consent must be sought from their parents or guardians. This rule might also apply to some adults who may not be able to give full informed consent because they have reduced abilities to make informed decisions – for example, those who have certain kinds of mental illness or learning difficulties or elderly patients suffering with certain kinds of dementias.

Dealing with deception

Many studies in psychology simply could not happen if there was fully informed consent, so it is perhaps not surprising that deception is the most frequent ethical issue arising from research. The psychologist must make a judgement as to whether the aims of the study justify the deception. Of course, the deception is often a very minor one, but even in these cases the participants should be informed, after the event, about what has happened and told that, if they wish, they can refuse to allow data gathered from them to be used.

Dealing with the right to withdraw

It is possible that a participant may become unhappy with continuing to take part in a study. It is important to make clear to participants at the outset that they are free to withdraw from the study at any time and for whatever reason (they are not bound to explain). It is also sometimes the case that having taken part, on reflection, a participant wishes they hadn't for some reason. Therefore, they should also be told that even after the data gathering is complete they still have the right to remove their data. Right to withdraw is a particularly important consideration in studies where participants have been paid to take part and so feel obligated to continue. It must be made clear to such participants that their right to withdraw is the same as though they had not been paid.

Dealing with confidentiality

Confidentiality is a relatively straightforward ethical issue to manage. Researchers need only gather personal information about participants which is considered important to the study. Also, participants can be given a unique number, meaning that their personal identities are hidden and comments regarding their performance only reference this anonymous number. Where research involves studying one person, it is usual to give a nom de plume (e.g. HM), so hiding

ETHICAL ISSUE	EXPLANATION
Informed consent	Participants must be told what they are doing and why they are doing it so they can provide 'informed' consent.
Deception	Deception usually involves withholding information about the aims of the study but it can also involve participants being deliberately misinformed. Deception mainly occurs because of difficulties caused by informed consent.
Right to withdraw	Participants should be free to leave the experiment at any time.
Confidentiality	Any information and data provided by the participant must be confidential.
Protection from harm	The safety and well-being of the participant must be protected at all times.

Table 3.4: Summary of ethical considerations when designing research.

their identity. Unusually, psychologists might encounter a situation where they have to break confidentiality. It may come about during a debrief, or during the procedure itself, that the participant is in need of specialist care that the psychologist is unable to give or that others need protection. If the participant reveals information of this nature to the psychologist, then they must seek advice and possibly reveal information about the participant to someone better situated or more qualified to help them.

Dealing with protection from harm

Whilst it is not always easy to predict the outcome and consequences of a study for participants, researchers have an obligation to do everything possible to ensure that participants leave the study in the same state as when they arrived. There are many ways in which harm can be caused in research, many of them very difficult to predict in advance. Protecting participants from physical harm should be relatively straightforward but protection from psychological harm is much more problematic. Detailed planning, full informed consent and careful debriefing are essential to avoid participants having their self-esteem negatively affected, being embarrassed or in any way disturbed by their experience.

Debriefing

Debriefing is the most common way of dealing with ethical issues that arise in psychological research. Indeed, it is argued that all research should be accompanied by some form of debriefing. After the data have been collected, the full aims of the research should be revealed and the participants given the opportunity to ask any questions. If a participant reports any reaction or distress because of taking part in research, then the researcher is responsible for correcting these consequences. This might require no more than discussing the rationale for the study and reassuring the participant about confidentiality. Sometimes, however, more lengthy procedures are needed to ensure that participants are left no worse for their experience.

Whilst desirable, debriefing may not be very effective in practice. For example, it assumes that any reaction immediately follows participation in the research, but in reality this might come much later on, once the experience has been given some consideration. The participant might also be reluctant to discuss their emotions or be unable to clearly express their thoughts. Care and effort is needed by researchers to ensure that debriefing is effective.

THE ROLE OF PEER REVIEW IN THE SCIENTIFIC PROCESS

When a psychologist completes a piece of research, it is written in a generally agreed format and then sent to a psychological journal for consideration. If the journal thinks the work is good enough they will publish it for all to see. The process of assessing whether it is good enough for publication is normally peer review. The work is sent to one or more established scientists with similar expertise (who usually remain anonymous) for them to read and perhaps criticise its method and thinking. It is then sent back to the researchers with recommendations for revision. If the work does not meet the standards of the peer reviewers it will not be published. This system ensures that standards of quality are maintained in research and that unsubstantiated claims are not made.

The peer review system is certainly very highly regarded but it is not without its critics.

For instance, just because something is not thought by a reviewer to be appropriate for publishing does not mean that others would feel the same way. It could be that the reviewer is providing a fair assessment, in which case the work should be rejected and looked at by the researchers again. It could be, however, that the reviewer is biased in some way. It may be that the paper under consideration is expressing an opinion that the reviewer disagrees with; if this is the case the reviewer may be approaching the research from a position of bias. In situations like these, research may not be widely seen by the community, just because of the opinions of a single reviewer.

There is also something called the 'file drawer problem', which is where there is a strong tendency for the publication of research with positive results (i.e. which supports the hypothesis). Non-significant findings rarely get published, so researchers file away research which has not rejected the null hypothesis, and

Despite numerous obstacles and sometimes long timescales involved, the publication of high quality psychological research is essential for the dissemination of knowledge in the international scientific community.

it is never seen by the scientific community. It is argued that this produces a bias in the research process where designs are tweaked to ensure positive results.

A related problem with peer review is that very few (a recent estimate was less than 2%) psychological publications were replications or partial replications of previous research. This is particularly worrying since replication is a cornerstone of science. A reluctance to publish replications, and especially failed replications (i.e. ones that did not get positive results), means that theories and concepts are not being properly scrutinised before becoming widely accepted.

Publication in peer reviewed journals can do a great deal to enhance the reputation of researchers. Not only are they more esteemed but, because of a good research and publication record, they also stand a better chance of obtaining funding for further research. Published research also provides enormous benefits for the institutions where the researchers work. Most research takes place in universities. The amount of money a university gets is partly based on periodic audits of the university's research output, including the amount of published work they generate (the process is called the Research Excellence Framework, or REF). The publication of journal articles is therefore of crucial importance to both the researcher and their respective institutions.

PSYCHOLOGICAL RESEARCH AND THE ECONOMY

Psychology is a vibrant subject at university and thus contributes to the many millions of pounds that universities provide to their local communities. However, psychological research makes its own contribution to the economy. Psychology has an extremely broad research focus – the impact of psychological research can be seen in almost any sphere where a human is involved, or where behaviour is developed or modified.

For instance, psychologists are likely to have been involved in advertising on television or in other media. This might involve designing persuasive ways of encouraging people to buy a certain product – for example, a particular car or products with apple symbols on the back. This kind of activity generates sales and builds companies so that they pay more taxes. It also helps them to employ more people on better wages, further contributing to the tax income of the government.

Any attempt at health intervention is also certain to have involved psychology at some point. This could be at the level of campaign design or it could be at a more theoretical level – research may have indicated the most effective ways of changing health-related behaviours. Smoking cessation and healthy eating campaigns are good examples of the contributions that health psychologists make to the economy by reducing the burden on the health service and increasing longevity so people are contributing to society for longer.

Some behaviours that psychologists aim to change through their research have more directly obvious economic benefits. A great deal of psychological research is aimed at improving the mental health of the population. When you consider that depression and other mood disorders are estimated to cost the UK economy £16 billion a year, the economic – let alone humane – advantages become obvious. Smoking is another example. It is an addictive behaviour that has huge implications for the National Health Service (NHS), which must help the people damaged through years of using tobacco. This money may be more usefully spent helping older people who, through no fault of their own, have problems that require treatment. The British government set up and now partly owns a 'company' called the Behavioural Insights Team (which was known previously as the Nudge Unit), whose role it is to look at applying research from a range of areas, including psychology, to 'nudge' or encourage certain behaviours and discourage others, like smoking. It is in places like this that research is being applied successfully in the economy, saving money and freeing up funds to be put to better use elsewhere.

The psychology research community treats the economic impact of research very seriously. Research Councils UK (RCUK) invests around £3 billion each year in university research, including psychological research. They define research impact as 'the demonstrable contribution that excellent research makes to society and the economy' which is 'of benefit to individuals, organisations and nations'. In order to attract money from the RCUK to do research, researchers must demonstrate in their application that what they propose to do will have 'impact'.

Psychological research into behaviour change has the potential to save government millions of pounds.

RELIABILITY

Reliability refers to the consistency of the research – how well the research can be replicated at another time, or if two researchers carried out observations how well their opinions of what was observed agree. Reliability is important in research because we can be more confident of research which is seen to have reliability. There are a number of types of reliability and ways to assess them.

Inter-observer reliability

A widely used method and technique in psychological research is observation. Here the researchers observe behaviour and record what they see. The results of such research will not be of much use if the observations are not done consistently, both across different observations and between different observers.

Improving inter-observer reliability

1. Correlate observations: Comparing the observations of observers is best done using correlation. This relatively simple statistical technique allows us to see how similar two sets of values are. A good positive correlation shows that the observers provided similar results and you can then claim with some confidence that there is good inter-observer reliability.

2. Training: If observers are able to easily identify the type of behaviours they are watching, then they will be able to record those behaviours accurately. Practice certainly makes perfect as observation is a great skill. Behaviours 'happen' fast and recording them can be very difficult. For this reason, carefully training the observers before the research begins is advisable as a means of ensuring that they are observing and recording in the same way.

3. Operationalisation: Observers have to be clear exactly what they are looking for – for instance, if they are observing 'helping' behaviours then they must agree what this means. How helpful does a behaviour need to be before they record it as 'helpful'? If the definitions of the behaviours to be observed are clear and carefully laid out, then observer reliability will be better than if categories of behaviour are badly defined.

4. View of the behaviours: Each observer must have the same opportunity to see the behaviours being observed. The best way to do this is to have them base their recordings on exactly the same video film of the behaviours. If the observations are recorded 'live', perhaps by watching behaviours in a school playground, then different sight lines may mean that incidences of a behaviour may be missed by one observer but recorded by the other. This would weaken the correlation between their results and so weaken inter-observer reliability.

Test reliability

Various tests (or instruments) are employed in psychological research to measure behaviour. For example, these instruments are often in the form of questionnaires and scales that require the participants to indicate opinions of things and how they might respond or behave in different situations. If an instrument has test–retest reliability then it will give similar results each time it is used with the same person (i.e. it gives consistent results).

Improving test–retest reliability

1. Test–retest: The test can be given again to the same participant on a different occasion. The participant's responses to the test on each occasion are compared, and if there is a strong positive correlation between the responses then we can say that there is a high level of test–retest reliability.

2. Altering the test to improve correlation:
If the test–retest correlation is low then the reliability of the test is in question. This means that the researchers must alter the test to improve this reliability. They can do this by looking carefully at the test itself and identifying the parts of it that did not correlate well on the two occasions it was given. They can then remove those components of the test that are weakening its reliability and replace them with alternative questions and tasks. This new test is then tested again using the test–retest correlation assessment to see whether reliability has improved. This process is repeated until a high level of test–retest reliability is shown by a strongly correlated first and second running of the test.

VALIDITY

Validity refers to the extent to which an instrument actually does what it claims to do. Having validity means that the data collected likely gives an accurate, or 'true', picture of what is being studied. We can be fairly sure that tools used in the physical sciences, such as thermometers, really are testing what they claim to test – in this instance, thermometers are valid tools for measuring temperature. However, in psychology we are often far less sure. For example, IQ (intelligence quotient) tests are used to measure intelligence. The problem is that there is considerable debate about whether or not IQ tests really do test intelligence – their validity is questioned. This is not a unique case. The nature of the phenomena of interest to psychology means that they can only be brought to light by the methods used to test them. For example, psychologists demonstrate aspects of human memory through the response of participants to particular kinds of memory task. If the test is flawed then it follows that the assumptions which are drawn from the results of the test must also be suspect.

The issue of validity is a crucial one for psychology. Researchers talk of validity in terms of the validity of the measures they are using in the study and in terms of whether the study itself has validity (i.e. is the study really doing what it claims to be doing?). In terms of the validity of the study, researchers must consider *internal* validity and *external* validity. There is internal validity to the extent that we can say our findings are to do with what we claim, rather than something we have not controlled for. For example, anything which influences the DV other than the IV reduces internal validity. External validity refers to whether the findings of research can be applied beyond the context of the study.

Ecological validity

This is a form of external validity and is a way of assessing the legitimacy of a study. It refers to the extent that findings can be generalised to situations outside of the setting in which the study was conducted. For instance, some work carried out in a laboratory may lack ecological validity because people may behave differently outside the carefully controlled environment of the laboratory.

Improving ecological validity

Having low ecological validity is not necessarily a bad thing – the results of some studies are not intended to be generalised beyond their specific setting. For example, if a psychologist was conducting research into stressors experienced by soldiers on active duty then it can hardly be criticised because it doesn't apply to other settings in which stressors occur. However, if the intention of a researcher is to generalise the findings to other settings beyond the research context then they need to make the study resemble those settings as much as possible. For example, the researcher might consider whether their laboratory experiment can be done as a field experiment or whether the materials and the tasks sufficiently resemble real life. Memory research has often been criticised for lack of ecological validity – the tasks that participants engage do not closely resemble the way that we use memory in everyday life (a great deal of our memory is prospective – thinking about things we are going to do, rather than retrospective – remembering things we have just done).

Temporal validity

This is a form of external validity and a way of assessing the legitimacy of a study. Behaviour is greatly affected by social mores and the *zeitgeist* – attitudes, opinions and behaviours change over time. This is particularly important for psychology. If psychologists are to produce convincing general laws of behaviour, then they have to show that their findings are not a product of the time period in which it took place. For example, Asch's famous studies into conformity were conducted in the United States of the 1950s. Subsequent studies have failed to replicate Asch's high levels of conformity and it has been suggested that this is due to high levels of social conformity at that time in US society.

Improving temporal validity

Researchers can *attempt* to design their research to minimise temporal validity, but it is extremely difficult to control for; all research ultimately reflects the period during which it was conducted. The main strategy is to *replicate* research. If we are able to show with periodic testing that a theory holds true, then it has some temporal validity. However, this has to be a continual process – what holds true now for something 50 years ago might not hold true in 50 years' time.

Population validity

This is a form of external validity and a way of assessing the legitimacy of a study. The results of our research have external validity if they can be generalised from our sample to the general population, in other settings beyond those in which the research was carried out and at different times. If research has high population validity then the findings can be said to relate to the general population. For instance, if a piece of research has used an opportunity sample of 10,000 people chosen from 20 countries worldwide, then its findings are more likely to be relevant to the whole population of the world than if the sample had been three people taken from a cafe in Bristol. If we can say confidently that something has high population validity, then similar research carried out on a different sample elsewhere should provide similar results.

Improving population validity

Population validity is improved by consideration of the population and the sampling method used. Carefully identifying the population is important as this is the target for generalising the results of the study. For example, the findings of a study of attitudes of students in south-east England can be generalised from the sample to the population of students in south-east England *only if* the sample is representative of this population. Good sampling methods are therefore crucial. Since we have identified our population as students in south-east England, we must also be cautious about generalising these findings to other student populations. Presumably, the sample population was restricted to this geographic region for a particular reason and these criteria may not apply elsewhere.

Concurrent validity

This is a form of internal validity and is used to assess the validity of a measure. A measure has concurrent validity when it produces the same (or very similar) outcome to an existing already validated measure.

Improving concurrent validity

When a comparison is made between two measures of a particular behaviour, one well-validated and well-established and the other new, if the results of the comparison show strong similarity, then the new test has validity – it is doing what it is supposed to be doing. If there are differences between them, then the new measure can be tweaked and then reassessed against the valid measure. This process can continue until there is close agreement.

Face validity

This is a form of internal validity used to assess the validity of a measure. It refers to how valid a test seems to be 'on the face of it' (i.e. does the measure appear to be assessing what it claims to?).

Improving face validity

The extent to which a measure has face validity depends to some extent on who is *claiming* face validity. Sometimes several theoretical expert views might be required, and if there is general agreement that the measure looks like it is doing what it claims then it has face validity. However, the 'expert' views need not be psychologists. For example, if you were interested in observing toddler behaviour during meal times in the average home, you would want to seek the views of parents of such toddlers to see whether you really are observing the right things.

PILOT STUDIES

A great deal of planning and preparation goes into good research. A trial run of a study using a small sample is sometimes a good idea to tidy up the fine details of the design and to see whether the procedure actually does what the researcher wants it to do. A pilot study is a good way of checking that the assessment tools work – that they do what we expect them to do and that they are giving consistent results. In other words, the *reliability* and *validity* of any measurements or tests being used can be checked. It is also a useful way of ensuring that the variables have been appropriately operationalised. For instance, if we are looking at the effects of noise on memory, then this is the chance to get the volumes right to get the effect we are interested in. Similarly, we might find out that the sound levels are just too loud for comfort! This is a very important point – ethical considerations mean that participants *must not be damaged* in any way, and that includes their hearing! A pilot study also provides an ideal opportunity to talk to a few participants about their experience of taking part. Such feedback can provide vital information about demand characteristics, investigator bias and the design of the study in general. After a careful check of the procedures and findings, problems can be ironed out and the research design amended, where necessary, before the study begins for real.

FEATURES OF SCIENCE

OBJECTIVITY AND THE EMPIRICAL METHOD

The goal of psychology is to describe and understand behaviour. This will ultimately allow us to predict, control or change the way people behave. Psychology *is* a science. This means that psychologists rely on scientific methods of acquiring knowledge in order to achieve their goals, and it is these methods that we will be describing in the following sections. These methods highlight the importance of evidence about human behaviour gathered by careful observation and measurement. This is called *empirical* evidence. An empirical approach assumes that observations are not influenced by emotions or personal opinions; they are *objective*. It is very difficult in psychology to be entirely objective about events – we all have ideas and expectations about people and why they behave the way they do, which are formed throughout our life before we begin to look at behaviour scientifically as psychologists. Because of this, psychologists have to be extremely careful and systematic about how they conduct their research. A good scientist should always be an objective scientist. This means that the findings of a piece of research should not depend on the person who did the research in the first place. The results should not be influenced by the ideas and feelings of the individual who designed the study, carried it out, analysed the results or drew the conclusions. A high level of objectivity increases other people's confidence in the results, as they are able to say that it would have made no difference who did the work, the results would have been the same.

REPLICABILITY AND FALSIFIABILITY

A theory is a way of describing a phenomenon which is based on evidence acquired through testing and retesting hypotheses. Once the theory is developed it continues to be tested – and this brings us to a very important point. The most important aspect of a scientific theory is that it must be testable and ultimately *falsifiable*. By this we mean that researchers must be able to develop ideas that can be tested against the claims of the theory. These ideas will either be supported, in which case the theory is rejected or adapted, or proved wrong, in which case the theory is strengthened. Theories that are unfalsifiable are not scientific. This is one of the criticisms of the theories developed by Sigmund Freud – for example, his theory of the subconscious being made up of three interacting components (the id, ego and superego) is unfalsifiable. It cannot be tested and as such is not regarded as truly scientific.

If the same research is conducted again at another time and the same or similar results are found, then we can say that the findings have been *replicated*. Being able to do this is extremely important in the scientific method. If we find something on Monday and carry out the same research on Wednesday but find a different result, we might, understandably, be a little cautious about Monday's hypothesis. After all, if we have found something on Monday, why *would* the effect not still be there on Wednesday? A high level of consistency (reliability) means that the audience for the research – fellow scientists – can be confident that the findings really do represent what they claim to, and they can then extend the research without having to constantly replicate the original research. Well-designed research with careful control of variables should increase replicability.

THEORY CONSTRUCTION AND HYPOTHESIS TESTING

The scientific method progresses by hypothesis testing. A hypothesis is a statement that can be tested by research. The aim is to prove the hypothesis wrong – if we cannot do that, despite our best efforts, then the hypothesis is supported. It was the philosopher Karl Popper who proposed this way of thinking about advancing scientific ideas through hypothesis testing and theory construction. He said that a theory must be falsifiable in order to be considered as scientific. His logic was that any amount of evidence can be presented to support a theory, but only a single piece of evidence is needed to show that a theory is incorrect. The efforts of scientists should therefore be directed at trying to falsify.

1. The hypothesis

The scientific process begins with the hypothesis. This is the statement (a prediction), based on the aims of our research, that will be tested.

2. Test hypothesis

Appropriate methods of investigation are chosen that allow us to test the hypothesis.

3a. Do not support the hypothesis

If the results of the tests are inconsistent with the hypothesis, and therefore do not allow us to support it, the hypothesis must be rethought. The procedure begins again, through steps 1, 2 and 3.

3b. Support the hypothesis

If the results of the test chosen in step 2 are consistent with the hypothesis, then we can accept it and move on to our final goal.

4. The theory

The findings of carefully constructed research that support the hypothesis allow us to form a theory or modify one that already exists.

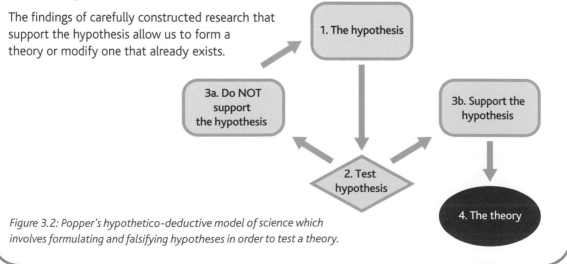

Figure 3.2: Popper's hypothetico-deductive model of science which involves formulating and falsifying hypotheses in order to test a theory.

PARADIGMS AND PARADIGM SHIFTS

A paradigm is basically a framework of assumptions – a way of thinking about something. Scientists working in one paradigm cannot provide evidence to falsify a theory in another paradigm because the principles upon which each paradigm is based are different. An example in psychology might be that research into the ideas of Freud under the paradigm of psychodynamics cannot falsify the research of biological psychologists working in the neuropsychological paradigm. This is because the psychodynamic paradigm assumes the existence of the subconscious, and it is partly upon this assumption that the research is built. The neuropsychological paradigm is concerned with the physical activity of the brain and does not accept that the subconscious exists. It

follows that information from the one paradigm cannot be used to falsify theories from the other.

According to the philosopher Thomas Kuhn, science progresses quite happily most of the time, testing hypotheses and developing theories within its own paradigms. Occasionally, however, science undergoes a sort of shake-up, which he described as a *paradigm shift*. For example, scientists have findings from research that cannot be explained by the accepted paradigm. Scientists are generally very attached to their paradigms and either ignore this evidence, make efforts to discredit it or prove it wrong. Eventually, though, a growing weight of evidence leads to a *scientific revolution* – the old paradigm is replaced by a new one. An example in psychology might be the shift away from the behavioural paradigm to a cognitive one, which began in the 1960s.

REPORTING PSYCHOLOGICAL INVESTIGATIONS

Once research is completed it needs to be written up for peer review and possible publication. There are certain conventions that should be followed when reporting psychological research, and the following structure is the one most commonly used.

1. Title: It is important that the title clearly expresses what the research is investigating.

2. Abstract: The abstract (sometimes called the summary) is a short (about 150 word) summary of the research paper placed at the very start. A good abstract should provide a little background, some details of the method, a statement of results and a short conclusion. It should provide the reader with all the essential details of the research.

3. Introduction: This presents the background to the research so that the results of the current study are placed in the right context. It is a review of previous research so that the scene is set for what is happening now. The introduction should start broadly, providing a general overview of key ideas, but become more specific as it progresses by considering research that is directly relevant. There should be a logical 'flow' towards a statement of aims and the hypotheses.

4. Method: A good method has just the right amount of information needed for someone who has never watched you work before, and who may never have carried out research in the area, to carry out a replication of the study. The following information would normally be included:

» *Design:* This might indicate the different conditions in the research and, if appropriate, you might say whether a repeated measures or independent samples design was used, or even include the independent and dependent variables.

» *Participants:* This section would give details of the sampling techniques employed, numbers of participants, target population and any other relevant participant details, such as numbers of males and females and age range.

» *Apparatus/materials:* Any materials used should be described (e.g. words lists or questionnaires) and any specialist apparatus identified and explained.

» *Procedure:* How the study was conducted is described here, including the order of events and any standardised instructions used.

5. Results: The presentation of results may be in the form of descriptive statistics, tables, graphs and also inferential statistics – whatever is most appropriate for the result. For example, results of qualitative analysis would likely be presented differently to those from quantitative analysis.

6. Discussion: The results are explained with reference to the hypothesis and in the context of the background presented in the introduction. For example, findings which lead to doubts about the claims of previous research will need to be explained. The study itself is critically reviewed here, with suggestions for improvements and suggestions for future research.

7. References: Full details of any research mentioned in the report are listed alphabetically here, normally using Harvard referencing style.

You are expected to know the purpose of each section of a psychological report, and you can expect to be asked about any or all of them! Often the best way to learn is to do, so you really should take any chance you get to write up a report of your own.

DATA HANDLING AND ANALYSIS

QUANTITATIVE AND QUALITATIVE RESEARCH

 Psychologists engage in both quantitative and qualitative research. The distinction between them appears straightforward enough – essentially, quantitative research is assigning numbers to things and qualitative research is to do with thoughts and feelings.

Quantitative research

There is an emphasis in psychological research on gathering numerical data. In doing this researchers are being *quantitative* – they are assigning numerical values to things. Quantitative research always involves measuring something in some way – for example, how many times you can hop in one minute, how many cars pass a local school, how far you can go in a car on a single litre of fuel. When these data are collected, statistical techniques are used to analyse them in order to find out if there are any numerical patterns or relationships. For many researchers this approach to investigating behaviour is the right one because it is regarded as the most scientific. It limits the amount of interpretation and opinion needed and therefore is more objective.

Qualitative research

Qualitative research gathers information which is *non-numerical*. For example, open-ended questions on questionnaires provide *qualitative* information. Qualitative research focuses on a person's *experience* and *feelings*, and is more concerned with uncovering the meaning of these things than with measuring behaviour.

Although this kind of information can be converted into quantitative data, it is often left and used as qualitative data (e.g. as quotes to support a point). Qualitative research:

» Describes events using words rather than numbers. It can provide extremely rich and detailed data of emotions and opinions.
» Takes the point of view of the participant, since their responses are not restricted in advance by the preconceptions of the researcher.
» Is less controlled and structured compared to quantitative research. Quantitative research is more concerned with issues of reliability. It is hard to assess reliability in qualitative research.
» Can be difficult and laborious to analyse, and it is often really difficult to see patterns in the data that would allow you to draw conclusions.

Quantitative or qualitative?

Whether or not a quantitative or qualitative approach is selected depends on the nature of the research and the interests of the researcher. For example, a researcher interested in a participant's subjective experience of an event would prefer a qualitative approach to gathering information. On the other hand, a researcher interested in measuring an aspect of human memory might prefer a quantitative approach. Qualitative data (e.g. from an interview) can also be converted into numbers (e.g. the number of times a particular view was expressed). What was essentially qualitative is now quantitative. However, quantitative and qualitative approaches are not necessarily exclusive – one can complement the other. This has led some researchers to use both approaches.

Analysing and interpreting qualitative data

Qualitative data is to do with quality (e.g. opinions, feelings). How, then, do you present qualitative data relating to things like thoughts and feelings? Consider the following example. A psychologist interested in communication is carrying out a kind of analysis called 'discourse' analysis on interviews with politicians, which involves investigating samples of speech. He is interested in seeing how often politicians comment on matters that are local to the UK or matters relating to international issues. The speeches of 10 politicians are identified and investigated.

Whilst listing comments might be interesting, it is not very well-organised. We can use a table to help present some of the data in such a way that the reader does not have to sort through a list to work out what has been said about the UK and what has been said about global issues. There may be many more comments, and these may be included in another table, but a good summary table with samples will be very useful to readers interested in seeing the kind of comments that have been made. The table may look like this:

The table makes it much easier and faster to find the relevant information. Tables like this might also include the total number of comments in each category which allows us to draw a graph.

It is immediately clear from Figure 3.3 that the speeches of the politicians used in this research had many more comments that directly related to UK issues than ones that dealt with international matters. This is a perfect example of what a graph is for: graphs allow readers to access a good summary of the data in an immediate, visual way.

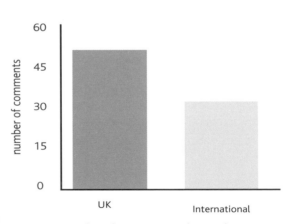

Figure 3.3: Number of comments made in each category.

CATEGORY	EXAMPLES
Comments directly relating to UK issues	'The Scottish parliament can work hand in hand with the parliament in Westminster.' 'House prices in the UK are, frankly, ridiculous.' 'The floods in the West Country were devastating. We must do all we can to stop this happening again.'
Comments directly relating to international issues	'The US elections have huge implications for the wars in the Middle East.' 'The crisis in Central Africa is worsening. I fear for the lives of these people.' 'Rebel fighters in parts of the Russian Federation have grown in strength over the last two years.'

PRIMARY AND SECONDARY DATA AND META-ANALYSIS

Primary data are those that are gained directly by the researcher. *Secondary* data are those that have already been collected but which are reused by the researcher. A case study is a good example of a methodology that uses both primary and secondary sources. For example, primary sources might come from interviews, assessments and observations of the individual or their family. Examples of secondary data might include school reports and medical records, or initial studies of the individual that may have been carried out by other researchers. The type of information collected will depend on what the researcher is trying to investigate. An example of a methodology that solely uses secondary data is a meta-analysis. This is the gathering of data from multiple studies on one topic/area of psychology that is then analysed to draw an overall conclusion about that topic or area.

	PRIMARY SOURCES	SECONDARY SOURCES
Advantages	The main advantage of a primary source is that you know that the data or information is unchanged and has not been manipulated by another researcher, so there is less chance of bias. It allows the researcher to collect data specifically related to the aim of the research, rather than relying on data that might have been collected based on a similar aim or topic.	Secondary sources reduce the amount of work that the researcher has to do on a topic as it has already been covered, so it allows you to cover a wider range of information faster than if you were to design and carry out methods to obtain all the data yourself!
Disadvantages	Because you, as the researcher, will be collecting and analysing the data, there is the risk of bias in interpreting that data. This is a time consuming technique because it takes time to locate your sample and collect the data; secondary sources will have already done this for you!	It is impossible to know everything about the secondary source as there is always the chance that the original authors left something out or interpreted the data incorrectly, leading to bias.

Table 3.5: Summary of the advantages and disadvantages of primary and secondary sources.

DESCRIPTIVE STATISTICS

Psychologists often end up with loads of numbers as a result of research. These numbers have to be presented to others in ways which make them clear and meaningful – it is usually impossible to make sense of lists of numbers (or *raw data*). Researchers use descriptive statistics to summarise their findings. However, descriptive statistics simply *describe* the raw data. They do not tell us what you did or whether your findings are reliable (i.e. would they be the same if you did the experiment again?) and they do not explain the result, type and size of the relationship you may have found.

Measures of central tendency

Measures of central tendency are sometimes referred to as *averages*. To find an average of a set of numbers is to calculate a single value that is representative of the whole set. That is, the average is said to be a score which is typical of the rest of scores. There are three measures of central tendency: *mean*, *median* and *mode*.

1. Mean

This measure of central tendency is calculated by adding all the scores in a set of scores together and dividing by the number of scores. For example, take the following raw data where we've measured the height of five people.

> Height/cm: 153, 146, 151, 170, 160
>
> *Step 1:* Add up all the heights to find the
>
> *Total:* (153 + 146 + 151 + 170 + 160) cm = 780 cm
>
> *Step 2:* Divide the *total* by the number in your sample (in this case 5): 780 cm divided by 5 (780/5) = 156 cm

The mean height of this sample is 156 cm.

Strengths and weaknesses of the mean

The mean is the most powerful measure of central tendency because it is the only one which uses all the numbers in its calculation. This, however, is also its weakness. Because the calculation uses all your numbers, one rogue number has a huge effect on your mean. For example, imagine if one of your five people was 234 cm in height. You now have six people in your sample.

Step 1: Add up all the heights to find the

Total: (153 + 146 + 151 + 170 + 160 + 234) cm = 1014 cm

Step 2: Divide the total by the number in your sample (now 6): 1014 divided by 6 (1014/6) cm = 169 cm

The mean height is now 169 cm.

The new mean height is not really typical of the heights of your sample. Five out of six of the people have heights that are lower than the mean. This is why it is a good idea, when using a mean, to also give some indication of how spread out your scores are by including a measure of dispersion, particularly the standard deviation.

Sometimes a mean simply does not make sense. For example, the mean number of children per family in the UK is 2.4. How can someone possibly have 2.4 children? In this case, another measure of central tendency might be preferable.

The mean height is quite typical of the heights of your sample. Three people are shorter and two are taller. It is pretty much in the middle – on the face of it, a good 'typical' mean.

2. Median

The median is the central number in a set of scores. In order to find the median, all the numbers in a set of scores need to be put in

Strengths and weaknesses of the median

The main strength of the median is that it is less affected by extreme scores than the mean. When put in order, extreme scores will be at either end of the list. Being at the centre of the list, the median is likely to be affected only by the extreme scores shifting the centre point slightly. However, it is not suited to being used with small sets of data, especially when these contain widely varying scores. For example:

7, 8, 9, 102, 121

The median here would be 9, which is neither central nor typical. A central number might be something between 9 and 102, maybe 60. In cases like this the median does not provide us with a very good measure of central tendency.

Strengths and weaknesses of the mode

The mode is useful when you want to know how often something occurs. For instance, we might want to know how many days off due to sickness most people take. The mode is usually unaffected by occasional extreme scores because they (usually) occur only once, and so will not be the most typical number and will not affect your assessment of the mode. However, the mode does not always provide a typical score – for example, in a small set of numbers when the most frequent number occurs at either end of a set of scores and is thus far from the central score. Take this set of data showing the number of holiday days taken:

1, 1, 1, 23, 24, 26, 27, 30, 33

The mode here is 1 day. Not really a 'central' measure, and not really informative about the whole set of data.

Also, sometimes a set of scores does not actually have a most frequent score – for example, everyone may take a different number of days off for sickness or holidays. In these cases there is no mode. The mode is therefore best used when there are lots of numbers in the set of data and there are likely to be lots of tied scores.

order and the *mid-point* found. If there is an odd number of scores (Example 1) then the number in the centre of the set, once you have put them in order, is the median. If there is an even number of scores (Example 2) then the median is the number midway between the two central numbers.

Example 1

Ages of employees/years: 21, 56, 44, 34, 29

Put them in order (youngest to oldest, or oldest to youngest, it doesn't matter which!):

21, 29, 34, 44, 56

The one in the middle is 34 years

The median age of the employees is *34 years*.

Example 2

Ages of employees/years: 21, 56, 48, 44, 34, 29

Put them in order (youngest to oldest, or oldest to youngest, it doesn't matter which!):

21, 29, 34, 44, 48, 56

Even number in the sample – two in the middle are 34 and 44 years

The median age of the employees is the midpoint of the two: *39 years*.

3. Mode

The mode is the most frequently occurring number in a set of scores. It is the score that appears most often in your data. For example, if our data is 'days off work because of sickness', we might have a set that looks like this:

3, 5, 6, 6, 6, 8, 9

Here, the mode would be 6 days off sick as it occurred most often (three times in total).

Sometimes a set of numbers gives us two modes, in which case the data are said to be *bimodal*. More than two modes would make the data *multimodal*. For instance, let's enlarge our 'days off work because of sickness' data set:

3, 3, 3, 5, 6, 6, 6, 8, 9

In this case, the numbers 3 and 6 occur just as often as each other. The data is *bimodal* which means it has two modes, 3 and 6.

Measures of dispersion

Whilst measures of central tendency give us a typical value, *measures of dispersion* tell us something about the spread of scores or how spread out they are. Whenever you give the measure of central tendency, you should also give a measure of dispersion, as both scores together tell us more about our numbers than either one alone does.

For example, the mean height of everyone in a large college might be 153 cm. This does not tell us anything about how spread out the heights are. If we just give the mean value, we are hiding the true nature of the data. We want to be able to give an idea of how spread out the heights are – how much shorter than 153 cm people might be and how much taller. You need to know about two measures of dispersion, *range* and *standard deviation*.

Each measure of central tendency (mean, median and mode) has an appropriate measure of dispersion. The mean is always associated with standard deviation (which uses the mean in its calculation).

1. Range

The range is the simplest measure of dispersion and is calculated by finding the lowest and highest scores in the data and subtracting the smallest from the biggest.

> ### Strengths and weaknesses of the range
>
> Using only two numbers, the range is a very easy figure to calculate. It also takes into consideration extreme scores. However, these are also its main weaknesses. In simply using two scores, the majority of scores are ignored. These two scores could also be particularly extreme, thus distorting the range.
>
> For example, the mean height may well be 153 cm, but the tallest may be 190 cm and the shortest may be 110 cm. Your range here would come out as 190 – 110 cm = 80 cm. This is not really a true reflection of the data. The majority of the heights, which cluster more closely around the mean of 153 cm, are ignored; they provide nothing to the range. The range tells us very little about the actual spread of scores – for example, how spread out or clustered they are.

For example, if the smallest person in the college is 135 cm and the tallest is 165 cm, the range is (165 – 135) cm = 30 cm.

2. Standard deviation

The standard deviation tells us the mean distance of scores from the mean of a set of scores. A large standard deviation tells us that scores are widely spread out above and below the mean, suggesting that the mean is not very representative of the rest of the scores. If there is a small standard deviation then the mean is representative of the scores from which it was calculated.

For example, take two sets of data, set A and set B. The mean of set A is 72 and the mean of set B is also 72. *But*, the standard deviation of set A is 14.2 whilst the standard deviation of set B is 3.2. What does this tell us? Whilst the mean scores are the same, the standard deviation tells us something about the quality of

Calculating the standard deviation

Calculating the standard deviation is not as difficult as it might seem. Just follow these steps and the worked example.

Step 1: Calculate the mean. This is written as an x with a line over it ($\bar{x}$). Mathematicians call this the x-bar.

Step 2: Get a sheet of paper. In a column (column 1) write down each value in your data set (in maths, each data value is referred to as *x*). Subtract the mean from it and write this value in the next column (column 2).

Step 3: Multiply each value in column 2 by itself and write the result next to it in column 3. The procedure is called *squaring* the value.

Step 4: Add up everything in column 3.

Step 5: Divide the value you get in step 4 by the number in your data set (*n*).

Step 6: Finally! Take the square root of the value you get from step 5. That's your standard deviation!

Calculation of Standard Deviation

Sample data: 1, 2, 3, 4, 5

Sample size = 5

Calculate the mean of the sample data

1+2+3+4+5 = 15 divided by 5 (number of items of data)

Therefore the mean = 3

Column 1 Number (x)	Column 2 Number – Mean	Column 3 (Number – Mean)^2	Column 4 Total of Column 3
1	= 1-3=-2	= -2 x -2 = 4	
2	= 2-3=-1	= -1 x -1 = 1	
3	= 3-3= 0	= 0 x 0 = 0	
4	= 4-3=1	= 1 x 1 = 1	
5	= 5-3= 2	= 2 x 2 = 4	= 10

10 divided by 5 = 2

square root of 2 = 1.41

Therefore the standard Deviation = 1.41

Strengths and weaknesses of the standard deviation

The standard deviation is the most sensitive measure of the spread of scores as it uses every score in its calculation and it is not heavily distorted by extreme scores. The standard deviation is closely related to the mean. Indeed, the mean is part of the standard deviation calculation. It is therefore the measure of dispersion to use whenever the mean is used as the measure of central tendency. However, even though it only involves relatively simple mathematics, it is still relatively laborious to calculate.

the mean in terms of how well it represents the rest of the scores. The first mean has a standard deviation of 14.2, demonstrating that there is a greater spread of scores around this mean. It is therefore less representative than the mean with a standard deviation of 3.2.

Percentages

Percentages can be a useful way of both displaying and comparing data. Statements on the news or in newspapers often use percentages to back them up – for example 'Health crisis! 55% of people are classed as obese', 'Nuclear option – at least 72% of people think nuclear power is safe'.

'Per cent' means 'number per 100', so 10% means 10 out of every 100, 95% means 95 out of every 100 and so on. So, '35% of the population voted *yes* to free ice creams' means that for every 100 people in the population, 35 said yes, which means 65 people said something else (no, maybe or don't know). Percentages are a useful way of standardising numbers so they can be compared.

Comparing descriptive statistics

Each measure of central tendency and dispersion has its good and bad points. A strong descriptive statistic is generally one that takes in a good deal of the raw data in its calculation. Each is appropriate in different circumstances, however, depending on the data you have and what you are looking for in your research.

	MEAN	MODE	MEDIAN	STANDARD DEVIATION	RANGE
Strength	Most powerful measure of central tendency as it uses all of the data.	The best measure to use if you want to know how often things happen.	Not heavily influenced by rogue scores.	Uses every value in the data set, is not heavily distorted by extreme values and is the most sensitive.	Takes extreme scores into consideration and is simple to calculate.
Weakness	One rogue score (large or small) can heavily influence it. For instance, the mean of 3, 4 and 8 is 5. The mean of 3, 4, 8 and 1005 is 255. The extreme value has seriously influenced the mean.	Sometimes a data set does not have a most common value and sometimes it has lots of common values.	Not good for using with small data sets. For instance, if you only have the numbers 1, 17 and 2000 in your data set the median is 17. Not very informative.	The most laborious of the measures of central tendency to calculate.	If either of the two scores are extreme, range will be distorted. It tells us little about how spread out or clustered together the data are.

Table 3.6: Strengths and weaknesses of descriptive statistics.

APPROPRIATE SELECTION OF GRAPHS

Just as statistics should be presented as simply and as clearly as possible, graphs should also be simple and clear, and should be the appropriate type of graph for the data. Poorly presented data can give a bad impression of what could otherwise have been clever and careful research. Professional researchers will tell you that when looking over the many hundreds of papers that are produced in their field each year, they first look at the title of the article, then the summary at the start and then the results section where the research data is presented. If they find the presentation of the data interesting then they may spend time reading the whole article from start to finish. If they do not find the presentation of the data clear then they may put the article to one side, maybe not returning to it at all. The importance of data presentation should not be underestimated.

Scattergraph

Scattergraphs are used when the study is correlational (i.e. investigating a relationship between variables). Drawing a scattergraph involves plotting two scores: one is measured along the horizontal (*x*) axis and the other on the vertical (*y*) axis. An 'x' (or plotting point) is placed where the two plots match. Sometimes a 'line of best fit' is added after all the data has been plotted. This straight line is to show a trend in the plots – it is an estimated line and it does not have to pass through any particular number of plotting points. Generally speaking, unless there is a specific need to draw attention to this line of best fit, it is better to leave it out. The pattern of plotting points represents a particular kind of correlation.

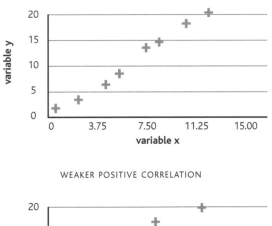

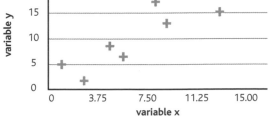

Figure 3.4a and 3.4b: As one variable increases, so too does another. The more the points resemble a straight line, the stronger the positive correlation.

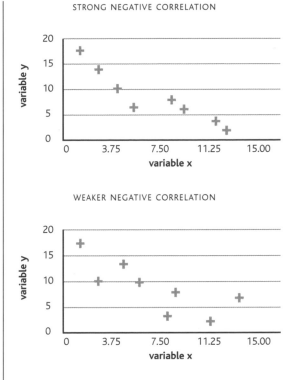

Figure 3.5a and 3.5b: As one variable increases the other decreases. As with positive correlations, the tighter the points cluster around a single straight line, the stronger the negative correlation.

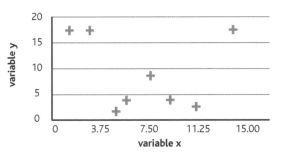

Figure 3.6: There appears to be no relationship between the variables.

ASK AN EXAMINER

In reality, it is not always easy to tell from a scattergraph the type of correlation indicated by the data. Examiners are not out to trick you however, so if you get an exam question involving a scattergraph the correlation should be readily identifiable.

Watch out for curvilinear relationships!

If you calculated the correlation coefficient for a *curvilinear* relationship, you'd probably find something close to zero. This is because for half of the time the relationship is positive (as *x* increases so too does *y*), but for the rest of the time it is negative (as one increases the other decreases). Taken together, they cancel each other out and you get a zero correlation. By looking at the correlation coefficient you may believe that there was no relationship between the two variables at all, but you would be wrong! There is a very interesting relationship indeed.

For example, in psychology there is a law called the Yerkes–Dodson law. It says that performance on a task will increase as the person becomes more alert. However, if they become too alert then performance will begin to get worse. Variable *x* in this case is 'level of alertness' and variable *y* is 'performance on a task'.

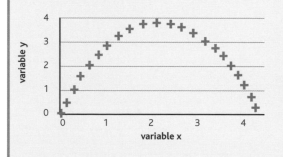

Figure 3.7: Curvilinear relationships.

ASK AN EXAMINER

You need to be able to select an appropriate graph for specific situations, draw graphs and identify types of graph. You also need to be able to read graphs, i.e. explain what they are saying about the data. It is well worth practicing these skills – students often over-estimate their skills in this area and come unstuck in an exam.

Bar chart

Bar charts use data which come in categories. Each thing you are counting up for these data can only fit into one category or another. We call this *discrete data*. For example, you may collect data on how many of each type of bird you see in your garden. The data are discrete – a sparrow can only be a sparrow. When drawing a bar chart, the vertical axis should show the score of a variable – for example, the mean or frequency (how often something occurred), whilst the horizontal axis should show the individual categories, or variables measured. The bars on the horizontal axis should be drawn separately with equal width and gaps.

Bar charts have:
» Gaps between the bars.
» Frequency (number) on the *y* axis.
» Category labels on the *x* axis.

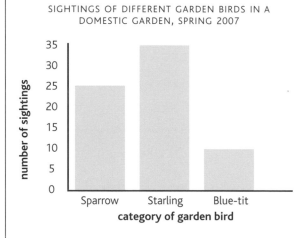

Figure 3.8: The bar chart need not show all the categories on the horizontal axis – it is acceptable to just show those of particular interest as a comparison. However, being selective in this way can be misleading so care must be taken. Only choosing to show certain categories does not tell the whole story.

Histogram

The histogram is similar in many ways to the bar chart and they are often confused. The major difference is that in a histogram the *x* axis does not depict discrete categories but rather a continuous scale – in our example, that scale is mass (kg). If, on the other hand, your data were concerned with temperature and fatigue, you would measure 'degrees Celsius' on the *x* axis.

Histograms have:

» No gaps between the bars.
» A continuous variable on the *x* axis.

NUMBER OF PUSH-UPS POSSIBLE AT DIFFERENT MASS

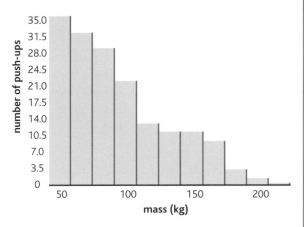

Figure 3.9: Unlike a bar chart, histograms do not have gaps between the vertical bars. This indicates that the horizontal axis has a continuous measure rather than distinct categories. The vertical axis represents the frequency of something – that is, the number of times something has occurred. The points on the vertical axis should be equal, as should the width of the columns.

Frequency polygon

The frequency polygon is very similar to the histogram. Imagine a histogram with a point drawn in the centre of the top of each bar. Now, remove all the bars and join up the points.

A frequency polygon has:

» A continuous variable on the *x* axis.
» A continuous line, no bars.

NUMBER OF PUSH-UPS POSSIBLE AT DIFFERENT MASS

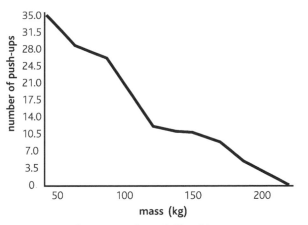

Figure 3.10: A frequency polygon is like a histogram except that a line joins the points where the summit of each bar would have been.

Tables

The whole point of a table is to present otherwise complicated information in as simple a way as possible. A table should allow readers to find the information they need with as little effort as possible. Tables can be large and contain lots of data, or they may be small and contain data in the form of summary statistics, such as mean, mode and median. When drawing a table, make sure you follow the most important rule: be as clear and straightforward as you can.

	CONDITION	
	Control condition	Experimental condition
Mean	9.7	14.2
Standard deviation	1.4	1.2

Table 3.7: Tables should be constructed so that they are clear and straightforward. Always remember to give your table a title, e.g. 'The mean and standard deviation for conditions in experiment'.

Data distributions

A normal distribution means that *most* people in a population (and therefore in the sample) on your particular measure fit somewhere around the middle: 50% of them score higher than the middle and 50% lower, but most of them fit more or less around the middle point. This is an important mathematical phenomenon and has a lot of applications in psychology.

For example, if you tested the IQ of 10 million people the average (mean) score would be 100. If we assume that IQ is distributed normally – and generally we can assume that 5 million people would have a higher IQ than 100 and 5 million a lower IQ – *very* few people would have a super-high IQ, like Stephen Hawking and us book authors, and *very* few people would have a super-low IQ. The *distribution* of IQs when mapped would look rather like the curve shown: a normal curve or a normal distribution (also sometimes referred to as a Gaussian curve, after its discoverer).

The mean is always the midpoint of the normal curve. The extreme right and left of the curve are described as the *tails* of the distribution (and, yes, that's where we get the phrase 'one-tailed' and 'two-tailed' hypotheses from).

A one-tailed hypothesis may be, for instance, that 'Women are cleverer than men'. This means that you are looking for a difference in a particular direction: you are looking to see that the IQ tests of the women you test are higher than those of the men – a *directional hypothesis*. The idea is that by measuring the IQ of loads of people, you are looking to see whether the tail (to the right here) is mostly women. A two-tailed hypothesis would be that 'The IQ of people depends on their gender'. You don't really know whether men or women will be cleverest, and so really you are looking to see whether either the tail on the right or the tail on the left is mostly men or mostly women – a *non-directional hypothesis*.

Not all data is in a normal distribution, sometimes it is *skewed*. On a graph, a skewed distribution is one that looks like it has been pushed a little to one end or the other of the horizontal axis.

A *negatively skewed distribution* means that there is more data in the left-hand, or negative tail. The result is that the mean value is higher than in a normal distribution and the tail is elongated. For instance, this might happen in Holland if you were plotting the height of people, as the Dutch are the tallest nation on earth. More people than you would expect from a normally distributed population would be a little taller, and so you would experience a negative skew.

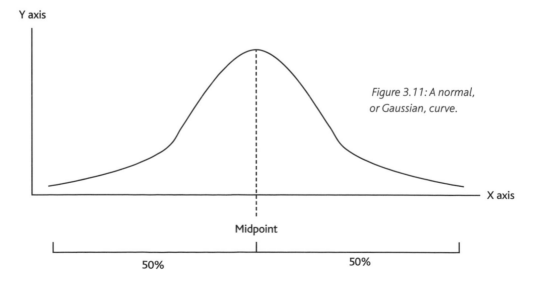

Figure 3.11: A normal, or Gaussian, curve.

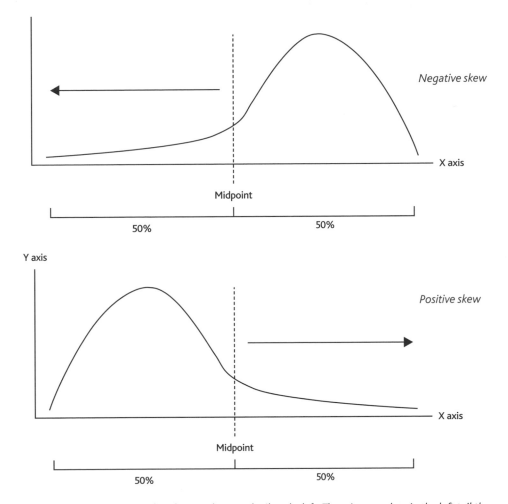

Figure 3.12: Skewed distribution. A negative skew has an elongated tail at the left. *There is more data in the left tail than would be expected in a normal distribution. A positive skew has an elongated tail at the* right. *There is more data in the right tail than would be expected in a normal distribution.*

A *positively skewed distribution* means that there is more data in the positive, right-hand tail. This results in a slightly lower mean than in a normal distribution. It's the type of thing you might see if you took 10,000 people to the top of a very tall mountain and then asked them to do as many sit-ups as possible in one minute. Because of the altitude, physical activity there would be much harder than at sea level, and so you would observe a slightly lower mean than you might expect from a normal distribution, and thus more people in the positive tail.

The implications of a skewed distribution mean that the assumptions of the parametric tests have been compromised (see page 238 for an explanation of what is meant by 'parametric'). Because the data are not normally distributed, the parametric test may give you a misleading and unreliable statistic that may mean you make a mistake in accepting or rejecting your hypothesis. There are ways of correcting the skew. These are called *transformations*, and sophisticated statistical computer programs can do this for us. However, it's not a technique that most psychologists need to use and is certainly not something you will need to know about until you do your psychology degree!

INFERENTIAL TESTING

PROBABILITY AND SIGNIFICANCE

Descriptive statistics are ways of presenting data in clear ways, but they do not necessarily say what the findings mean. They may not tell us, for example, if one set of numbers is likely to be dependably bigger than another set of numbers, or whether one measured variable is reliably correlated with another. For this we need to turn to another type of statistic – *inferential statistics*. The main purpose of inferential statistics is to show the extent to which the results might have occurred by chance. When we do inferential analysis, the end result (adding, multiplying, dividing, etc.) is a single important number, which is referred to as p. It stands for 'probability'.

The p-value gives us an idea of how likely it is that our results happened by chance. The p-value can be anywhere between 0 and 1. A p of 1 means that something is definitely, absolutely going to happen. For instance, there is a probability of 1, an absolute certainty, that in the UK Christmas Day will follow Christmas Eve. A p of 0 means that something is never ever going to happen. For instance, there is a probability of 0 that this book will turn into a badger. The nearer to 1 your value of p, the more likely it is that the results happened by chance. The smaller the value of p, the more likely it is that we can confidently accept our hypothesis and reject our null hypothesis. A p of 1 means that we are 100% certain that something will happen. A p of 0.9 means that we are 90% certain that something will happen by chance. A p of 0.8 means we are 80% certain

that something will happen by chance and so on. The smaller the p, the less likely it is that something will happen by chance. Remember:

> Small p – Good
>
> Big p – Bad

If we can reject our null hypothesis we can say that our results were *significant*. By this we mean that our findings did not occur by chance. Statistics lets us measure how significant our results are. Statistical tests are used to analyse the data gathered in research to tell us the p-value (we will describe these tests in more detail shortly). The smaller the p-value, the more significant the result. For example, the statistical analysis might tell us that we have a p-value of 0.02. This is the significance level. When we report p in research papers and books, it is more often than not written like this: $p \leq 0.02$. What this means is that the level of p we have found is less than or equal to 0.02. This means that we are at least 98% certain that our results did not happen by chance. Is 98% enough though? For this we need to check the level of significance selected for our research, and this is given by a number referred to as *alpha* (*a*).

Alpha

It is important to decide just how sure we need to be that our results did not occur by chance for us to go ahead and conclude that the hypothesis is to be supported and the null hypothesis rejected. In other words, just how small does p need to be? The level that p needs to be for us to accept it is called the alpha level. In psychology we say that we need to be at least 95% certain that our results did not happen by chance; 95% certainty translates to a p of 0.05. This means that if our p-value is less than or equal to 0.05 then we can reject our null hypothesis and say that our results are significant at the 0.05 level.

You may ask why it is that we choose an alpha of 0.05. The answer is that this level is an accepted convention right across the behavioural sciences as it gives us the best chance of avoiding errors (see box 'Type 1 and type 2 errors'). In some cases, however, we might want to be even stricter. For instance, in situations where people's quality of life may be harmed if we are not completely sure that our results did not happen by chance, we may choose an alpha of 0.01. That is to say, we would need to be at least 99% certain that our results did not happen by chance. This would allow us to say that our results were significant, not only at the 0.05 level but also at the more demanding 0.01 level. You might employ an alpha like this, for instance, if you had been investigating how well an experimental drug influenced the memory of elderly people with Alzheimer's disease. In order to put your drug on to the market and allow people to start taking it, you need to be very sure that it does what it is supposed to do.

If the p-value you find does not fall at or below your chosen alpha, then you are unable to accept your hypothesis. In effect, you are unable to reject the null hypothesis and you cannot say that your results were significant. In these circumstances, you have to say that your results were non-significant. This is quite different from *insignificant* by the way! Your findings were not at all insignificant. Even a result that does not support the hypothesis is interesting to scientists, but statistically speaking it is a non-significant result.

Type 1 and type 2 errors

After you have carried out a statistical test you must decide whether you accept or reject the null hypothesis. There are two major errors that can be made when doing this. These are described rather confusingly as type 1 and type 2 errors.

Type 1 error

This is also known as the 'false positive' error. It is the mistake of rejecting the null hypothesis when it is actually true. You have made the decision to accept your hypothesis by mistake. A very strict alpha value makes this kind of mistake less likely.

Type 2 error

This is also known as the 'false negative' error. This is the mistake of accepting the null hypothesis when it is in fact false, and you should have rejected it in favour of your hypothesis. A very strict alpha value makes this kind of mistake more likely.

Things happen by chance!

Things happen by chance all the time. For instance, you might recover from a cold the day after you happened to have a banana for breakfast. Does this mean that the banana caused the cold to go away, or did it just happen by chance? You would need to do some research to see. Let's say you have carried out your research and done the descriptive statistics. From what you can see the results seem conclusive – more people who had a banana recovered than people who did not have a banana. It really does look as if bananas are the elusive cure for the common cold. However, you cannot conclude anything yet as you are not sure that your result did not happen just by chance. It may look as though a chance result is very unlikely, but you need to demonstrate this – and we do this by significance testing.

INVESTIGATION	HYPOTHESIS AND NULL HYPOTHESIS	ALPHA	CALCULATED P-VALUE	CORRECT DECISION
Does eating crisps make you feel sick?	Hypothesis: The more crisps you eat, the sicker you feel. Null hypothesis: You do not feel sicker by eating more crisps.	0.05	$p \leq 0.02$ (p is less than or equal to 0.02)	The p-value is less than alpha. We can reject the null hypothesis and say that the result supports our hypothesis. We can confidently say that we are 95% certain that our results did not occur by chance. Our results are significant.
Does wearing perfume make females more attractive to males?	Hypothesis: Wearing perfume makes females more attractive to males. Null hypothesis: Wearing perfume does not make females more attractive to males.	0.05	$p \leq 0.09$ (p is less than or equal to 0.09)	The p-value is larger than alpha. We cannot accept our hypothesis and must retain our null hypothesis. We can only say with 91% confidence that our results did not occur by chance. Our results are non-significant.
Should we prescribe a potentially dangerous experimental drug to those with schizophrenia?	Hypothesis: Treatment with the experimental drug improves the quality of life of those suffering with schizophrenia. Null hypothesis: Treatment with the experimental drug does not improve the quality of life of those suffering with schizophrenia.	0.01	$p \leq 0.0017$ (p is less than or equal to 0.0017)	The p-value is less than alpha. We can reject the null hypothesis and say that the result supports our hypothesis. We can coincidentally say that we are 99% certain that our results did not occur by chance. Our results are significant at the 0.01 level.

Table 3.8: Examples of significance testing.

THE SIGN TEST

There are a lot of inferential tests available, but one of the very simplest for comparing two sets of scores is called the *sign test*. As with most things to do with research methods, the best way to explain it is with an example.

Imagine you were interested in seeing whether drinking a certain brand of drink actually did make you feel more energised. The best way to do it is to arrange for some people to come into your testing room and ask them to say, on a scale of 1 to 100 (1 being not energised at all and 100 being super-energised), how energised they feel. Then give them a nice glass of 'energy' drink and ask them 20 minutes later how energised they now feel, again on a scale of 1 to 100. Your hypothesis is a directional hypothesis based on all the marketing for the energy drink you have seen on the television and all over those Formula 1 cars: Drinking the 'energy' drink will make a person feel more 'energised'.

Your results might just look like this:

PERSON NUMBER	ENERGY BEFORE DRINK	ENERGY AFTER DRINK
1	63	59
2	40	43
3	12	25
4	25	27
5	33	45
6	26	26
7	15	9
8	82	77
9	72	58
10	34	36
Mean	40.2	40.5
Standard deviation	22.87	19.11

At first glance, the means are quite similar and so are the standard deviations, so your first conclusion may be that the energy drink made no difference whatsoever. However, you have a sneaky feeling that something is going on here, and so you decide on a quick sign test.

Redraw the table but add two columns and calculate the difference between the 'before' and 'after' scores for each person. The most important column, and the one that gives the test its name, is the final one – the 'sign' of the difference (e.g. for participant 1, 63 minus 59 leaves us with $+4$ – the plus sign that is recorded in the final column).

The next step is to calculate the sign (S) by adding up the number of least frequent signs. There are 4 pluses and 5 minuses, so $S = 4$. We also need to calculate N – this is just the number of signs (ignoring zeros). Here, $N = 9$. The final step is to check if the result of this test is significant so that, if it is, we can reject the null hypothesis that the energy drink makes no difference at all to how energised people feel.

Significance testing and the use of critical values

Statistical tests have tables that are used to check the *significance* of the findings. To check the significance of the findings of the sign test, three pieces of information are needed:

1. How many signs there were – $N = 9$.

2. How many less frequent signs there were – $S = 4$.

3. The alpha – the usual one for behavioural sciences being 0.05.

PARTICIPANT	ENERGY BEFORE DRINK (A)	ENERGY AFTER DRINK (B)	(A)–(B)	SIGN OF DIFFERENCE (– OR +)
1	63	59	4	+
2	40	43	−3	−
3	12	25	−13	−
4	25	27	−2	−
5	33	45	−12	−
6	26	26	0	0
7	15	9	6	+
8	82	77	5	+
9	72	58	14	+
10	34	36	−2	−

How to read the table

Look for the *N* column which equals 9. Next to it is the *S* column (look carefully – this goes down the column from 0 to 4. It only goes as far as 4 because this is the maximum number of least frequent signs when you have N = 9. Think about it!).

Go down the *S* column until you come to *S* = 4 (notice across from this in the final column is 5 – the number of negative signs you had! So, you had 4 positives and 5 negatives).

Read off the number in the *p* column which is across from 4 – you should see that it is 0.5000. This is called a *critical value*, and 0.5000 is our critical value of *p*.

For the sign test to show a significant result, the critical value *must be smaller than alpha*. In this case *it is not*: the selected alpha was 0.05, and the critical value is 0.5000 – bigger. This means you *cannot* be confident that your results did not occur by chance. You must reject your hypothesis and accept the null hypothesis: Drinking the 'energy' drink does not make a person feel more 'energised'.

If the critical value was smaller than the alpha, this would mean that you were able to reject the null hypothesis, drinking the 'energy' drink will make a person feel more 'energised'.

N	S	p	
9	0	0.0020	9
	1	0.0195	8
	2	0.0898	7
	3	0.2539	6
	4	0.5000	5
10	0	0.0010	10
	1	0.0107	9
	2	0.0547	8
	3	0.1719	7
	4	0.3770	6
	5	0.6230	5
11	0	0.0005	11
	1	0.0059	10
	2	0.0327	9
	3	0.1133	8
	4	0.2744	7
	5	0.5000	6

Table 3.9: A section of the sign test table. You can find full versions of the table on the internet by searching for 'sign test table'.

Doing a sign test

A psychologist was interested in discovering whether words and images together would be more easily recalled than words alone. She gave participants a memory test. In one condition (A), they were given a list of 10 words, each with an associated image (e.g. 'tree' below a line drawing of a tree). In another condition (B) the participants were given a different set of words, this time with no associated image. The recall of participants in each condition was as follows:

Condition A: 7, 8, 6, 5, 5, 6, 6, 7, 7, 4

Condition B: 5, 6, 6, 4, 4, 5, 5, 7, 8, 4

Analyse the data using a sign test. Use the sign test table to check for significance and state the result in terms of its *p* value.

The sign test is the only statistical test that you are expected to have experience of doing. Practice doing them. This will help you enormously to grasp the logic of inferential testing, and will be particularly helpful to your understanding of significance and probability.

THE CHOICE OF CORRECT STATISTICAL TEST

The choice of statistical test is influenced by the type of research you have done and the level of measurement being used. You can't just choose any test. They are designed for a particular purpose and a particular job. It's a bit like choosing a screwdriver to iron with – it would be a pointless process and would not help in solving your problem of creased clothes! A knowledge of experimental design, types of data and levels of measurement used will lead you to the appropriate statistical test.

Levels of measurement

There are three types of measurement you can make in psychological research. These are *nominal*, *ordinal* and *interval*. The best way to describe each is with an example.

1. Nominal level: If you have nominal data you have data that can be classified in categories. By this we mean that if something is in one category, it cannot be in another category also. For instance, if you are counting up the number of men and women at a rugby match, you cannot have someone who counts as a man and as a woman – they exist as discrete categories. If your data is like this, it is described as nominal level data.

2. Ordinal level: The clue for this one is in the name. Ordinal suggests that there is an *order*. Horse racing is a good example. Horses are recorded as finishing first, second, third, fourth and so on. The order in which they finish is the important thing, not the distance between them. If your data is like this, in some kind of order, rank or scale, then it is described as ordinal level data.

3. Interval level: If you are measuring something and you are able to take one measurement from another then you are using an interval scale. Time, temperature, weight and height are all examples of interval levels of measurement.

Parametric and non-parametric data

Some tests make assumptions about the data in that they expect the data to meet certain conditions, or have certain *parameters*. The ones that make assumptions are called *parametric tests*. They are called this because they test parametric data. The ones that do not make assumptions are called *non-parametric tests* – they test non-parametric data.

Parametric tests are quite flexible and durable – they are described as 'robust' in that it is acceptable to assume that the parameters are met.

Three things make data parametric:

1. The data are normally distributed.

2. The data are evenly distributed around the mean.

3. There is at least some interval data. This is absolutely crucial, as the type of maths required for parametric tests means that nominal and ordinal data just won't do.

Choosing the test

Three pieces of information are needed in order to select the appropriate statistical test:

1. What kind of data do I have? Is the data parametric? The key criterion is interval data – if you do not have that then you do not have parametric data. If the level of measurement is not interval, is it nominal?

2. Is the study looking for a relationship between variables (i.e. is it correlational)? Or is it looking for a difference between conditions (i.e. is it experimental)?

3. If it is an experiment, what is the experimental design? Is it independent groups design, yes or no?

The answers to these questions can be applied to the flow chart. For example, you have done a study where the data is non-parametric (i.e. it does not have an interval level of measurement).

» Is it nominal data? ➔ No.
» Is it a correlational study? ➔ No.
» Is it independent groups design? ➔ Yes.
» The correct test to use is a Mann–Whitney test.

You don't need to have done any statistical test other than the sign test for A level. However, you must be aware of a range of tests and the circumstances in which they might be selected to analyse data. For example, you might be asked what test should be used given certain data, or to justify the selection of a particular test. Learn the flow chart and you will have the core knowledge needed to tackle most questions.

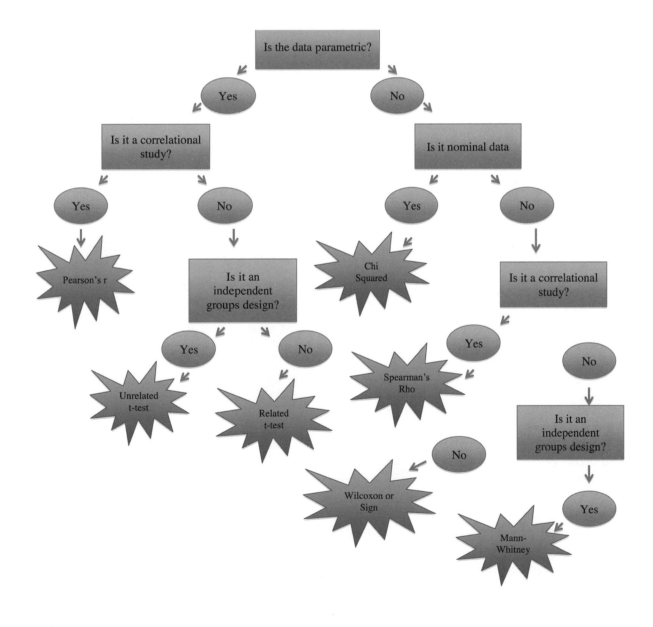

Section 4
Your Exam

Your Exam

This book gives you all the information you need to get top grades at both AS and A level. However, having the knowledge content to hand is one thing but doing an exam is quite another! We think that exam success is down to one key thing – good preparation. It puzzles us how few students we speak to and teach prepare themselves properly for their exams. If you were going for a driving test wouldn't you have practised driving a bit?

Maybe looked at what the test involves? Learned the theory and practised tests over and over? It's a pretty simple message, really, isn't it – exam success is very highly correlated with good preparation. Unfortunately for some, this means working consistently and, sometimes, working quite hard. Maybe this is the answer to our puzzlement!

> Preperation – the (not very) secret key to exam success
>
> Know your stuff
>
> +
>
> Know your exam   = good preperation
>
> +
>
> Know how to revise

ASK AN EXAMINER

Look for yourself!
You can get lots of information about your exam from www.aqa.org.uk. This includes specifications, specimen exam papers and mark schemes.

You will hear a lot about things called 'assessment objectives' (or AOs) on internet forums, in textbooks, from AQA and (alas) from your teachers. However, the reality is that other than describing the three skills you will need to demonstrate in an exam, *they have very little relevance to you as a student!* We have spent years and years advising teachers to develop the three skills (of course, they're really important) but to dump the jargon. Focus on learning and enjoying the psychology. Put the effort into becoming a good student of psychology rather than a dodgy examiner (and to any teacher reading this – yes, Rob had years of great success as an A level teacher without *ever* filling his students' heads with AO1, AO2 and AO3 junk). We suspect that teachers drill this into their students more to reduce their own anxieties than to benefit their students.

So what do you really need to know about assessment objectives? When you are asked to describe a theory, read or draw a graph, or comment on the value of a piece of research, you are demonstrating these skills. Your exam is highly structured – you will have lots of (fairly short) questions and spaces in an answer book in which to write your answer. For the most part, you just answer the question – in doing this, you are demonstrating a skill. For example, if you are asked to explain how social influence leads to social change by answering a question, you are demonstrating an AO2 skill. Would it help you to know that in advance? No, of course not. It was a question you had to answer, end of. The same applies to a question that asks you to outline and evaluate something. Answer the question and you will do okay; ignore the request to outline *and* evaluate and you won't. The outline and the evaluation are things you learn from the content of psychology and with the assistance of your teacher. A good teacher will plan their learning and teaching to develop these three main skills, and whilst it is worth being *aware* of them, please don't become *fixated* on the jargon.

The only time you really need to be aware of different skills is when you come to extended writing questions (8 or more marks). It will sometimes be obvious that you have two things to do (e.g. when you are asked to outline *and* evaluate). Sometimes it will be less clear (e.g. when you are asked to discuss). Extended writing questions will always require an equal balance of AO1 (descriptive) and AO3 (evaluative) skills.

AO1	AO2	AO3
Demonstrate knowledge and understanding of scientific ideas, processes, techniques and procedures.	Apply knowledge and understanding of scientific ideas, processes, techniques and procedures in handling qualitative and quantitative data in theoretical and practical contexts.	Analyse, interpret and evaluate scientific information, ideas and evidence, including making judgements and reaching conclusions and doing research.

Here are the assessment objectives for your psychology examination. Okay, hands up, who really feels better for knowing this? Who really understands it? You do? Great, go explain it to your teacher!

Question styles

MULTIPLE CHOICE

These require you to make a selection from a range of possible answers. Read the question carefully!

Example:

Tick three of the boxes below to indicate which of the following concepts relate to the multi-store model of memory. *(3 marks)*

❏ Sensory memory

❏ Articulatory loop

❏ Long-term memory

❏ Short-term memory

❏ Visuo-spatial sketchpad

APPLICATION QUESTIONS

You will need to carefully read a scenario and apply your knowledge as requested. Remember to place your answer in the context of the scenario! Example:

Kelly talks all the time in class. She never seems to stop. Whenever Sophie sits next to Kelly in class she has trouble following what the teacher is saying and concentrating on her work.

Use your knowledge of the working memory model to explain why Sophie is having difficulty following, listening and concentrating whilst sat next to Kelly. *(4 marks)*

EXTENDED WRITING QUESTIONS

These are worth up to 12 marks for AS and up to 16 marks for A level. Remember, two skills are needed in your answer.

Examples:

- Describe and evaluate animal studies of attachment. *(10 marks)*

- Discuss factors affecting the accuracy of eyewitness testimony. *(12 marks)*

- Discuss the influence of early attachment on adult relationships. *(16 marks)*

SHORT ANSWER QUESTIONS

These are never worth more than 8 marks each. You might need to describe/outline, to evaluate or to do both.

Examples:

- Outline **one** definition of abnormality. *(2 marks)*

- Evaluate cognitive-behavioural therapy (CBT) as a treatment for depression. *(6 marks)*

- Explain **one** strength and **one** limitation of laboratory experiments. *(4 marks)*

- Outline and evaluate the multi-store model of memory. *(8 marks)*

THE AS EXAMINATIONS

Topics in this book highlighted in pale yellow are A level *only* – you do not need them for the AS exam. However, you will need to know this should you wish to go on to do the full A level – your teacher will be able to advise you on this.

Paper 1 (72 marks, 50% of total marks)	1½ hours
Introductory Topics in Psychology	
Section A	Social influence
Section B	Memory
Section C	Attachment

Paper 2 (72 marks, 50% of total marks)	1½ hours
Psychology in Context	
Section A	Approaches
Section B	Psychopathology
Section C	Research methods

THE A LEVEL EXAMINATIONS

Paper 1 (96 marks, 33% of total marks)	2 hours
Introductory Topics in Psychology	
Section A	Social influence
Section B	Memory
Section C	Attachment
Section D	Psychopathology

If you are doing a two year A level course, this book contains all you need for the first two examinations (Paper 1 and Paper 2) – that is, two thirds of your A level. The final third (Paper 3) is covered in the companion Book 2.

Paper 2 (96 marks, 33% of total marks)	2 hours
Psychology in Context	
Section A	Approaches
Section B	Biopsychology
Section C	Research methods

Paper 3 (96 marks, 33% of total marks)	2 hours
Section A	Issues and debates in psychology
Section B	Relationships *or* gender *or* cognition and development
Section C	Schizophrenia *or* eating behaviour *or* stress
Section D	Aggression *or* forensic psychology *or* addiction

Mathematical content for AS and A level

At least 10% of the marks across the whole of AS, or the whole of A level, are given for mathematical skills. It is at least the standard of higher tier GCSE mathematics. As in GCSE maths exams you are allowed to use a calculator if you need to. The kinds of things you might be asked to do include calculating measures of central tendency and dispersion (mean, median, mode, range), calculate percentages, understand ratios and fractions (as used in probability and significance), do a sign test and use critical tables. This is explained in more detail on the AQA specification. The list looks daunting at first, but a careful read will tell you that there is very little you would not have done already prior to AS/A level and it will all be planned for by your teacher and covered in your lessons.

REVISION

There is a difference between *learning* and *revision*. Learning is what you do as you go along. You work in class, you do assignments, you regularly review the work you have done so far on the course and organise your notes and hand-outs. And you will also have done a lot of reading. Revision is the process of 'fixing' the information in your mind so that you can remember it in the exam. It is an individual thing: what works well for one person might not work so well for another. Regardless of what approach to revision you adopt, done properly it will take time, planning and self-discipline. You have to ask yourself something and answer it honestly – how much do you want success, and what are you willing to sacrifice for it?

The first steps

You need to find a place to revise quietly and without disruption. We know it's not always easy, but there is always somewhere you can go for some quality revision time. Get yourself organised – you can't revise until you've sorted yourself out with material (pens, paper, etc.) and learning matter (notes, books, etc.). We can assure you that the more organised you are, the more likely you are to get good grades.

Manage your time

Spaced practice is an effective way to approach revision. Don't study all the time, and take time out to relax and have fun, but when you do settle to revise, make sure that you really *do* work at it (just sitting there chewing your pen does not constitute real revision!). It is vital that you keep track of your revision. We cannot stress enough the benefits of a revision timetable. This will help you to monitor what you need to revise, what you have revised and what you need to return to. A revision timetable reminds you how little time you have left and how much you still have left to do. This can

help motivate you to, perhaps, waste less time and invest more of what you have into revision.

The hard bit

Passively sitting and reading will do you little good when it comes to revision. Some students even seem to think that holding a book will cause the contents to somehow seep up their arm. *Learning* is about *doing* – it is not a passive process. However, doing requires effort and motivation, so it's not as simple as sitting there staring at a book. There are some things you can do to make your revision time more effective.

Practice

Skills are acquired through practice, and answering exam questions is a skill. Therefore, the more you practice, the better you get. Practise answering questions and planning answers – there are questions in this book to have a go at and plenty more to be found elsewhere.

Flashcards

Reduce your notes to essential key points. These can then be written on index cards (6" x 4" work well). Use colour, **embolden** or CAPITALISE key words and phrases and use images. Don't put too much information on each card – less is more. Use one side of the card for a single topic. You can carry some around with you and flick through them when you have a moment. Don't worry if things don't stick straight away; the more frequently you look at your cards, the more familiar the contents will become.

Mind maps

Mind mapping is a very useful strategy for revision because of the thinking and effort that goes into producing one. Use words, colours, images and spatial connections. There are plenty of guides on how to create mind maps on the internet.

BIBLIOGRAPHY

Adorno, T. E., Frenkel-Brunswik, E. and Levinson, D. (1950). *The Authoritarian Personality*. New York: Harper.

Aggleton, J. P. and Waskett, L. (1999). The ability of odours to serve as state-dependent cues for real-world memories: can Viking smells aid the recall of Viking experiences? *British Journal of Psychology*, 90, 1–7.

Ainsworth, M. D. S. and Bell, S. M. (1970). Attachment, exploration, and separation: illustrated by the behavior of one-year-olds in a Strange Situation. *Child Development*, 41, 49–67.

Ainsworth, M. D. S., Blehar, M. C., Waters, E. and Wall, S. (1978). *Patterns of Attachment: A Psychological study of the Strange Situation*. Hillsdale, NJ: Erlbaum.

Allen, V. L. and Levine, J. M. (1968). Creativity and conformity. *Journal of Personality*, 36(3), 405–419.

Anderson, M. C. and Neely, J. H. (1996). Interference and inhibition in memory retrieval. In E. L. Bjork and R. A. Bjork (eds.), *Memory: Handbook of Perception and Cognition* (2nd edn). San Diego, CA: Academic Press, pp. 237–313.

Andrés, P. (2003). Frontal cortex as the central executive of working memory: time to revise our view. *Cortex*, 39(4–5), 871–895.

Arnold, P. D., Sicard, T., Burroughs, E., Richter, M. A. and Kennedy, J. L. (2006). Glutamate transporter gene SLC1A1 associated with obsessive-compulsive disorder. *Archives of General Psychiatry*, 63(7), 769–776.

Aronson, E. (1976). *The Social Animal*. New York: Freeman.

Asch, S. E. (1951). Effects of group pressure upon the modification and distortion of judgements. In H. Guetzkow (ed.), *Groups, Leadership and Men*. Pittsburgh, PA: Carnegie Press.

Asch, S. E. (1955). Opinions and Social Pressure. *Scientific American*, 193(5), 31–35.

Asch, S. E. (1956). Studies of independence and conformity: a minority of one against a unanimous majority. *Psychological Monographs*, 70 (whole no. 416).

Aschoff, J., Gerecke, U. and Wever, R. (1967). Desynchronization of human circadian rhythms. *Japanese Journal of Physiology*, 17(4), 450–457.

Atkinson, R. C. and Shiffrin, R. M. (1968). Human memory: a proposed system and its control processes. In K. W. Spence and J. T. Spence, *The Psychology of Learning and Motivation* (Vol. 2). New York: Academic Press, pp. 89–195.

Baddeley, A.D. (1986). *Working Memory*. Oxford: Clarendon Press.

Baddeley, A. D. and Hitch, G. H. (1974). Working memory. In G. H. Bower (ed.), *The Psychology of Learning and Motivation: Advances in Research and Theory* (Vol. 8). New York: Academic Press, pp. 47–89.

Baddeley, A. D. and Hitch, G. H. (1976). Verbal reasoning and working memory. *Quarterly Journal of Experimental Psychology*, 28(4), 603–621.

Baddeley, A. D., Thomson, N. and Buchanan, M. (1975). Word length and the structure of short term memory. *Journal of Verbal Learning and Verbal Behavior*, 14, 575–589.

Bahrick, H. P., Bahrick, P. O. and Wittlinger, R. P. (1975). Fifty years of memory for names and faces: a cross-sectional approach. *Journal of Experimental Psychology: General*, 104(1), 54–75.

Bandura, A., Ross, D. and Ross, S. A. (1961). Transmission of aggression through imitation of aggressive models. *Journal of Abnormal and Social Psychology*, 63, 575–582.

Banse, R. (2004). Adult attachment and marital satisfaction: evidence for dyadic configuration effects. *Journal of Social and Personal Relationships*, 21(2), 273–282.

Bareggi, S. R., Bianchi, L., Cavallaro, R., Gervasoni, M., Siliprandi, F. and Bellodi, L. (2004). Citalopram concentrations and response in obsessive-compulsive disorder. *CNS Drugs*, 18(5), 329–335.

Bastani, B., Nash, J. F. and Meltzer, H. Y. (1990). Prolactin and cortisol responses to MK-212, a serotonin agonist, in obsessive-compulsive disorder. *Archives of General Psychiatry*, 47(9), 833–839.

Beck, A. T. (1967). *Depression – Clinical Experimental and Theoretical Aspects*. New York: Harper and Row.

Bedny, M., Konkle, T., Saxe, R. and Pascual-Leone, A. (2010). Sensitive period for a multi-modal response in human visual motion areas MT/MST. *Current Biology*, 20, 1900–1906.

Bellodi, L., Sciuto, G., Diaferia, G., Ronchi, P. and Smeraldi, E. (1992). Psychiatric disorders in the families of patients with obsessive-compulsive disorder. *Psychiatry Research*, 42, 111–120.

Belsky, J., Rovine, M. and Taylor, D. G. (1984). The Pennsylvania Infant and Family Development Project, III. The origins of individual differences in infant–mother attachment: maternal and infant contributions. *Child Development*, 55, 718–728.

Bickman, L. (1974). The social power of a uniform. *Journal of Applied Social Psychology*, 85, 87–92.

Blackburn, I. and Moorhead, S. (2000). Update in cognitive therapy for depression. *Journal of Cognitive Psychotherapy*, 14(3), 305–311.

Bowlby, J. (1951). *Maternal Care and Mental Health*. Geneva: WHO; London: HMSO.

Bowlby, J. (1958). The nature of the child's ties to his mother. *International Journal of Psychoanalysis,* 39, 350–371.

Brazelton, T. B. (1984). Four early stages in the development of mother–infant interaction. In N. Kobayashi and T. B. Brazelton (eds.), *The Growing Child in Family and Society: An Interdisciplinary Study in Parent–Infant Bonding*. Tokyo: University of Tokyo Press, pp. 19–34.

British Psychological Society (2001). *Code of Conduct, Ethical Principles, & Guidelines*. Leicester: BPS.

Brooks, L. (1968). Spatial and verbal components of the act of recall. *Canadian Journal of Psychology*, 22, 349–368.

Burger, J. M. (2009). Replicating Milgram: would people still obey today? *American Psychologist*, 64(1), 1–11.

Bushnell, I. W. R., Sal, F. and Mulhn, J. T. (1989). Neonatal recognition of the mother's face. *British Journal of Developmental Psychology*, 7, 3–15.

Carey, G. and Gottesman, I. I. (1981). Twin and family studies of anxiety, phobic and obsessive disorders. In D. Klein and J. Radkin (eds.), *Anxiety: New Research and Changing Concepts*. New York: Raven Press.

Cassidy, J. (1999). The nature of the child's ties. In J. Cassidy and P. R. Shaver (eds.), *Handbook of Attachment: Theory, Research, and Clinical Applications*. New York: Guilford Press, pp. 3–20.

Chase, W. G. and Simon, H. A. (1973). Perceptions in chess. *Cognitive Psychology*, 4, 55–81.

Cho, K. (2001). Chronic 'jet lag' produces temporal lobe atrophy and spatial cognitive defects. *Nature Neuroscience*, 4, 567–568.

Choy, Y., Fyer, A. J. and Lipsitz, J. D. (2007). Treatment of specific phobia in adults. *Clinical Psychology Review*, 27, 266–286.

Collins, N. L. and Feeney, B. C. (2004). Working models of attachment shape perceptions of social support: evidence from experimental and observational studies. *Journal of Personality and Social Psychology*, 87, 363–383.

Coltheart, M. (2004). Brain imaging, connectionism and cognitive neuropsychology. *Cognitive Neuropsychology*, 2, 21–25.

Conrad, R. (1964). Acoustic confusions in immediate memory. *British Journal of Psychology*, 55, 75–84.

Crutchfield, R. (1955). Conformity and character. *American Psychologist*, 10, 191–198.

Cyranowski, J. M. and Andersen, B. L. (1998). Schemas, sexuality, and romantic attachment. *Journal of Personality and Social Psychology*, 74, 1364–1379.

D'Astous, M., Cottin, S., Roy, M., Picard, C. and Cantin, L. (2013). Bilateral stereotactic anterior capsulotomy for obsessive-compulsive disorder: long-term follow-up. *Journal of Neurology, Neurosurgery and Psychiatry*, 84(11), 1208–1213.

D'Esposito, M., Detre, J. A., Alsop, D. C., Shin, R. K., Atlas, S. and Grossman, M. (1995). The neural basis of central execution systems of working memory. *Nature*, 378, 279–281.

Darwin, C. J., Turvey, M. T. and Crowder, R. G. (1972). An auditory analogue of the Sperling partial report procedure: evidence for brief auditory storage. *Cognitive Psychology*, 3, 255–267.

Davey, G. (2008). *Psychopathology: Research, Assessment and Treatment in Clinical Psychology*. Oxford: Wiley.

Davey, G., Dash, S. and Meeten, F. (2014). *Obsessive Compulsive Disorder*. Basingstoke: Palgrave.

David, D., Aurora, S., Lupu, V. and Cosman, D. (2008). Rational emotive behavior therapy, cognitive therapy, and medication in the treatment of major depressive disorder: a randomized clinical trial, posttreatment outcomes, and six-month follow-up. *Journal of Clinical Psychology*, 64(6), 728–746.

Deater-Deckard, K., Scarr, S., Mccartney, K. and Eisenberg, M. (1994). Paternal separation anxiety: relationships with parenting stress, child-rearing attitudes, and maternal anxieties. *Psychological Science*, 5(6), 341–346.

DeCasper, A. J. and Spence, M. J. (1986). Prenatal maternal speech influences newborns' perception of speech sounds. *Infant Behavior and Development*, 9(2), 133–150.

Delgado, P. L. and Moreno, F. A. (1998). Hallucinogens, serotonin and obsessive-compulsive disorder. *Journal of Psychoactive Drugs*, 30(4), 359–366.

DeRubeis, R. J., Hollon, S. D., Amsterdam, J. D., Shelton, R. C., Young, P. R., Salomon, R. M., O'Reardon, J. P., Lovett, M. L., Gladis, M. M., Brown, L. L. and Gallop, R. (2005). Cognitive therapy vs. medications in the treatment of moderate to severe depression. *Archives of General Psychiatry*, 62, 409–416.

DeVeaugh-Geiss, J., Moroz, G., Biederman, J., Cantwell, D., Fontaine, R., Greist, J. H. et al. (1992). Clomipramine hydrochloride in childhood and adolescent obsessive-compulsive disorder: a multicenter trial. *Journal of the American Academy of Child and Adolescent Psychiatry*, 31, 45–49.

Di Nardo, P. A., Guzy, L. T., Jenkins, J. A., Bak, R. M., Tomasi, S. F. and Copland, M. (1988). Etiology and maintenance of dog fears. *Behaviour Research and Therapy*, 26, 241–244.

Downes, C. (1992). *Separation Revisited*. Aldershot: Ashgate.

Eich, E. and Metcalfe, J. (1989). Mood dependent memory for internal versus external events. *Journal of Experimental Psychology: Learning, Memory and Cognition*, 15(3), 443–455.

Ellis, A. (1962). *Reason and Emotion in Psychotherapy*. New York: Lyle Stuart.

Ellis, N.C. and Henelly, R.A. (1980) A bilingual word-length effect: Implications for intelligence testing and the relative ease of mental calculation in Welsh and English. *British Journal of Psychology*, 71(1), 43–51.

Erickson, M. F., Sroufe, L. A. and Egeland, B. (1985). The relationship between quality of attachment and behavior problems in preschool in a high-risk sample. *Monographs of the Society for Research in Child Development*, 50(1/2: Growing Points of Attachment Theory and Research), 147–166.

Evans, M. D., Hollon, S. D., DeRubeis, R. J., Piasecki, J. M., Grove, W. M., Garvey, M. J. and Tuason, V. B. (1992). Differential relapse following cognitive therapy and pharmacotherapy for depression. *Archives of General Psychiatry*, 49, 802–808.

Evans, J., Heron, J., Lewis, G., Araya, R. and Wolke, D. (2005). Negative self-schemas and the onset of depression in women: longitudinal study. *British Journal of Psychiatry*, 186(4), 302–307.

Farran, D. C. and Ramey, C. T. (1977). Infant day care and attachment behavior toward mothers and teachers. *Child Development*, 48, 1112–1116.

Fisher, R. P., Chin, D. M. and McCauley, M. R. (1990). Enhancing eyewitness recollection with the cognitive interview. *National Police Research Unit Review*, 6, 3–11.

Fisher, R. P., Geiselman, R. E., Raymond, D. S., Jurkevich, L. M. and Warhaftig, M. L. (1987). Enhancing enhanced eyewitness memory: refining the cognitive interview. *Journal of Police Science and Administration*, 15, 291–297.

Fontenelle, L. F., Mendlowicz, M. V., Soares, I. D. and Versiani, M. (2004). Patients with obsessive-compulsive disorder and hoarding symptoms: a distinct clinical subtype? *Comprehensive Psychiatry*, 45, 375–383.

Foroushani, P. S., Schneider, J. and Assareh, N. (2011). Meta-review of the effectiveness of computerised CBT in treating depression. *BMC Psychiatry*, 11, 131–137.

Freud, A. and Dann, S. (1951). *An Experiment in Group Upbringing: The Psychoanalytic Study of the Child* (Vol. 6). New York: International Universities Press.

Fullana, M., Vilagut, G., Rojas-Farreras, S., Mataix-Cols, D., de Graaf, R., Demyttenaere, K. and Alonso, J. (2010). Obsessive compulsive symptom dimensions in the general population: results from an epidemiological study in six European countries. *Journal of Affective Disorders*, 124(3), 291–299.

Garry, M., Manning, C. G. and Loftus, E. F. (1996) Imagination Inflation: Imagining a Childhood Event Inflates Confidence that it Occurred. *Psychonomic Bulleting and Review*, 3(2), 208–214.

Gazzaniga, M. S. (1967). The split brain in man. *Scientific American*, 217, 24–29.

Gehring, W. J., Goss, B., Coles, M. G. H., Meyer D. E. and Donchin, E. (1993). A neural system for error detection and compensation. *Psychological Science*, 4, 385–390.

Geiselman, R. E. and Fisher, R. P. (1997). Ten years of cognitive interviewing. In D. Payne and F. Conrad (eds.), *Intersections in Basic and Applied Memory Research*. New York: Lawrence Erlbaum, pp. 291–310.

Geiselman, R. E., Fisher, R. P., MacKinnon, D. P. and Holland, H. L. (1985). Eyewitness memory enhancement in the police interview: cognitive retrieval mnemonics versus hypnosis. *Journal of Applied Psychology*, 70, 401–412.

Geiselman, R. E., Fisher, R. P., MacKinnon, D. P. and Holland, H. L. (1986). Enhancement of eyewitness memory with the cognitive interview. *American Journal of Psychology*, 99, 385–401.

Geschwind, N. (1970). The organization of language and the brain. *Science, New Series*, 170 (3961), 940–944.

Goldfarb, W. (1943). The effects of early institutional care on adolescent personality. *Journal of Experimental Education*, 12(2), 106–129.

Gonzalez, J. E., Nelson, R. J., Gutkin, T. B., Saunders, A., Galloway, A. and Shwery, C. S. (2004). Rational emotive therapy with children and adolescents: a meta-analysis. *Journal of Emotional and Behavioral Disorders*, 12(4), 222–235.

Goodwin, D. W., Powell, B., Bremer, D., Hoine, H. and Stern, J. (1969). Alcohol and recall: state-dependent effects in man. *Science*, 163(3873), 1358–1360.

Gougoux, F., Zatorre, R. J., Lassonde, M., Voss, P. and Lepore, F. (2005). A functional neuroimaging study of sound localization: visual cortex activity predicts performance in early-blind individuals. *PLoS Biology*, 3: e27.

Greist, J. H., Marks, I. M., Baer, L., Parkin, J. R., Manzo, P. A., Mantle, J. M., Wenzel, K. W., Spierings, C. J., Kobak, K. A., Dottl, S. L., Bailey, T. M. and Forman, L. (1998). Self-treatment for obsessive compulsive disorder using a manual and a computerized telephone interview: a US–UK study. *MD Computing*, 15, 149–157.

Gross, S. R., Jacoby, K. J., Matheson, D. J. and Montgomery, N. (2005). Exonerations in the United States 1989 through 2003. *Journal of Criminal Law and Criminology*, 95(2), 523–560.

Grossmann, K., Grossmann, K. E., Spangler, G., Suess, G. and Unzner, L. (1985) Maternal Sensitivity and Newborns' Orientation Responses as Related to Quality of Attachment in Northern Germany. *Monographs of the Society for Research in Child Development*, 50(1/2): *Growing Points of Attachment Theory and Research*, 233–256.

Grossmann, K., Grossmann, K. E., Fremmer-Bombik, E., Kindler, H., Scheuerer-Englisch, H. and Zimmermann, P. (2002). The uniqueness of the child–father attachment relationship: fathers' sensitive and challenging play as the pivotal variable in a 16-year longitudinal study. *Social Development*, 11, 301–337.

Gusella, J., Muir, D. W. and Tronick, E. (1988). The effect of manipulating maternal behavior during an interaction on three- and six-month-olds' affect and attention. *Child Development*, 59, 1111–1124.

Hammen, C. L. and Krantz, S. E. (1976). Effects of success and failure on depressive cognitions. *Journal of Abnormal Psychology*, 85, 577–586.

Harlow, H. F. (1958). The nature of love. *American Psychologist*, 13, 673–685.

Harlow, H. F. and Harlow, M. (1962). Social deprivation in monkeys. *Scientific American*, 207, 136–146.

Harrist, A. W., Pettit, G. S., Dodge, K. A. and Bates, J. E. (1994). Dyadic synchrony in mother–child interaction: relation with children's subsequent kindergarten adjustment. *Family Relations*, 43, 417–424.

Harrist, A. W. and Waugh, R. M. (2002). Dyadic synchrony: its structure and function in children's development. *Developmental Review*, 22, 555–592.

Haslam, S. A. and Reicher, S. D. (2012). Contesting the 'nature' of conformity: what Milgram and Zimbardo's studies really show. *PLoS Biology*, 10, e1001426.

Hauari, H. and Hollingworth, K. (2009). *Understanding Fathering: Masculinity, Diversity and Change*. York: Joseph Rowntree Foundation.

Hazan, C. and Shaver, P. (1987). Romantic love conceptualized as an attachment process. *Journal of Personality and Social Psychology*, 52, 511–524.

Hemmings, S. M., Kinnear, C. J., Lochner, C., Niehaus, D. J., Knowles, J. A., Moolman-Smook, J.C., Corfield, V. A. and Stein, D. J. (2004). Early- versus late-onset obsessive-compulsive disorder: investigating genetic and clinical correlates. *Psychiatry Research*, 128, 175–182.

Hensley, P. L., Nadiga, D. and Uhlenhuth, E. H. (2004). Long-term effectiveness of cognitive therapy in major depressive disorder. *Depression and Anxiety*, 20, 1–7.

Hess, E. H. (1958). 'Imprinting' in animals. *Scientific American*, 198(3), 81–90.

Hess, E. H. (1961). Imprinting, an effect of early experience, imprinting determines later social behaviour in animals. *Science*, 130, 3368, 133–141.

Hess, E. H. (1972). 'Imprinting' in a natural laboratory. *Scientific American*, 227(2), 24–31.

Hobson, J. A., McCarley, R. W. and Wyzinski, P. W. (1975). Sleep cycle oscillation: reciprocal discharge by two brainstem neuronal groups. *Science*, 189, 55–58.

Hofling, C. K., Brotzman, E., Dalrymple, S., Graves, N. and Pierce, C. M. (1966). An experimental study in nurse-physician relationships. *Journal of Nervous Mental Disease*, 143, 171–180.

Hökfelt, T., Johansson, O. and Goldstein, M. (1984). Chemical anatomy of the brain. *Science*, 225, 1326–1334.

Hollander, E., DeCaria, C. M., Nitescu, A., Gully, R., Suckow, R. F., Cooper, T. B., Gorman, J. M. Klein, D. F. and Liebowitz, M. R. (1992). Serotonergic function in obsessive-compulsive disorder: behavioural and neuroendocrine response to oral m-chlorophenylpiperazine and fenfluramine in patients and healthy volunteers. *Archives of General Psychiatry*, 49, 21–28.

Holt, N., Bremner, A., Sutherland, E., Vliek, M., Passer, M. and Smith, R. (2012). *Psychology: The Science of Mind and Behaviour* (2nd edn). London: McGraw-Hill.

Howes, C. (1999). Attachment relationships in the context of multiple caregivers. In J. Cassidy and P. R. Shaver (eds.), *Handbook of Attachment Theory and Research*. New York: Guilford, pp. 671–687.

Hrdy, S. B. (1999). *Mother Nature: A History of Mothers, Infants, and Natural Selection*. New York: Pantheon Books.

Irons, C. (2014). *Depression*. Basingstoke: Palgrave.

Isabella, R. A., Belsky, J. and von Eye, A. (1989). Origins of infant–mother attachment: an examination of interactional synchrony during the infant's first year. *Developmental Psychology*, 25, 12–21.

Jacob, S., Spencer, N. A., Bullivant, S. B., Sellergren, S. A., Mennella, J. A. and McClintock, M. K. (2004). Effects of breastfeeding chemosignals on the human menstrual cycle. *Human Reproduction*, 19, 422–429.

Jahoda, M. (1958). *Current Concepts of Positive Mental Health*. New York: Basic Books.

Jenkins, J. and Dallenbach, K. (1924). Obliviscence during sleep and waking. *American Journal of Psychology*, 35, 605–612.

Jenness, A. (1932). The role of discussion in changing opinion regarding matter of fact. *Journal of Abnormal and Social Psychology*, 27, 279–296.

Jordan, L. C. and Hillis, A. E. (2005). Aphasia and right hemisphere syndromes in stroke. *Current Neurology and Neuroscience Reports*, 5(6), 458–464.

Joy-Bryant, R. (1991). The effects of stress on reciprocal matching behaviors of preterm infants and their caregivers. Unpublished doctoral dissertation, University of Texas at Austin.

Jung, H. H., Kim, S. J., Roh, D., Chang, J. G., Chang, W. S., Kweon, E. J., Kim, C-H. and Chang, J. W. (2014). Bilateral thermal capsulotomy with MR-guided focused ultrasound for patients with treatment-refractory obsessive-compulsive disorder: a proof-of-concept study. *Molecular Psychiatry*, 171(24), 5881–5897.

Kebbell, M. and Milne, R. (1998). Police officers' perception of eyewitness factors in forensic investigations. *Journal of Social Psychology*, 138, 323–330.

Keller, H. (2013). Attachment and culture. *Journal of Cross-Cultural Psychology*, 44(2), 175–194.

Keller, H. and Otto, H. (2011). Different faces of autonomy. In X. Chen and K. H. Rubin (eds.), *Socioemotional Development in Cultural Context*. New York: Guilford, pp. 164–185.

Kelman, H. C. (1958). Compliance, identification, and internalization: three processes of attitude change. *Journal of Conflict Resolution*, 2(1), 51–60.

Kendrick, K. M., Haupt, M. A., Hinton, M. R., Broad, K. D. and Skinner, J. D. (2001). Sex differences in the influence of mothers on the sociosexual preferences of their offspring. *Hormones and Behaviour*, 40, 322–338.

Kermoian, R. and Leiderman, P. H. (1986). Infant attachment to mother and child caretaker in an East African community. *International Journal of Behavioral Development*, 9(4), 455–469.

Kerns, K. A., Klepac, L. and Cole, A. (1996). Peer relationships and preadolescents' perceptions of security in the child-mother relationship. *Developmental Psychology*, 32, 457–466.

Kessler, R. C., Stang, P., Wittchen, H-U., Stein, M. and Walters, E. E. (1999). Lifetime co-morbidities between social phobia and mood disorders in the US National Comorbidity Survey. *Psychological Medicine*, 29(3), 555–567.

Kinderman, P., Schwannauer, M., Pontin, E. and Tai, S. (2013). Psychological processes mediate the impact of familial risk, social circumstances and life events on mental health. *PLoS One*, 8, e76564.

Kirkpatrick, L. A. and Davis, K. E. (1994). Attachment style, gender, and relationship stability: a longitudinal analysis. *Journal of Personality and Social Psychology*, 66, 502–512.

Kirschbaum, C., Wolf, O. T., May, M., Wippich, W. and Hellhammer, D. H. (1996). Stress- and treatment-induced elevations of cortisol levels associated with impaired declarative memory in healthy adults. *Life Science*, 58, 1475–1483.

Klaus, M. H. and Kennell, J. H. (1976). *Maternal-Infant Bonding*. St Louis, MO: C. V. Mosby.

Kolb, B. and Wishaw, I. Q. (2001). *Fundamentals of Human Neuropsychology*. New York: Worth.

Kotelchuck, M. (1976). The infant's relationship to the father: experimental evidence. In M. E. Lamb (ed.), *The Role of the Father in Child Development*. New York: Wiley, pp. 329–344.

Krackow, A. and Blass, T. (1995). When nurses obey or defy inappropriate physician orders: attributional differences. *Journal of Social Behavior and Personality*, 10, 585–594.

Kupfer, D. J. and Frank, E. (2001). The interaction of drug- and psycho-therapy in the long-term treatment of depression. *Journal of Affective Disorders*, 62, 131–137.

LaFreniere, P. J. and Sroufe, L. A. (1985). Profiles of peer competence in the preschool: interrelations between measures, influence of social ecology, and relation to attachment history. *Developmental Psychology*, 21, 56–69.

Lamb, M. E. (1977). The development of mother–infant and father–infant attachments in the second year of life. *Developmental Psychology*, 13, 637–648.

Lenane, M. C., Swedo, S. E., Leonard, H., Pauls, D. L., Sceery, W. and Rapoport, J. (1990). Psychiatric disorders in first-degree relatives of children and adolescents with obsessive-compulsive disorder. *Journal American Academy of Child and Adolescent Psychiatry*, 29, 407–412.

Leonard, H. L., Lenane, M. C., Swedo, S. E., Rettew, D. C., Gershon, E. S. and Rapoport, J. L. (1992). Tics and Tourette's disorder: A 2- to 7-year follow-up of 54 obsessive-compulsive children. *American Journal of Psychiatry*, 149, 1244–1251.

LePort, A. K., Mattfeld, A. T., Dickinson-Anson, H., Fallon, J. H., Stark, C. E., Kruggel, F., Cahill, L. and McGaugh, J. L. (2012). Behavioral and neuroanatomical investigation of highly superior autobiographical memory (HSAM). *Neurobiology of Learning and Memory*, 98, 78–92.

Lewis, C. and Lamb, M. E. (2003). Fathers' influence on children's development: the evidence from two-parent families. *European Journal of Psychology of Education*, 28(2), 211–228.

Loftus, E. F. (1979). *Eyewitness Testimony*. Cambridge: Harvard University Press.

Loftus, E. F. (2003) Our changeable memories: legal and practical implications. *Nature Reviews: Neuroscience*, 4, 231–234.

Loftus, E. and Burns, T. (1982). Mental shock can produce retrograde amnesia. *Memory & Cognition*, 10 (4), 318–323.

Loftus, E. F. and Ketcham, K. (1994) *The Myth of Repressed Memory*. New York: St. Martin's Press.

Loftus, E., Loftus, G. R. and Messos, J. (1987). Some facts about weapon focus. *Law and Human Behavior*, 11(1), 55–62.

Loftus, E. F. and Palmer, J. E. (1974). Reconstruction of automobile destruction: an example of the interaction between language and memory. *Journal of Verbal Learning and Verbal Behavior*, 13, 585–589.

Lorenz, K. (1935). Der Kumpan in der Umwelt des Vogels. Der Artgenosse als auslösendes Moment sozialer Verhaltensweisen. *Journal für Ornithologie*, 83, 137–215, 289–413.

Main, M. and Solomon, J. (1990). Procedures for identifying disorganized/disoriented infants during the Ainsworth Strange Situation. In M. Greenberg, D. Cicchetti and M. Cummings (eds), *Attachment in the Preschool Years*. Chicago, IL: University of Chicago Press, pp. 121–160.

Main, M. and Weston, D. (1981). The quality of the toddler's relationship to mother and to father: related to conflict behaviour and the readiness to establish new relationships. *Child Development*, 52, 932–940.

Marks, I., Boulougouris, J. and Marset, P. (1971). Flooding vs. desensitization in the treatment of phobic patients: a cross-over study. *British Journal of Psychiatry*, 119, 353–375.

Marshall, W. L. (1985). The effects of variable exposure in flooding therapy. *Behavior Therapy*, 16, 117–135.

McBride, D. M. and Cutting, J. C. (2015). *Cognitive Psychology: Theory, Process, and Methodology*. London: Sage.

McClelland, J. L. (2009). The place of modeling in cognitive science. *Topics in Cognitive Science*, 1(1), 11–38.

McClintock, M. K. (1971). Menstrual Synchrony and Suppression. *Nature*, 229, 244–245.

McGeoch, J. A. and McDonald, W. T. (1931). Meaningful relation and retroactive inhibition. *American Journal of Psychology*, 43, 579–588.

McGuire, P. K., Bench, C. J., Frith, C. D., Marks, I. M., Frackowiak, R. S. and Dolan, R. J. (1994). Functional anatomy of obsessive-compulsive phenomena. *British Journal of Psychiatry*, 164, 459–468.

McLeod, J. (2009). *An Introduction to Counselling*. Milton Keynes: Open University Press.

Meehan, C. L. (2005). The effects of maternal residential locality on parental and alloparental caregiving among the Aka foragers of central Africa. *Human Nature*, 16, 62–84.

Meins, E., Fernyhough, C., Russell, J. and Clark-Carter, D. (1998). Security of attachment as a predictor of symbolic and mentalising abilities: a longitudinal study. *Social Development*, 7, 1–24.

Meltzoff, A. N. and Moore, M. K. (1977). Imitation of facial and manual gestures by human neonates. *Science*, 198, 75–78.

Milgram, S. (1963). Behavioural study of obedience. *Journal of Abnormal and Social Psychology*, 67, 371–378.

Milgram, S. (1974). *Obedience to Authority: An Experimental View*. New York: Harper and Row.

Miller, G. W. (1956). The magical number seven, plus or minus two: some limits on our capacity for processing information. *Psychological Review*, 63, 81–97.

Milner, B. (1962). Physiologie de l'hippocampe. In P. Passouant (ed.), *Colloques Internationaux 1961*. Paris: Centre National de la Recherche Scientifique, pp. 257–272.

Mitchell, K. J., Livosky, M. and Mather, M. (1998). The weapon focus effect revisited: the role of novelty. *Legal and Criminological Psychology*, 3, 287–303.

Mogilner, A., Grossmant, J. A. I., Ribary, U. R. S., Joliot, M., Volkmann, J., Rapaportt, D., Beasley, R. W. and llinas, R. R. (1993). Somatosensory cortical plasticity in adult humans revealed by magnetoencephalography (somatosensory cortex/brain mapping). *Proceedings of the National Academy of Science*, 90, 3593–3597.

Moore, R. Y. (1973). Retinohypothalamic projection in mammals: a comparative study. *Brain Research,* 51, 403–409.

Moscovici, S. (1976). *Social Influence and Social Change*. London: Academic.

Moscovici, S., Lage, E. and Naffrechoux, M. (1969). Influence of a consistent minority on the responses of a majority in a colour perception task. *Sociometry*, 32, 365–380.

Mowrer, O. H. (1951). Two-factor learning theory: summary and comment. *Psychological Review*, 58, 350–354.

Mowrer, O. H. (1960). *Learning Theory and Behavior* (vol. xiv). Oxford: Wiley.

Mugny, G. and Papastamou, S. (1982). Minority influence and psycho-social identity. *European Journal of Social Psychology*, 12, 379–394.

Murdock, B. (1962). Serial position effect of free recall. *Journal of Experimental Psychology,* 64(2), 482–488.

Nemeth, C. and Wachtler, J. (1974). Creating the perceptions of consistency and confidence: a necessary condition for minority influence. *Sociometry*, 37(4), 529–540.

Nestadt, G., Grados, M. and Samuels, J. (2010). Genetics of obsessive-compulsive disorder. *Psychiatric Clinics of North America*, 33(1), 141–158.

O'Connor, E. and McCartney, K. (2006). Testing associations between young children's relationships with mothers and teachers. *Journal of Educational Psychology*, 98, 87–98.

O'Connor, T. G., Rutter, M. and the English and Romanian Adoptees Study Team (2000). Attachment disorder behavior following early severe deprivation: extension and longitudinal follow-up. *Journal of the American Academy of Child and Adolescent Psychiatry*, 39, 703–712.

Organisation for Economic Cooperation and Development (OECD) (2011). Fathers' Leave, Fathers' Involvement and Child Development: Are They Related? Evidence from Four OECD Countries. OECD Social, Employment and Migration Working Papers no. 140.

Orne, M. T. and Holland, C. H. (1968). On the ecological validity of laboratory deceptions. *International Journal of Psychiatry*, 6, 282–293.

Öst, L. G. and Hugdahl, K. (1981). Acquisition of phobias and anxiety response patterns in clinical patients. *Behaviour Research and Therapy*, 15, 231–238.

Parker, E. S., Cahill, L. and McGaugh, J. L. (2006). A case of unusual autobiographical remembering. *Neurocase*, 12(1), 35–49.

Paul, G. L. (1966). *Insight versus Desensitization in Psychotherapy: An Experiment in Anxiety Reduction*. Stanford, CA: Stanford University Press.

Pena-Garijo, J., Barros-Loscertales, A., Ventura-Campos, N., Ruipérez-Rodríguez, M.Á., Edo-Villamon, S. and Ávila, C. (2011). Involvement of the thalamic-cortical-striatal circuit in patients with obsessive-compulsive disorder during an inhibitory control task with reward and punishment contingencies. *Revista de Neurologia*, 53, 77–86.

Perrin, S. and Spencer, C. P. (1981). Independence or conformity in the Asch experiment as a reflection of cultural and situational factors. *British Journal of Social Psychology*, 20(3), 205–209.

Peters, D. P. (1988). Eyewitness memory and arousal in a natural setting. In M. Gruneberg, P. Morris and R. Skyes (eds.), *Practical Aspects of Memory: Current Research and Issues* (Memory in Everyday Life, Vol. 1). Chichester: Wiley, pp. 89–94.

Peterson, L. R. and Peterson, M. J. (1959). Short-term retention of individual verbal items. *Journal of Experimental Psychology*, 58, 193–198.

Quinton, D. and Rutter, M. (1976) Early hospital admissions and later disturbances of behaviour: an attempted replication of Douglas' findings. *Development Medicine and Child Neurology*, 18, 447–459.

Rank, S. G. and Jacobsen, C. K. (1977). Hospital nurses' compliance with medication overdose orders; a failure to replicate. *Journal of Health and Social Behaviour*, 18, 188–193.

Rapoport, J. (1990). *The Boy Who Couldn't Stop Washing*. New York: Penguin Books.

Rasmussen, T. and Milner, B. (1977). The role of early left-brain injury in determining lateralization of cerebral speech functions. *Annals of the New York Academy of Science*, 299, 355–369.

Rauch, S. L. and Jenike, M. A. (1993). Neurobiological models of obsessive-compulsive disorder. *Psychosomatics*, 34, 20–32.

Rauch, S. L., Jenike, M. K., Alpert, N. M., Baer, L., Breiter, H. C. R., Savage, C. R. and Fischman, A. J. (1994). PET Regional cerebral blood flow measured during symptom provocation in obsessive-compulsive disorder using oxygen 15-labeled carbon dioxide and positron emission tomography. *Archives of General Psychiatry*, 51, 62–70.

Reynolds, M. and Salkovskis, P. M. (1992). Comparison of positive and negative intrusive thoughts and experimental investigation of the differential effects of mood. *Behaviour and Research Therapy*, 30, 273–281.

Richter, C. P. (1968). Inherent twenty-four hour and lunar clocks of a primate – the squirrel monkey. *Communications in Behavioural Biology*, 1, 305–332.

Robertson, J. and Bowlby, J. (1952) Responses of young children to separation from their mothers. *Courrier of the International Children's Centre, Paris*, II, 131–140.

Rogers, C. R. (1942). *Counseling and psychotherapy: Newer Concepts in Practice*. Boston, MA: Houghton Mifflin.

Rohrer, J. H., Baron, S. H., Hoffman, E. L. and Swander, D. V. (1954). The stability of autokinetic judgments. *Journal of Abnormal and Social Psychology*, 49(4/1), 595–597.

Rose-Krasnor, L., Rubin, K. H., Booth, C. L. and Coplan, R. (1996). The relation of maternal directiveness and child attachment security to social competence in preschoolers.

International Journal of Behavioral Development, 19(2), 309–325.

Rosenbaum, R. S., Köhler, S., Schacter, D. L., Moscovitch, M., Westmacott, R., Black, S. E., Gao, F. and Tulving, E. (2005). The case of K.C.: contributions of a memory impaired person to memory theory. *Neuropsychologia,* 43, 989–1021.

Rosenberg, J. and Wilcox, W. B. (2006). *The Importance of Fathers in the Healthy Development of Children: Fathers and Their Impact on Children's Well-Being.* US Children's Bureau, Office on Child Abuse and Neglect.

Rosenhan, D. L. and Seligman, M. E. P. (1989). *Abnormal Psychology.* New York: W.W. Norton.

Rotter, J. B. (1966). Generalised expectancies for internal versus external control of reinforcement. *Psychological Monographs: General and Applied,* 80, 1–28.

Russell, M. J., Switz, G. M. and Thompson, K. (1980). Olfactory influences on the human menstrual cycle. *Pharmacology, Biochemistry and Behaviour,* 13, 737–738.

Rutter, M. (1981). *Maternal Deprivation Reassessed.* London: Penguin.

Rutter, M. (1997). Nature–nurture integration: the example of antisocial behavior. *American Psychologist,* 52(4), 390–398.

Rutter, M., Beckett, C., Castle, J., Colvert, E., Kreppner, J., Mehta, M., Stevens, S. and Sonuga-Barke, E. (2007). Effects of early profound institutional deprivation: an overview of findings from a UK longitudinal study of Romanian adoptees. *European Journal of Developmental Psychology,* 493, 332–350.

Salkovskis, P. M. (1985). Obsessive-compulsive problems: a cognitive-behavioural analysis. *Behaviour Research and Therapy,* 23, 571–583.

Saxena, S., Brody, A. L., Schwartz, J. M. and Baxter, L. R. (1998). Neuroimaging and frontal-subcortical circuitry in obsessive-compulsive disorder. *British Journal of Psychiatry Supplement,* 35, 26–37.

Schaffer, H. R. (ed.) (1983). Nuevas perspectivas en psicologia del descarrollo en lengua Inglesa (New perspectives in psychological development in the English language). *Infancia y Apredizaja* (Madrid, Monograph no. 3).

Schaffer, H. R. (1996). *Social Development.* Oxford: Blackwell.

Schaffer, H. R. and Emerson, P. E. (1964). The development of social attachment in infancy. *Monographs of the Society for Research in Child Development,* 29(3), serial no. 94.

Schernhammer, E. S. and Hankinson, S. E. (2003). Light at night: a novel risk factor for cancer in shift workers? *Clinics in Occupational and Environmental Medicine,* 3, 263–278.

Schernhammer, E. S., Laden, F., Speizer, F. E., Willett, W. C., Hunter, D. J., Kawachi, I. and Colditz, G. A. (2001). Rotating night shifts and risk of breast cancer in women participating in the nurses' health study. *Journal of the National Cancer Institute,* 93, 1563–1568.

Seligman, M. E. P. (1970). On the generality of the laws of learning. *Psychological Review,* 77, 406–418.

Seligman, M. E. P. (1971). Phobias and preparedness. *Behaviour Therapy,* 2, 307–320.

Senchak, M. and Leonard, K. E. (1992). Attachment styles and marital adjustment among newlywed couples. *Journal of Social and Personal Relationships,* 9, 51–64.

Shallice, T. and Warrington, E. K. (1970). Independent functioning of verbal memory store: neuropsychological study. *Quarterly Journal of Experimental Psychology,* 22, 261–273.

Shallice, T. and Warrington, E. K. (1974). The dissociation between short term retention of meaningful sounds and verbal material. *Neuropsychologia,* 12(4), 553–555.

Shaw, P. (1979). A comparison of three behaviour therapies in the treatment of social phobia. *British Journal of Psychiatry,* 134(6), 620–623.

Sheridan, C. L. and King, R. G. (1972). Obedience to authority with an authentic victim. *Proceedings of the Annual Convention of the American Psychological Association*, 80, 165–166.

Sherif, M. A. (1935). A study of some social factors in perception. *Archives of Psychology*, 27, 1–60.

Shih, R. A., Belmonte, P. L. and Zandi, P. P. (2004). A review of the evidence from family, twin and adoption studies for a genetic contribution to adult psychiatric disorders. *International Review of Psychiatry*, 16(4), 260–283.

Shipley, R. and Boudewyns, P. (1980). Flooding and implosive therapy: are they harmful? *Behaviour Therapy*, 11, 503–508.

Siffre, M. (1975). Six months alone in a cave. *National Geographic*, March, 426–435.

Skene, D. J., Lockley, S. W., Thapan, K. and Arendt, J. (1999). Effects of light on human circadian rhythms. *Reproduction Nutrition Development*, 39, 295–304.

Skinner, B. F. (1940). The nature of the operant reserve. *Psychological Bulletin*, 37, 270–277.

Slade, A. (1987). The quality of attachment and early symbolic play. *Developmental Psychology*, 23, 78–85.

Sluckin, W. (1965). *Imprinting and Early Learning*. Chicago, IL: Aldine.

Smith, E. R., Mackie, D. M. and Claypool, H. M. (2015). *Social Psychology* (4th edn). London: Psychology Press.

Smith, P. B. and Bond, M. H. (1996). *Social Psychology Across Cultures*. London: Prentice Hall.

Smith, S. M. (1979). Remembering in and out of context. *Journal of Experimental Psychology: Human Learning and Memory*, 5, 460–471.

Sperling, G. (1960). The information available in brief visual presentations. *Psychological Monographs*, 74, 1–29.

Stang, D. J. (1976). Group size effects on conformity. *Journal of Social Psychology*, 98(2), 175–181.

Stein, L. and Memon, A. (2006). Testing the efficacy of the cognitive interview in a developing country. *Applied Cognitive Psychology*, 20(5), 597–605.

Steketee, G. and Barlow, D. H. (2004). Obsessive-compulsive disorder. In D. H. Barlow (ed.), *Anxiety and Its Disorders: The Nature and Treatment of Anxiety and Panic*. New York: Guilford Press, pp. 516–550.

Stephan, F. K. and Zucker, I. (1972). Circadian rhythms in drinking behavior and locomotor activity of rats are eliminated by hypothalamic lesions. *Proceedings of the National Academy of Sciences USA*, 69, 1583–1586.

Sutton, R. and Douglas, K. (2013). *Social Psychology*. Basingstoke: Palgrave.

Swerdlow, A. (2003). Shift Work and Breast Cancer: A Critical Review of the Epidemiological Evidence. Sudbury Health and Safety Executive. Research report 132, 1–28.

Thomas, A. and Chess, S. (1977). *Temperament and development*. New York: Brunner/Mazel.

Tizard, B. and Hodges, J. (1978). The effect of early institutional rearing on the development of 8 year-old children. *Journal of Child Psychology and Psychiatry*, 19, 99–118.

Tomarken, A. J., Mineka, S. and Cook, M. (1989). Fear-relevant selective associations and covariation bias. *Journal of Abnormal Psychology*, 98, 381–394.

Tronick, E. Z., Adamson, H. A. and Brazelton, T. B. (1975). Infant emotions in normal and perturbated interactions. Presentation at the biennial meeting of the Society for Research in Child Development, Denver, CO, April.

Tronick, E. Z. and Cohn, J. F. (1989). Infant-mother face-to-face interaction: age and gender differences in coordination and the occurrence of miscoordination. *Child Development*, 60(1), 85–92.

Tronick, E. Z., Morelli, G. A. and Ivey, P. K. (1992). The Efe forager infant and toddler's pattern of social relationships: Multiple and simultaneous. *Developmental Psychology*, 28(4), 568–577.

True, M. M., Pisani, L. and Oumar, F. (2001). Infant–mother attachment among the Dogon of Mali. *Child Development*, 72(5), 1451–1466.

Tulving, E. (1972). Episodic and semantic memory. In E. Tulving and W. Donaldson (eds.), *Organization of Memory*. New York: Academic Press, pp. 381–402.

Tulving, E. and Thomson, D. (1973). Encoding specificity and retrieval processes in episodic memory. *Psychological Review*, 80(5), 352–373.

Turner, J. C. (1991). *Social Influence*. Belmont, CA: Wadsworth.

Van Ijzendoorn, M. H. and Kroonenberg, P. M. (1988). Cross-cultural patterns of attachment: a meta-analysis of the Strange Situation. *Child Development*, 59, 147–156.

Wade, K. A., Garry, M., Read, J. D. and Lindsay, D. S. (2002) A picture is worth a thousand lies: Using false photographs to create false childhood memories. *Psychonomic Bulletin and Review*, 9, 597–603.

Watson, J. B. and Rayner, R. (1920). Conditioned emotional reactions. *Journal of Experimental Psychology*, 3(1), 1–14.

Weisner, T. S. and Gallimore, R. (1977). My brother's keeper: child and sibling caretaking. *Current Anthropology*, 18, 169–190.

Wendland, J. R., Kruse, M. R., Cromer, K. C. and Murphy, D. L. (2007). A large case–control study of common functional SLC6A4 and BDNF variants in obsessive-compulsive disorder. *Neuropsychopharmacology*, 32, 2543–2551.

West, K. W., Mathews, B. L. and Kerns, K. A. (2013). Mother–child attachment and cognitive performance in middle childhood: an examination of mediating mechanisms. *Early Childhood Research Quarterly*, 28, 259–270.

Wickens, D. D. (1972). Characteristics of word encoding. In A. W. Melton and E. Martin (eds.), *Coding Processes in Human Memory*. Washington, DC: Winston & Sons.

Wolpe, J. (1969). *The Practice of Behavior Therapy*. New York: Pergamon Press.

Yuille, J. C. and Cutshall, J. L. (1986). A case study of eyewitness memory of a crime. *Journal of Applied Psychology*, 71(2), 291–301.

Zeanah, C. H., Nelson, C. A., Fox, N. A., Smyke, A. T., Marshall, P., Parker, S. W. and Koga, S. (2003). Designing research to study the effects of institutionalization on brain and behavioral development: the Bucharest Early Intervention Project. *Development and Psychopathology*, 15, 885–907.

Zeitzer, J. M., Dijk, D. J., Kronauer, R. E., Brown, E. N. and Czeisler, C. A. (2000). Sensitivity of the human circadian pace-maker to nocturnal light: melatonin phase resetting and suppression. *Journal of Physiology*, 526, 695–702.

Zimbardo, P. G. (2007). *The Lucifer Effect: Understanding How Good People Turn Evil*. New York: Random House.

Zimbardo, P. G., Haney, C., Banks, W. C. and Jaffe, D. (1973). The mind is a formidable jailer: a Pirandellian prison. *New York Times Magazine* (8 April), Section 6, 38–60.

Zohar, J., Greenberg, B. and Denys, D. (2012). Obsessive-compulsive disorder. *Handbook of Clinical Neurology*, 106, 375–390.

APPENDIX OF URLS

SOCIAL INFLUENCE

p. 12 Asch conformity experiment: https://www.youtube.com/watch?v=TYIh4MkcfJA

p. 16 The Stanford Prison Experiment: https://www.youtube.com/watch?v=L_LKzEqlPto

p. 17 BBC prison study experiment: https://www.youtube.com/watch?v=ZaXXqrUzKHw

p. 17 Philip Zimbardo – the psychology of evil: https://www.youtube.com/watch?v=OsFEV35tWsg

p. 19 Milgram obedience study: https://www.youtube.com/watch?v=fCVlI-_4GZQ

p. 26 Rosa Parks and the Montgomery Bus Boycott: https://www.youtube.com/watch?v=pxTWb38NERg

p. 27 Votes for women 1906 to 1918: https://www.youtube.com/watch?v=kBhP-j5evYI

MEMORY

p. 33 The multi-store model of memory: https://www.youtube.com/watch?v=I2BK8JAn1LA

p. 34 Sensory memory: https://www.youtube.com/watch?v=sXphKw1BPBw

p. 37 Memory loss: https://www.youtube.com/watch?v=Vwigmktix-2Y&list=PL5614B161DFA03590

p. 38 HM: https://www.youtube.com/watch?v=SQASyR0w8Qo

p. 39 Mirror drawing: https://www.youtube.com/watch?v=Nz_FVxYU74Y

p. 40 Working memory: https://www.youtube.com/watch?v=UWKvpFZJwcE

p. 43 Retroactive and proactive interference: https://www.youtube.com/watch?v=jyXbdLIBhQo

p. 46 Misleading information: https://www.youtube.com/watch?v=PB2OegI6wvI

p. 50 Cognitive interview: https://www.youtube.com/watch?v=jyMLDN9UOrE

ATTACHMENT

p. 58 Still face experiment: https://www.youtube.com/watch?v=apzXGEbZht0

p. 62 The role of the father: https://www.youtube.com/watch?v=BJh3qF5Ab14

p. 63 Konrad Lorenz and imprinting: https://www.youtube.com/watch?v=CayHUn6z_Is

p. 63 The barnacle goose: https://www.youtube.com/watch?v=0_JoetV3ZTQ

p. 65 Harlow's monkeys: https://www.youtube.com/watch?v=OrNBEhzjg8I

p. 66 Bowlby's monotropic theory: https://www.youtube.com/watch?v=zcnIo0NZrcw

p. 71 The Strange Situation: https://www.youtube.com/watch?v=s608077NtNI

p. 72 Secure attachment: https://www.youtube.com/watch?v=9a6I6xXJ0Lw

p. 72 Insecure anxious/ambivalent attachment: https://www.youtube.com/watch?v=3UW6R7JVE8M

p. 72 Insecure anxious/avoidant attachment: https://www.youtube.com/watch?v=FD771ASTMes

p. 75 Cultural differences in attachment: https://www.youtube.com/watch?v=6po5tV4tKgw

p. 77 Rutter's criticism of maternal deprivation theory: https://www.youtube.com/watch?v=igC9R45TS5E

p. 78 Romanian orphans: https://www.youtube.com/watch?v=bvL_DGjGuhA

p. 83 Attachments and adult relationships: https://www.youtube.com/watch?v=2xOziE-Jlac

PSYCHOPATHOLOGY

p. 89 Defining abnormality: https://www.youtube.com/watch?v=cwKJ0juPIrQ

p. 93 Depression: https://www.youtube.com/watch?v=fWFuQR_Wt4M

p. 94 Beck's theory of depression: https://www.youtube.com/watch?v=CAofO0-gvCY

p. 95 Cognitive behaviour therapy: https://www.youtube.com/watch?v=0ViaCs0k2jM

p. 96 Beating the blues: https://www.youtube.com/watch?v=pVdyNzP41yM

p. 97 Ellis's ABC model: https://www.youtube.com/watch?v=WRRdSm4ZjX4

p. 99 Brain chemistry and depression: https://www.youtube.com/watch?v=KispXWwDaOc

p. 100 Phobia: https://www.youtube.com/watch?v=ZcARwov3HpI

p. 102 Systematic desensitization: https://www.youtube.com/watch?v=sRaeMTVGurY

p. 103 Virtual reality SD: https://www.youtube.com/watch?v=co7BWWoF-5I

p. 103 Exposure therapy (flooding): https://www.youtube.com/watch?v=zKTpecooiec

p. 104 Baby Albert Experiments https://www.youtube.com/watch?v=FMnhyGozLyE

p. 105 OCD: https://www.youtube.com/watch?v=DhlRgwdDc-E

p. 106 Biological explanation of phobia: https://www.youtube.com/watch?v=hP2COYrpW8A

APPROACHES IN PSYCHOLOGY

p. 121 Pavlov and classical conditioning: https://www.youtube.com/watch?v=hhqumfpxuzI

p. 122 Skinner box: https://www.youtube.com/watch?v=MOgowRy2WC0

p. 123 Social learning theory: https://www.youtube.com/watch?v=eqNaLerMNOE

p. 125 The cognitive revolution: https://www.youtube.com/watch?v=AeoyzqmyWug

p. 126 Schemas: https://www.youtube.com/watch?v=Xj0CUeyucJw

p. 128 Cognitive neuroscience: https://www.youtube.com/watch?v=Y1XbOjGALfo

p. 131 Phineas Gage: https://www.youtube.com/watch?v=NFO6ts6vZic

p. 140 Humanistic psychology: https://www.youtube.com/watch?v=XhQhBtHjqAA

BIOPSYCHOLOGY

p. 151 The neuron: https://www.youtube.com/watch?v=6qS83wD29PY

p. 153 Synaptic transmission: https://www.youtube.com/watch?v=WhowH0kb7n0

p. 155 Divisions of the nervous system: https://www.youtube.com/watch?v=q3OITaAZLNc

p. 156 Fight-or-flight response: https://www.youtube.com/watch?v=FBnBTkcr6No

p. 158 Split brain: https://www.youtube.com/watch?v=lfGwsAdS9Dc

p. 162 Language and the brain: https://www.youtube.com/watch?v=5k8JwC1L9_k

p. 164 Plasticity: https://www.youtube.com/watch?v=Wn08mkGbGnQ

p. 165 Dissecting brains: https://www.youtube.com/watch?v=OMqWRlxo1oQ

p. 166 Electroencephalogram (EEG): https://www.youtube.com/watch?v=I3j2VrhqTAA

p. 167 fMRI: https://www.youtube.com/watch?v=lLORKtkf2n8

p. 168 Circadian rhythms: https://www.youtube.com/watch?v=UbQ0RxQu2gM

RESEARCH METHODS

p. 181 The experimental method: https://www.youtube.com/watch?v=qtLnBz6lbRQ

p. 181 The IV and the DV: https://www.youtube.com/watch?v=s-fVRJyEvS0

p. 182 The experimental method: causality: https://www.youtube.com/watch?v=DMJciSKsX-M

p. 182 Variable: https://www.youtube.com/watch?v=Qe7wN8qT8ic

p. 191 Questionnaire design: https://www.youtube.com/watch?v=HfGyiRBwSec

p. 195 Correlations: https://www.youtube.com/195?v=jUPkkiW-Q80

p. 200 The scientific method: https://www.youtube.com/watch?v=tJVxPwe3kz0

p. 216 Features of science: https://www.youtube.com/watch?v=qVDKhiH7ZWI

p. 219 Types of data: https://www.youtube.com/watch?v=--r9_R60Jws

p. 222 Mean, median, mode: https://www.youtube.com/watch?v=yv8DrOkQqYg

INDEX

IMAGE CREDITS

p. 4 © Katie Jenkins. pp. 6–7 © agsandrew, fotolia. p. 8 © alswart, fotolia. p. 10 © imageegami, fotolia. p. 11 © pushba, fotolia. p. 18 © Sergey Nivens, fotolia. p. 19 From the film *Obedience*, © 1968, Stanley Milgram. Distributed by Alexander Street Press. p. 27 © Bill Perry, fotolia. p. 30 © olllinka2, fotolia. p. 32 © Werner Dreblow, fotolia. p. 33 © ivan kmit, fotolia. p. 37 © mitrija, fotolia. p. 38 © Gabriele Rohde, fotolia. p. 39 © Nigel Holt. p. 40 © ilarialapreziosa, fotolia. p. 43 © olly, fotolia. p. 46 © rudall30, fotolia. p. 49 © JRB, fotolia. p. 54 © Paul Hakimata, fotolia. p. 56 © ellisia, fotolia. p. 57 © Monkey Business, fotolia. p. 58 @ Andrew Meltzoff from A.N. Meltzoff and M.K. Moore, 'Imitation of facial and manual gestures by human neonates'. Science, 1977, 198, 75-78. p. 59 © Lsantilli, fotolia. p. 62 © Magalice, fotolia. p. 63 © Science Photo Library. p. 64 © scabrn, fotolia. p. 65 © Science Source/Science Photo Library. p. 66 © sonsedskaya, fotolia. p. 68 © Andrey Kiselev, fotolia. p. 70 © Monkey Business, fotolia. p. 74 © paulmz, fotolia. p. 76 © Julija Sapic, fotolia. p. 79, 80 © Action Press/Rex Shutterstock. p. 81 © Oksana Kuzmina, fotolia. p. 82 © Finanzfoto, fotolia. p. 86 © BortN66, fotolia. p. 88 © Photographee.eu, fotolia. p. 89 © Sergey Nivens, fotolia. p. 93 © George.M., fotolia.

p. 100 © pcgbes, fotolia. p. 103 © techbommer, fotolia. p. 105 © karenfoleyphoto, fotolia. p. 106 © Brian Evans, Science Photo Library. p. 108 © Andres Rodriguez, fotolia. p. 110 © nofear4232, fotolia. pp. 114–115 © tashatuvango, fotolia. p. 116 © kubko, fotolia. p. 118 © Photographee.eu, fotolia. p. 119 © minibytes01, fotolia. p. 120 © aga7ta, fotolia. p. 121 © Les Evans. p. 123 © Les Evans. p. 125 © pathdoc, fotolia. p. 126 (l) © Nikolai Tsvetkov, fotolia. p. 126 (m) © cynoclub, fotolia. p. 126 (r) © Vera Kuttelvaserova, fotolia. p. 127 © katusha161107, fotolia. p. 128 © Dr. Scott T. Grafton, Visuals Unlimited/Science Photo Library. p. 130 © maya2008, fotolia. p. 131 © Jacopin/Science Photo Library. p. 132 © Paulista, fotolia. p. 135 (t) © nuvolanevicata, fotolia. p. 135 (b) © Comugnero Silvana, fotolia. p. 136 © adimas, fotolia. p. 140 (t) © beeboys, fotolia. p. 140 (b) © marcociannarel, fotolia. p. 148 © adimas, fotolia. p. 150 © daboost, fotolia. p. 151 © vitstudio, fotolia. p. 152 (t) © blueringmedia, fotolia. p. 152 (table) © designua, fotolia. p. 153 © rob3000, fotolia. p. 154 © ram69, fotolia. p. 156 © Les Evans. p. 157 © Drivepix, fotolia p. 158 © shumpc, fotolia. p. 159 © Les Evans. p. 160 (t) © yodiyim, fotolia. p. 160 (b) © Les Evans. p. 161 (t) © Les Evans.

p. 161 (b) ©St Bartholomew Hospital/Science Photo Library. p. 163 © Les Evans. p. 165 (t) © EPSTOCK, fotolia. p. 165 (b) © psdesign1, fotolia. p. 166 © neurobite, fotolia. p. 167 © Zephyr/Science Photo Library. p. 168 © nikjvt, fotolia. p. 170 © mgkuijpers, fotolia. p. 171 © salajean, fotolia. p. 173 (t) © valentina morri, fotolia. p. 173 (b) © Photobank, fotolia. pp. 176–177 © freshidea, fotolia. p. 178 © kbuntu, fotolia. p. 180 © KM Sands, fotolia. p. 181 © madamsaffa, fotolia. pp. 184–186 © Les Evans. p. 188 © igor, fotolia. p. 191 © Rawpixel, fotolia. p. 193 © vadymvdrobot, fotolia. p. 194 © Photographee.eu, fotolia. p. 195 (t) © JenkoAtaman, fotolia. p. 195 (b) © thinglass, fotolia. p. 198 © olly, fotolia. p. 199 © dessauer, fotolia. p. 200 © Monkey Business, fotolia. p. 202 © James Steidl, fotolia. p. 208 © Feng Yu, fotolia. p. 209 © Christian Müller, fotolia. p. 210 © Sondem, fotolia. p. 214 © djedzura, fotolia. p. 215 © tiero, fotolia. p. 217 © rolffimages, fotolia. p. 219 © tostphoto, fotolia. p. 221 © Jakub Jirsák, fotolia. p. 232 © ag visuell, fotolia. pp. 240–241 © chrisdorney, fotolia. p. 242 © Drivepix, fotolia. p. 246 © ptnphotof, fotolia. p. 247 © christianchan, fotolia.

A level year 2
AQA Psychology

Nigel Holt and Rob Lewis

ISBN: 978-184590991-8

Crown House Publishing Limited
www.crownhouse.co.uk